Power Transitions

Power Transitions: Strategies for the 21st Century

Ronald L. Tammen
Jacek Kugler
Douglas Lemke
Allan C. Stam III
Mark Abdollahian
Carole Alsharabati
Brian Efird
and
A.F.K. Organski

CHATHAM HOUSE PUBLISHERS

SEVEN BRIDGES PRESS, LLC

NEW YORK • LONDON

Seven Bridges Press, LLC
135 Fifth Avenue
New York, NY 10010

Publisher: Robert J. Gormley
Managing Editor: Katharine Miller
Cover Design: Andrea Barash Design
Composition: ediType
Printing and Binding: Victor Graphics, Inc.

Library of Congress Cataloging-in-Publication Data

Power transitions : strategies for the 21st century / Ronald L. Tammen
. . . [et al.].
    p. cm.
    Includes bibliographical references and index.
    ISBN 1-889119-43-1
    1. United States – Foreign relations – 1989 – Forecasting. 2. World
politics – 1989 – Forecasting. 3. United States – Foreign
relations – 1989-. 4. United States – Foreign relations – 1945-1989. 5.
World politics – 1989-. 6. World politics – 1945- I. Tammen, Ronald L.,
1943-
E840 .P66 2000
327.1′01 – dc21
                      99-50686

*To an extraordinary man
with extraordinary ideas —
A.F.K. Organski*

Contents

List of Figures

Preface

The purpose of this book is to help bridge the gap between the academic and policy communities in world politics. We recognize the magnitude of that task and the modest role we hope to play in the process. We also understand that this may be an exercise that will not be welcomed by some authorities on both sides. There may be those in the academic community who would have preferred that we had devoted this entire volume to the purpose of the first chapter — codifying and unifying Power Transition theory by integrating its various strands and themes and by adding the conclusions of formal proofs. And there may be those in the policy community who will find the introduction of theoretical terms and tests to be less than useful in an operational setting. In a sense, it is this membrane of ignorance that keeps us apart, diluting the rich intellectual promise of the former and handicapping the strategic thinking of the latter.

Despite these anticipated obstacles, we designed this book with both constituencies in mind. The importance of the practical applications of the theory motivates us to speak to the policy community. The importance of the academic implications of a unified theory motivates us to extend and rectify the various strands of Power Transition research. We ask policymakers to be patient with the theoretical chapters and theoreticians to be patient with the policy chapters. Scholars will find many of their questions addressed in the more detailed endnotes. Policymakers looking for a set of tools to address critical problems of the twenty-first century may safely pass over many of these academic references without losing the thrust of our argument.

The arguments presented herein are a coherent compilation and extension of the academic tradition of Power Transition theory. The authors represent three intellectual generations of that theory, including A.F.K. Organski, who invented the theory in 1958; Jacek Kugler, who collaborated with Organski in an empirical evaluation of the theory; and Douglas Lemke, who extended it beyond merely great power interactions. Ronald L. Tammen and Allan Stam, also in the Organski lineage, have published articles that apply Power Transition concepts in policy settings. Mark Abdollahian, Carole Alsharabati, and Brian Efird have added formal tests and theoretical extensions to the theory. This book represents the latest, and in some ways the most aggressive, step in a continuing forty-year research project.

Those years have produced a theory unusual among academic products in that it offers clear and relevant implications for policymakers concerned with the management of international politics. This is a propitious moment for this theory to be extended into policy terms. The theory has now progressed far enough to offer refined policy advice. And there is a demand for new ideas to guide foreign policies at the start of the new century.

This book explains how the international system is organized. It discusses when, how, and why wars occur at the great power and regional power levels. It provides guidance for policymakers about managing the international system to avoid war. It offers a general theory of international politics that ties together both economic and security considerations. It also provides a guide to understanding peace as a product of economic and political integration.

Our ideas are first presented theoretically. The theory subsequently becomes a framework for the applications, but only after being subjected to empirical validation by testing against the historical record. Following this foundation, current policy implications are discussed and analyzed. Future extensions are elaborated as a guide to systematic long-term policy development. The final chapter offers a theoretically informed walk into the future.

The policy chapters address the fundamental challenges of the international system. In the aftermath of the Cold War, regional conflicts have been elevated in importance. We deal with these issues directly in chapter 3. Despite the ascendancy of regional issues, nuclear weapons and strategy retain a position of national importance. Therefore, nuclear deterrence and proliferation are discussed in chapter 4. With the downgrading of major power conflict propensity, the focus of major power relations also has shifted to economic interactions. In this arena there are two trends, one toward integration and consolidation and a second involving sanctions and trade wars. Chapter 5 discusses these issues in detail. Having looked at current regional, nuclear, and economic issues, we move to the challenges faced by decision makers looking forward in time. Chapters 6 through 8 formulate specific policy recommendations for the future relations of the great powers of the twenty-first century: the United States, China, the European Union, Russia, and India.

In the policy chapters we focus first on how NATO expansion, perhaps to include Russia, could affect worldwide power distributions. In the early decades of this century, the British failed to construct a coalition to preserve stability and peace in the face of the German-led challenge to the international order. The United States has the opportunity to avoid the mistakes of the 1930s by structuring a more successful coalition. The United States can also maintain peace and stability by successfully managing the future transitions with China and India. The coalition option is discussed in chapter 6, the Chinese and Indian power transitions are discussed in chapter 7, and the shape of the next international hierarchy is projected in chapter 8.

The concept of this book was born in a typhoon in Tokyo, where Organski, Kugler, and Tammen found themselves isolated by the forces of nature. Released from the tyranny of their schedules, they outlined the organization of this volume with the purpose of translating Power Transition from its theoretical base to policy prescriptions. We hope this is just the first step in this evolution. Being individuals, not to mention academics, we may disagree on some nuances or colorings in this volume, but we share a common dedication to the Power Transition tradition and to the proposition that, where possible, academic research should be utilized in the policy world. To do less is to waste a significant resource and to place the United States at a competitive disadvantage in the international marketplace of ideas.

Acknowledgments

This is a jointly authored book, an undertaking designed to demonstrate the broad appeal of Power Transition theory. All authors contributed to each chapter, an exercise that proved intellectually stimulating and remarkably collegial. For organizational purposes, some individuals assumed leadership for particular chapters as follows: chapter 1, Kugler, Lemke, and Tammen; chapter 2, Abdollahian; chapter 3, Lemke; chapter 4, Alsharabati and Kugler; chapter 5, Efird and Kugler; chapter 6, Stam (an earlier version of this chapter was coauthored with Bruce Russett); chapter 7, Tammen; and chapter 8, Kugler, Lemke, and Tammen. Kenneth Organski, of course, lives on in every page.

The Earhart Foundation, led by Secretary and Director of Program Antony T. Sullivan, was generous in providing funding for our research, including two conferences, one at the National War College (NWC), the other at the Monterey Institute for International Studies (MIIS). We thank Provost Steve Baker and Dean Phil Morgan of MIIS and Dean David Tretler of NWC for hosting us at their institutions and for providing sabbatical support to Ron Tammen, which facilitated the organization of this effort. The National Defense University Foundation administered the Earhart Foundation grant. We enjoyed the strong support and exceptional service provided by James V. Dugar and Tom Gallagher, the president and executive director, respectively, of that Foundation. Bob Gormley, the publisher of Chatham House, has become a friend and key adviser in this project. The importance of his firm commitment to our goal of reaching both the academic and policy communities cannot be overstated. Katharine Miller has added immeasurably to the quality of this book. We thank her not only for her editorial skills but for her patience in dealing with multiple authors. We also wish to thank Sarah Mikels, Library Director, and Jeannemarie Faison, Reference Librarian, at the National Defense University. Their expertise and assistance proved invaluable.

A number of individuals reviewed portions or all of our drafts and provided important insights and welcome criticisms. With apologies to anyone we may have accidentally omitted, we specifically wish to thank Bruce Bueno de Mesquita, Glenn Palmer, Yi Feng, Paul Zak, Marina Arbetman, Thomas Willett, Woosang Kim, Frank Zagare, Charles Doran, Randy Siverson, Sherry Bennett, Jim Rosenau, George Graham, Richard Rosecrance, Siddharth Swaminathan, Michelle Benson, and Kenneth Osterkamp. A special appreciation to Bruce Russett, with whom Allan Stam collaborated for chapter 6.

All of our spouses deserve special commendation for tolerating us during the often inconvenient process of writing this book. We therefore gratefully acknowledge Cheryl Kugler, Jill Lemke, B.B. Stam, Danny Al-sharabati, and, in particular, Susan Tammen, who not only graciously invited an army of us to occupy her home on several occasions but also was influential in the selection of our book title. Patricia Organski supported us every step of the way, even through the most difficult of times. Patricia, you are always in our hearts.

As one of our authors is an employee of the U.S. government, we must state that nothing contained in this volume should be construed as representing the views of the Department of Defense or the executive branch more generally. That said, clearly we believe that one day this volume *should* represent those views.

A Tribute to A.F.K. Organski

This work was inspired by the brilliant theoretical contributions of A.F.K. Organski, who died on 6 March 1998, while this project was in progress. In addition to his profound intellect and originality, Kenneth Organski will be remembered for his zest for life, love of language, and gift for friendship. The magnetic force that surrounded him inexorably drew students and colleagues into his vortex. He was a devoted husband, father, and grandfather who will be missed beyond measure by his family, colleagues, and generations of devoted students.

Kenneth was an academic's academic who made major contributions to the study of world politics. At a time when it was considered heresy, he challenged the realism school of Hans Morgenthau by detailing its inconsistencies. Later, he pioneered the use of empirical evidence to test propositions when other scholars relied on instinct or authority. With an uncanny ability to identify and restructure central issues in the field, Kenneth was a galvanizing figure of his generation. His impact on the profession has many measures but perhaps the most important is that he inspired generations of students to advance the frontiers of knowledge. AFKO did not believe in sterile academic accomplishments. If possible, he urged, research should be put to use for the benefit of mankind. Thus he strongly supported the transfer of academic research into the policy world.

This extraordinary political scientist, practitioner, and educator was born in Rome in 1923, where he attended the Ginnasio Liceo Torquato Tasso. He came to the United States fleeing the anti-Jewish laws of the Mussolini regime. He served with the American armed forces in the Pacific theater from 1943 to 1945. (Later in his life, when lecturing before senior military officials, Kenneth would gleefully recount that as a private he had hated officers and that he now took great pleasure telling them what to do!) After World War II, he settled in New York, where he became an American citizen in 1944 and earned his B.A. (1947), M.A. (1948), and Ph.D. (1951) degrees from New York University. In 1952 he started teaching at Brooklyn College, moving in 1964 to the University of Michigan, where most recently he was professor of political science and senior research scientist in the Institute for Social Research. In addition to his long and extraordinary teaching and research career, he was also chairman of the board of Decision Insights, a consulting firm. He cofounded this company in order to introduce scientific rigor to the execution of policy and decision making in government and business.

A.F.K. Organski will long be remembered for a series of extraordinary intellectual contributions. His influential ideas on power hierarchies in world politics were introduced in *World Politics* and extended in *The War Ledger*, coauthored with Jacek Kugler. His powerful insights on national development were set forth in *Population and World Power*, coauthored with Katherine Davis Fox, advanced in *Stages of Political Development*, and documented in *Birth, Death and Taxes*, which was written with several of his students. In *The $36 Billion Bargain*, Kenneth outlined the prospects and possibilities for peace in the Middle East. In these works and countless articles and presentations, he advanced new ideas about the future of world politics and applied these notions to real problems. He was the rare innovative academic who involved and inspired others to further elaborate his insights and to apply these new angles of vision to resolve problems. His willingness to take risks in the pursuit of knowledge was a distinguishing characteristic of his career. Organski's honors included the Distinguished Faculty Achievement Award from the University of Michigan, the lifetime achievement award from the Conflict Processes Section of the American Political Science Association, and the Cavalieri de la Republica from the government of Italy.

Above all, Kenneth Organski was a superb educator. His lectures at the University of Michigan were, without exaggeration, legendary. He would light up a room with his intellectual force and with the passion and humor of his charismatic personality. Some will remember him telling students: "math, math, math" and "write, write, write." Others will remember his authoritative voice and presentation style and his ability to focus intently on each individual as if no one else mattered. Through his writings and through his students, Kenneth Organski achieved immortality. He counted among his students many who became prominent authorities in the profession, including Aaron Wildavsky, Bruce Bueno de Mesquita, Jacek Kugler, Youssef Cohen, Allan Lamborn, Allan Stam, Glenn Palmer, and Ellen Lust-Okar. In turn they taught and inspired others, including Douglas Lemke, Marina Arbetman, Suzanne Werner, Frank Zagare, James Morrow, David Lalman, Woosang Kim, Mark Abdollahian, Carole Alsharabati, Vesna Danilovic, Brian Efird, and Ben Hunt — all dedicated to extending our knowledge of development and war and peace, and all keepers of the Organski flame. Other students chose to hone their talents in the policy world, including Ronald L. Tammen, Arthur House, Robert Hormats, and Ajaj Jarrouj. There they applied Organski insights on Capitol Hill, in the executive branch, and in the business and financial communities.

In Kenneth's memory, we have constructed an "Organski Tree" at the Internet site Powertransitions.com. This genealogy depicts the successive generations of Organski students who have continued to advance his Power Transition theory. The tree is a first and very limited effort to visually catalog the "Organski Effect." We invite all who have been associated with Kenneth's Power Transition work to contact Ron Tammen at that site so that we can add names to this lineage.

This book represents our — his students' — immeasurable debt of gratitude. Thank you, Kenneth.

Part I

Foundations

CHAPTER 1
Power Transition Theory for the Twenty-first Century

Never before has there been such utter confusion in the public mind with respect to U.S. foreign policy. The President doesn't understand it; Congress doesn't understand it; nor does the public, nor does the press. They all wander around in a labyrinth of ignorance and error and conjecture, in which truth is intermingled with fiction at a hundred points, in which unjustified assumptions have attained the validity of premises, and in which there is no recognized and authoritative theory to hold on to. — GEORGE F. KENNAN

The United States is engaged in a quiet war. It is the intellectual war between those who favor the expansion of American influence abroad and those who reject involvement in distant lands with strange names for purposes having little apparent linkage to their daily lives. It is a war that goes far beyond the old descriptions of "internationalist" and "isolationist" or the more modern terms of "engagement" and "retrenchment." It is a war fought with words, ideas, public opinion, and legislation as each side attempts to mobilize its resources within the interested public. Often operating as the subtext of national debates, this battle for primacy represents the single most important decision the United States faces today. Fundamentally, it is a struggle over no less than the defining role of the United States in the third millennium.

Will the United States retrench, withdraw, retreat into the perceived security of noninvolvement, or will it recognize the impending power shifts and make the policy choices necessary to meet these new conditions? It is a decision critical not only to the economic well-being and security of the United States, but to that of the international system it informally leads. It is a question central to this book.

Intellectually the United States is ill prepared for this challenge. From 1945 to 1990, American elites and the informed public were unified in their worldview. The single exception was the Vietnam War in its later stages. The United States was unified because of a common, documented threat. To meet that threat, American policy intellectuals, political leaders, and military officials fashioned a series of strategies with the common goal of defending the United States from the ideological and military challenges of communism as represented by the USSR. The single-mindedness of this effort, its narrow but necessary perspective, masked emerging trends in world power that will have a profound impact on the international system in this twenty-first century.

From the mid-1900s on, American strategists forged consensus based on perceptions of the threat. Then the dissolution of the Soviet Union undercut the intellectual and public support for the U.S. role in the world. In a phrase, it changed everything. The nature of the threat, the so-called bipolar world, the East-West blocs, all melted into history. In the aftermath, it is as if an intellectual void has been created, filled ad hoc by the threat of the day or the sum of all new threats. What has been missing is the theoretical and practical foundation upon which policy can be established. The purpose of this book is to offer a new perspective of the world based on a coherent and validated theory that bridges the theoretical-policy gap.

This book deals with the fundamental shifts in world power — power transitions — that have been submerged by the U.S.-USSR competition. It provides a theory, a worldview that not only explains the rise of the United States as the dominant power but also projects that role into this century. Laying out the future challenges to American leadership, it offers not only an intellectual foundation for anticipating these events but suggests specific management tools that could be utilized to ensure a peaceful evolution among the great powers.

This is a book about theory in policy terms and policy in theoretical terms. It unifies Power Transition theory and applies it to the central questions of the next decades. How should the United States attempt to manage world politics, particularly the challenge of China? How will critical alliances such as the North Atlantic Treaty Organization (NATO) evolve in the future? What is the nature and scope of regional instability? How can regional conflicts be managed? How will nuclear proliferation affect the stability of deterrence? What are the global economic effects of integration, trade, and growth? How will economic patterns influence international power relationships? This book offers a bridge whereon practitioners and theorists may meet to evaluate these issues and walk together into the new century.

The Search for New Explanations

The economic collapse and political dissolution of the Soviet Union has left policymakers and scholars searching for new fundamental truths about the nature of the international system. For many, the Cold War era was the supreme threat to international peace and security, but in hindsight, it was also intellectually comfortable. The nature of the threat was known. It was a powerful mobilizing tool for government, business, and society.

The loss of that threat has created conditions, for the first time in more than fifty years, favorable to an open, unconstrained assessment of how the international system operates without first being viewed through the prism of the Cold War.

The absence of a monolithic threat has forced policymakers to search for explanations that fit the new international circumstances without violating old, cherished concepts. The U.S. foreign policy community has gone through a difficult and wrenching exercise in the past ten years. The Department of Defense has identified a new set of transnational threats — including international crime, drugs, terrorism, biological and chemical weapons, and proliferation of nuclear weapons and delivery systems — that, in many ways, are less powerful for mobilizing political support, yet more complex and challenging than the brute force specter of Soviet aggression. Similarly, U.S. foreign policy has undergone a systematic realignment, substituting an economic focus for the political and military imperative of meeting communist challenges in the developing world.

The sense of uncertainty about the look of the new world stems not just from the radical changes it has undergone, but equally from the realization that the old theories did not predict and cannot explain why this dramatic transformation occurred.[1] Why is it that the world seems safer without two great superpowers balancing each other — the mutual deterrence that secured global peace? Was our notion of peace and balance of power misplaced? If so, that misjudgment may well represent the single most important intellectual and policy failure of the post–World War II era.

This chapter is designed to accomplish two goals. First, it offers the reader a composite picture of Power Transition theory by integrating the various extensions and amplifications into a coherent whole.[2] It brings together that new research and weaves it into the rich text of the underlying theory. By providing a systematic outline of the hierarchical relationship among power, satisfaction, and the choice of peace and conflict, Power Transition theory offers a foundation for exploring international politics.

Second, this chapter translates Power Transition theory into policy-relevant terms. Despite extensive empirical validation, the theory has been inaccessible to the policy community, in part because of its specialized use of language and in part because of its academic focus. For the policy-oriented reader, therefore, we keep the theoretical arguments cogent and readable. For the academic specialist, we provide detailed citations and discuss various nuances, colorings, and controversies in the endnotes.

The heart of this chapter is devoted to the three components of Power Transition theory: structure, dynamics, and policy. The structural aspect of the theory is explored first since it provides an understanding of the nature of power, power relationships among nations, and the characteristics of the international system linking nations. With the international structure in place, the theory then accounts for the most important dynamics in the system. Of all theories at the international level, Power Transition has the most tightly integrated and internally consistent explanation for why, how, and when wars occur. In addition, it provides evidence about the costs, intensity, duration, and consequences of war.

Having described the international system and how it deals with conflict, this chapter continues by exploring how the theory addresses the major policy issues facing the world. With the structural and dynamic components in place, the theory is in position to deal with the management of alliances and international organizations, coalition building, political economy concerns, and threats to international order — such as nuclear proliferation and local wars. Finally, the chapter ends with a look beyond the present, based upon the Power Transition view of our future.

The Structure of Power Transition Theory

In a theoretical sense, Power Transition defies traditional typecasting. It is neither realist nor idealist, though some scholars have placed it in the former category.[3] We prefer to call it *rationalist*. That is, it is structural, yet dynamic, since it recognizes that policy interests are at the core of all disputes. Subject to empirical testing, it meshes well with objective conclusions flowing from history. Thus, it marries empirical evidence with traditional scholarly research and sound policy advice. It is a theory that lends itself to a blend of the empirical and policy worlds.

Hierarchies

Power Transition theory describes a hierarchical system. All nations recognize the presence of this hierarchy and the relative distribution of power therein. The distribution of power is uneven and is concentrated in the hands of a few. A dominant nation sits at the top of this system (see figure 1.1). That nation controls the largest proportion of resources within the system. Yet this nation, despite our description as dominant, is not a hegemon. It cannot single-handedly control the actions of other powerful nations. It maintains its position as dominant power by ensuring power preponderance over potential rivals and by managing the international system under rules that benefit its allies and satisfy their national aspirations.

As we can see in figure 1.1, the category of great powers resides below the dominant nation, each having a significant proportion of the power of ·the leader. Currently the great powers are China, Japan, Germany or the European Union (EU) in toto, and Russia (assuming recovery). Their role, in most circumstances, is to share in the allocation of resources and to help maintain the international system. Among great powers one occasionally finds nations, such as China or India, that are not fully integrated into the

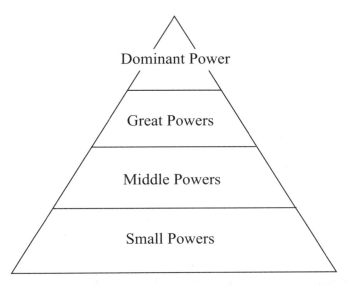

Figure 1.1 Classic Power Pyramid

dominant power's regime. On occasion a potential challenger arises out of this pool. Challengers are defined as those with 80 percent or more of the dominant country's power. Today, only China represents a potential challenger to the United States, and then only if it remains dissatisfied with its international role. In the distant future India could also play this role. Dissatisfied challengers and their supporters are the initiators of war.

Beneath the great powers are the middle powers, substantive states of the size of France, Italy, or Brazil, with resources that cannot be dismissed but with insufficient power to challenge the dominant power for international control. The largest number of nations resides farther down the pyramid: small powers with few resources relative to the middle and great powers. They pose no threat to the dominant nation's leadership of the international system.

New research has shown that hierarchies also exist at regional levels.[4] Within each region, such as South America or the Middle East, there are regional hierarchies, with their own sets of dominant powers, great powers, and lesser powers. These regional hierarchies are influenced by the global hierarchical system but cannot, in turn, control that larger system. Figure 1.2 (p. 8) suggests the relative power distributions in the global system and in a few regional systems.

Note that the distribution of power clearly makes the regional hierarchies subordinate to the global hierarchy. These regional hierarchies function in the same manner and operate under the same power rules as the global hierarchy. In all cases, the dominant power in the regional hier-

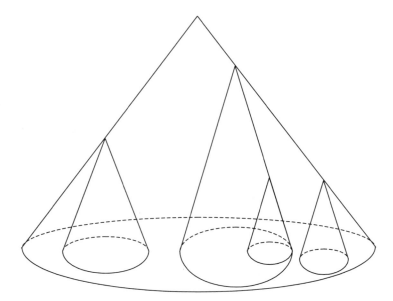

Figure 1.2   Hierarchies in the International System

archy is subordinate to the influences of the global dominant power and the
great power structure. Relative power establishes the relationships within
regional hierarchies and determines the spheres of influence that link the
global and regional hierarchies. Power Transition anticipates that wars will
diffuse downward from the global to the regional hierarchies but will not
diffuse upward from regional to global. For this reason, World Wars I and
II, which were major conflicts for the great powers of the international
system, diffused to include almost every regional hierarchy. Limited wars
involving the major global powers, such as the wars in Korea, Vietnam,
and Afghanistan, remained confined to their regions, despite fears to the
contrary.

Power

Defining power is central to the theory of Power Transition as relative
power establishes the precondition for war and peace in the international
system. Power is defined as the ability to impose on or persuade an opponent to comply with demands.[5] In the lexicon of Power Transition theory,
power is a combination of three elements: the number of people who can
work and fight, their economic productivity, and the effectiveness of the
political system in extracting and pooling individual contributions to advance national goals. How much "power" these capabilities endow a state

with generates the ability to project influence beyond its borders. Population is an essential component but cannot alone confer international power, as can be seen by the relative weakness of Bangladesh, Indonesia, or Brazil. In order to be truly powerful the population also must be productive. For this reason developed countries have far more influence than their developing counterparts. That is why the United States dominates China today. But those advantages cannot be realized without political capacity, defined as the ability of governments to extract resources to advance national goals. Politically capable governments garner relatively more resources and thereby expand national power. For this reason North Vietnam defeated the more populous and affluent South Vietnam in spite of the United States' massive help to the South.

Satisfaction and Dissatisfaction

The motivation driving decisions for war and peace is relative satisfaction with the rules of the global or regional hierarchy. While parity defines the structural conditions where war is most likely, conflicts are generated by the desire of a nation to improve its political position in the hierarchy. Dissatisfied nations challenge the status quo. Conflict does not occur frequently at the great power level because most of these nations are relatively satisfied and support the existing rules of the international system. Instead, these status quo nations seek cooperative solutions to problems that enhance their economic and security gains.

Nations at the top of the hierarchy (figure 1.3, p. 10) set the rules in place and are more likely to be more satisfied with those rules than those lower in the global hierarchy. This should not come as a surprise since the great powers control most of the wealth, enjoy most of the prosperity, and wield most of the power in the international system. By definition, the dominant power is satisfied, and specifically so in the absence of open conflict challenging its dominance. The dominant nation is the defender of the status quo. After all, it creates and maintains the global or regional hierarchy from which it accrues substantial benefits.[6]

The few dissatisfied nations at the top and many at the bottom of the hierarchy view the international system as not conferring benefits equal to their expectations and long-term interests. They consider the international system to be unfair, corrupt, biased, skewed, and dominated by hostile forces. Their rationale or grievance may be historical (Germany prior to World Wars I and II), ideological (Soviet Union), religious (Iran), territorial (Israel), personal (Libya and Iraq), or cultural (China). Despite different perspectives, dissatisfied nations all view the global status quo as unfavorable. They are dissatisfied with established international leadership, its rules and norms, and wish to change them. The largest proportion of dissatisfied nations likely resides in the small power category, nations with minimal

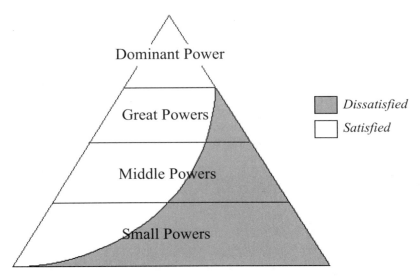

Figure 1.3   Distribution of Satisfaction

influence in the international system who often consider themselves the victims of more powerful neighbors. Occasionally a great power — like Germany or the Soviet Union — is dissatisfied with its role and status in the international system. If it is growing at a fast rate and extracting resources for use at the national level, that nation may become a challenger to the dominant nation.

Dynamics of Satisfaction and Dissatisfaction

The horizontal axis of figure 1.4 illustrates the relationship between the satisfaction or dissatisfaction of two countries with either a global or regional status quo. The vertical axis describes the type of relationship, by degree of cooperation, within the same dyad of nations. Jointly satisfied nations interact cooperatively. Examples are long-term security communities, such as NATO with the United States and any number of European actors and economic integration, as is occurring within the European Union. Deterioration in the degree of cooperation implies that one of the states may be becoming dissatisfied. Thus, the dyadic relationship is becoming more competitive.

The second column illustrates the relationship within a satisfied-dissatisfied dyad. Nations cooperate under these conditions when the satisfied power anticipates that the other is becoming satisfied. This is a transitional stage that should be temporary at best. The most prevalent relationship is confrontational competition. Given parity within this col-

Joint Status Quo Evaluation

	Satisfied-Satisfied	Satisfied-Dissatisfied	Dissatisfied-Dissatisfied
Cooperative	Security communities Economic integration	Competitive-Improving	Collusive partnership
Non-cooperative	Competitive-Deteriorating	Confrontational Competition Hierarchical Reordering war	Escalating war

Type of Relationship is shown along the vertical axis spanning Cooperative and Non-cooperative.

Figure 1.4   Degree of Cooperation and Joint Status Quo Evaluations

umn, the extreme form of noncooperation is a war to reorder the global or regional hierarchy — the source of the challenger's dissatisfaction.

The final column represents interactions between two dissatisfied nations. If two nations are dissatisfied with the status quo for the same reason, that is, they both would like to institute the same changes to the status quo, the result may be a collusive partnership in which the dissatisfied states align against the satisfied coalition. However, nations can be dissatisfied with the status quo for different reasons; that is, they would like to institute different and perhaps incompatible changes to the status quo. In such cases their relations will be very noncooperative, and there may be a high probability that they will resort to war.

Figure 1.5 (p. 12) summarizes the relationship between the probability and intensity of conflict between different types of dyads. These factors are interrelated and can reinforce or defuse confrontations. For simplicity we center on the security dimension only, but an equivalent analysis applying to economic concerns is the topic addressed in chapter 5. The reader should note that in figure 1.5 or in the text, specific cases are offered as examples illustrating the highlighted relationships. None of the figures are presentations of empirical data, although extant empirical research justifies the examples we employ.

Figure 1.5 illustrates the influence of status quo evaluations on the probability and severity of conflict. Jointly satisfied nations are expected to be the most cooperative and to face the lowest probability of conflict. In the rare event that a conflict should occur, it is anticipated to be of the mildest severity. Satisfied nations do not engage in continuous, noncooperative behavior because they resolve disputes through negotiation. Indeed, the difference in relations between Germany and France before and after

Joint Status Quo Evaluation

		Satisfied-Satisfied	Satisfied-Dissatisfied	Dissatisfied-Dissatisfied
Type of Relationship	Cooperative	No war/No disputes	Rare low-level, short disputes	No war/No disputes
	Non-cooperative	Rare, low-moderate severity disputes, short to medium duration	Many sub-war disputes, any duration possible, any severity possible Cold War Rare, intense war, long duration, ends with defeat (Western front of WWII)	Moderate amount of medium-high disputes, duration varies Rare, intense, long duration, total war, ends in annihilation (Eastern front of WWII)

Figure 1.5   War Occurrences and Joint Status Quo Evaluations

World War II can be attributed directly to a change from noncooperative to cooperative interactions as the pair moved from the satisfied-dissatisfied to satisfied-satisfied columns. Today, the EU is the most visible satisfied coalition. As common wisdom indicates, relations between satisfied and dissatisfied nations dominate world politics. Interactions produce a Cold War when the dissatisfied nation has insufficient resources to directly challenge the dominant one. In such situations relations are stable but confrontational. Under the rare circumstances of an overtaking, the probability of major wars — such as World War I or II — is at its highest. The satisfied-dissatisfied dyads seldom cooperate. Cooperation between such states is anticipated to be episodic at best and is perhaps most likely when the dissatisfied state is perceived to be changing its evaluation of the status quo. An example might be provided by U.S.-Soviet cooperation after 1989. As such transitory situations clarify, the satisfied nation will either continue to cooperate because it accrues gains — as is the case after World War II with the Marshall Plan — or will retreat from cooperation — illustrated by the emergence of the Iron Curtain in Eastern Europe. Thus, either the pair moves firmly into the satisfied-satisfied column or the cooperation diminishes.

Finally, jointly dissatisfied nations can collude when they concur about their opposition to the status quo. Such similar dissatisfaction was the basis for the alliance between Mussolini and Hitler. Alternatively, jointly dissatisfied states engage in the most severe noncooperation or outright conflict because they reject the international arrangements and also oppose the vision provided by the other dissatisfied nation. We believe this was the situation between Nazi Germany and the Soviet Union after Operation Barbarossa, the German invasion of Russia in 1941.

Figure 1.5 also provides a glimpse into relations between the United States and China. Immediately after World War II, these two nations were at odds and pursued noncooperative strategies. Despite its relative weakness compared to the United States, China intervened in the Korean conflict in 1950. Following Nixon's historic visit to China in 1972, relations improved to the point that extreme noncooperation was reduced. If this relationship follows the path exemplified by British-German or German-French relations in the post–World War II era, both parties could cooperate to their mutual advantage. On the other hand, if differences between them increase, they are likely to employ noncooperative tactics that in the long term will increase overall tensions in world politics. As China moves toward parity with the United States, the possibility of war increases.

Alliances

Power Transition argues that the stability of alliances reflects the similarity of interests and the degree of agreement about the status quo among allies. Nations that share common preferences will form stable alliances, such as NATO. Nations with incompatible preferences will create alliances that are likely to be broken when the immediate security danger that prompted the agreement disappears. This was the case with the Allied agreement with the USSR in World War II. From a long-term dynamic perspective, alliances cannot be treated as if they are simply responses to security threats. Long-lasting alliances are based on policy compatibility among the parties and joint commitment or opposition to the status quo. Short-term agreements drawn among opponents are based only on external threats. Because Power Transition concentrates on long-term dynamics, the relevant alliances are stable and with few defections. Figure 1.6 (p. 14) illustrates the conditions for stable and unstable alliances that can be established within either a global or a regional hierarchy.

Enduring and well-formed alliances are formed among nations that share a common commitment to the status quo and cooperate with each other. Indeed, the special relationship between the United States and Britain cannot be understood in any other terms. These two nations have coordinated policies even when the gains from such efforts were not clear for both sides. Recall that the United States violated the principles of the Monroe Doctrine and a long-standing anticolonialist policy when it sided with England during the Falkland-Malvinas War. Policy analysis at the time suggested that the United States could gain far more by supporting Argentina, because the weaker side would be far more willing to reward the United States for neutrality or support. Yet, despite minimal gains the United States

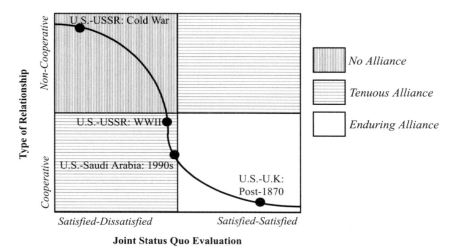

Figure 1.6   Alliances and Joint Status Quo Evaluations

favored Britain because it anticipated that in the future Britain would recip-
rocate. This was an accurate assessment. Britain has been an unwavering
supporter in the United Nations, the most important defender and participant in U.S.-led actions against Iraq following Desert Storm, and our
strongest ally during the Kosovo crisis. Cooperation builds trust, and trust
results in stable agreements.

Nations that do not share a common view of the status quo may still
enter into alliances, but they will be less stable. Indeed, the dictum that
"the enemy of my enemy is my friend" accurately describes short-lived alliances of convenience. For example, during World War II the United States
and the USSR joined forces to wage war against Germany, only to turn on
each other once the Nazi threat was defeated. Power Transition theory anticipates that such alliances will persist only as long as necessary and will
be broken in response to changes in the short-term calculations. Alliances
between nations that do not share common preferences but nevertheless
cooperate are far less stable and are consequently easy to unravel. For example, the alliance between the United States and Saudi Arabia is clearly
not based on shared preferences, yet economic interactions and regional
goals preserve it. The commitment to defend Saudi Arabia from potential
harm from Iraq is credible. A similar commitment in the event of conflict
with Israel is far less likely.

Figure 1.7 shows the potential contribution of alliance members and
the resulting stability of such alliances in the face of war.[7] Alliances established beneath the 45-degree line are stable and enduring. This condition
flows from the combination of a positive valuation of the status quo and

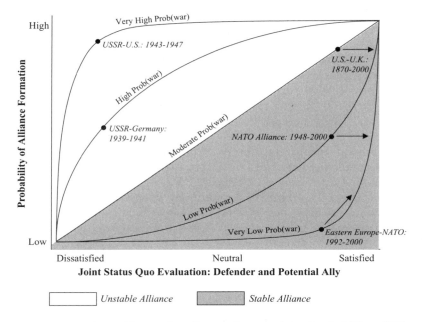

Figure 1.7 Alliance Formation, Status Quo, and the Probability of War

the low probability of conflict. During peacetime, these alliances are initiated and maintained by the shared policy goals of the nations. NATO, for example, was formed after World War II, aided in part by the Marshall Plan but also by the shared goals imprinted on the vanquished by an occupying force. It is specifically for this reason, shared policy goals, that democracies do not fight other democracies, and autocracies do not fight other autocracies.

Alliances formed above our 45-degree line are created in the shadow of war and thus are alliances of necessity. Nations maximize their relative power advantage to prevent defeat. The USSR and Western Allies entered into such an agreement to defeat Nazi Germany during World War II, but that alliance did not last beyond the war and eventually mutated into open hostility. Likewise, the Russian-German alliance lasted only a few years until Hitler chose to challenge the Russians.

Dynamics of Power

Power Transition postulates that a country's power is a function of population, productivity, and relative political capacity.[8] Power is measured by these three key elements, each with a different timing impact. Population size is relatively fixed and difficult to change in the short term. Economic growth changes more rapidly and affects power in the medium term. Finally, political capacity, which can be highly volatile, affects power in the short term.

The power measure advocated in Power Transition research is dynamic. Extensive tests show that this measure accurately accounts for the outcome of conflicts waged among fully committed competitors. Unlike alternate measures it accounts with equivalent accuracy for the outcome of conflicts between developed contenders and developed and developing opponents.

A number of competing conceptualizations of power or national capabilities are available, but most fail the twin tests of access to measurement and accounting for dynamic movement.[9] The most widely used measure in world politics is an aggregate of demographic, economic, and military components. National capability measures are effective in ranking the relations between nations but fail to capture the dynamics of power change.

Economic Growth

The foundation for economic growth described in figure 1.8 is adapted from current and future capital accumulation dynamics. Capital for our purpose is effectively reflected by national income and measured by gross domestic product (GDP) per capita. Political capacity, detailed below, is the ability of governments to extract resources from their populations in order to advance the policy goals of the government. Note that nations with limited GDP and low political capacity may fall into a "poverty trap." On the other hand, as economic growth starts, prompted by changes in political capacity, rapid economic growth is achieved. For this reason, fast rates of output change are concentrated among developing societies. When nations achieve relatively high levels of capital accumulation and maintain political capacity at average rates, output growth stabilizes and produces sustained growth at moderate levels.

Endogenous growth theory refines the characteristics of the stages of development originally proposed by Organski, reinforcing the tenets of Power Transition.[10] Endogenous growth theory shows that the technological revolution combined with political changes will help developed societies maintain steady growth rates, but will not allow them to remain ahead of rapidly developing countries. The dynamics of endogenous growth suggest that the distribution of capital and labor across societies will force output convergence because societies with relatively low rates of per-capita GDP will, if they avoid the poverty trap, enjoy high growth rate. Thus, efficient distribution of resources in market economies eventually will lead to convergence among all economies with sustained growth.

Figure 1.8 illustrates possible growth paths for societies at different stages in their economic growth.[11] Note that countries with different levels of political capacity have different growth trajectories. Nations with

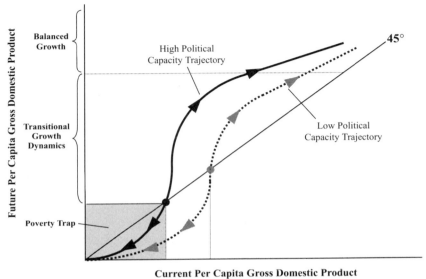

Figure 1.8 The Endogenous Growth Trajectory

high political capacity grow rapidly and achieve sustained growth much earlier. On the other hand, low political capacity governments maintain lower rates of economic growth and continue to flirt with the possibility of falling into the poverty trap. Figure 1.8 also illustrates the distinction between the direction of the growth path (indicated by the arrows located on the growth trajectories). Countries are either headed into the poverty trap (the lower left corner of the figure) or toward sustained economic growth (the upper right corner of the figure). For the path that leads to a poverty trap, political capacity and initial physical or human capital is so low that the economy will be caught in a low-income developmental trajectory. That is, when there is a paucity of physical and human capital, birth rates will be so high that human capital deaccumulates over generations. As a result, output will contract.[12]

Power Transition shows that the shifts in power associated with such dynamics have serious consequences for stability. The dynamics of national power growth cannot be changed dramatically by international interventions. Over the long term, political factors prompt changes in physical and human capital driven by technology and lead to economic convergence in per-capita terms. When societies with similar populations are at different stages in their growth paths, one dominates the other. When they are at the same stage, they achieve parity. From the perspective of war, the most potentially dangerous condition in the international system occurs when a society at the top of the global hierarchy, with a smaller population that has already achieved sustained growth, is passed by a rapidly growing nation with a much larger population. Such an overtaking greatly increases the likelihood of major war. Indeed, the story of the Western world can be summarized effectively by exploring the overtaking between, first, France and England, then England and Germany, and more recently the unsuccessful overtaking by the USSR of the United States (see chapter 2).

Despite the technological advantages of developed nations, challengers with high growth rates will rise in the international system due to the dynamics of convergence. The high differential in per-capita GDP between the United States and China clearly is a temporary condition that accounts for the current substantial power advantage of the United States. But American annual economic growth rates compare poorly with those of China, which are two to three times higher. Short of partition or decentralization, China eventually will become the world's largest economy. This process is no different than the several overtakings of the United Kingdom by Germany. Note that in two occasions world wars were fought, but following the last conflict, the EU emerged. An overtaking can produce war or peace, but it always changes the structure of the hierarchy. These dynamics have important policy ramifications for U.S.-Chinese relations, and future relations among China, the United States, and eventually India (see chapters 6 and 7).

Population

Of the three power variables, population is the sine qua non for great power status. Population is the potential resource pool that a nation can begin to mobilize through economic development. Productivity can be altered over the long run and relative political capacity can be changed in the short run by the imposition of new, more effective political controls. But without a large population, a nation cannot hope ever to become either a great power or a dominant nation. Population is not identical to great or dominant power status, but, if mobilized into a productive force and extracted for use at the national level, large populations offer enormous potential resources. Of the three variables, population is the least susceptible to rapid change. Governments can intervene economically to alter national productivity and politically to enhance the relative political capacity side of the equation, but in the short term, population growth rates are difficult to manage by government policy.[13]

The size of populations ultimately determines the power potential of a nation. Population is the element that determines in the long run which nations will remain major powers. France, England, and Germany were great powers when the rest of the world had not joined the industrial revolution. Today these nations no longer can hope to challenge individually for dominance in the global hierarchy. Despite their economic productivity, their population base is no longer sufficient to compete with national populations the size of those in the United States, Russia, China, or India.

A second aspect of population is critical in understanding how power grows in the international system. As figure 1.8 (see p. 17) suggests, mature developed nations have stable populations. These nations have fully undergone the demographic transition and are unlikely to expand their population base internally. Their only option for growth is through immigration. The major European nations and Japan have moved through this demographic transition. Some nations, such as France, Japan, and even Italy, may well have *declining* populations in this century. Developing nations, on the other hand, are still undergoing the demographic transition, and their populations continue to grow for twenty years or so even when fertility patterns are altered. As implied in figure 1.8, capable government creates an environment conducive to a demographic transition, thus boosting human capital and economic growth. Governments in developing nations that can increase government capacity will take control of the population expansion, accelerate investment in human capital, and attain self-sustaining growth.

While developing nations are able to reduce populations through a combination of political intervention and economic prosperity, it is very hard to increase a population in a developed society that already has undergone a power transition and has reached steady-state economic expansion. The most important implication of such power dynamics is that it is very difficult to reverse a power overtaking. Once France lost its premier position in Europe after Napoleon, it could no longer challenge Britain and Germany because both had the advantages of far larger populations. Likewise, England and Germany could no longer compete for world leadership when their colonies underwent the industrial revolution and became independent. Neither could confront the more populous Russia and the United States.

In the long run, the already prosperous United States cannot remain the dominant nation in the international system because both China and India have populations four times larger. This population gap cannot be bridged by a developed society. Therefore, because of the constraints that stable populations impose on the expansion of power in developed societies once Asian nations modernize and overtake the United States, no new transitions are anticipated. If the current roster of nations remains in place, it appears China and eventually India will become future dominant nations. Unless failed empires regenerate, no new subsequent overtakings will take place since no existing nations will have the potential to challenge either China or India and their overwhelming population advantages.

Political Capacity

The final component of national power is relative political capacity. Remembering that relative political capacity is the ability of governments to extract resources from their populations, the question is, which countries will be able to translate their economic vitality into national power? Focusing on the endogenous growth trajectory in figure 1.8, let us examine the possibilities.

Countries at the bottom of this growth trajectory with low levels of economic development have difficulty extracting resources from their populations, since individuals consume most if not all resources to support their daily existence. As nations develop, however, it does not necessarily follow that power increases either directly or proportionally. Among low and early growing nations, there is substantial variation in national ability to extract resources. Nations with strong political controls have leverage and can mobilize potential population resources into actual national power.

The Vietnam War provides a good example of the differences between potential and actual power. By virtue of effective political controls, North Vietnam extracted a higher proportion of resources from a smaller base population during the conflict. South Vietnam, with weak political controls yet a larger economic and demographic base, could not. Even substantial U.S. assistance and direct military intervention in support of the South Vietnamese could not give South Vietnam the edge.[14]

For countries with large populations and improving productivity on the steep portion of the growth trajectory, relative political capacity becomes the crucial variable for how powerful the state becomes. For example, should India, with a population of 1 billion, increase its per-capita productivity and then efficiently extract resources from its population, it would be on a trajectory to eventually challenge international leadership in the latter half of the twenty-first century. On the other hand, if Iraq were to undergo economic modernization and increase productivity, that nation could only aspire to challenge for dominance in its regional hierarchy due to the relatively small Iraqi population of about 20 million.

Countries at the top of the endogenous growth trajectory have mobilized most of the population and economic resources in their society and face increased costs for any marginal addition. It is physically impossible, for example, to double the extraction of resources in Sweden when the government already takes more than half of the available gross domestic product. Subsequently, these mature societies expand slowly both in economic and political development due in large part to technological advances. The lens of Power Transition allows a scholar or policymaker to see that political and economic changes are inescapably linked.

Why Conflict Arises in the International System

Overtaking

Most theories explain how and why conflict emerges in the international system only in the most generalized sense. Power Transition, however, has logical structures linking the core issues of conflict in the international system: the timing, initiation, costs, duration, and consequences of war. As such, it is unrivaled in scope and reach. It not only offers an explanation of why conflict occurs, but also describes and anticipates the characteristics of conflict and provides advice on how to manage conflict.

Two concepts define the structural conditions that greatly increase the probability of war. The first is *parity*. In Power Transition theory, parity exists in a hierarchy when a great power becomes a potential challenger and develops more than 80 percent of the resources of the dominant nation. Parity ends when the challenger exceeds the resources of the dominant nation by 20 percent.[15]

The second concept is *overtaking*, pictured generically in figure 1.9 (p. 22). Overtaking occurs when a rising power enters the steep growth portion of the endogenous growth trajectory and develops economically at a faster rate than the dominant power. In the overtaking process, the rising nation achieves parity either through increased productivity and/or political capacity and is poised to overtake the dominant nation in terms of relative power. This event greatly increases the probability of conflict.

Figure 1.9 displays the dynamics of Power Transition by illustrating the relative power relationships of a challenger and dominant nation over time. The solid line is the power trajectory of the defender/dominant power, and the dotted line is the power trajectory of the challenger. During the early time period, the dominant power has unambiguous power preponderance over the potential challenger, a superiority that is recognized by both sides. Note that the growth of the dominant power is relatively slow compared to that of the rising challenger because the dominant power has a mature economy. Under such conditions, war is highly unlikely; the expected outcome is peace. When a potential challenger is dissatisfied with the distribution of resources in the global or regional hierarchy but is incapable of altering the existing regime and its rules, it chooses peace over war.

This type of structural condition is depicted by relations in the Korean peninsula today. Despite its isolation and dissatisfaction with the existing order, North Korea can no longer challenge South Korea as it did in 1950. Although both nations argue that division is unacceptable, they have not reconciled governmental structures and continue to threaten each other across the demilitarized zone. Peace is preserved because South Korea now holds a preponderant advantage over the North and could compel the North in case of war. Indeed, assuming that third parties — such as the United States, China, or Russia — are not involved, any conflict on the Ko-

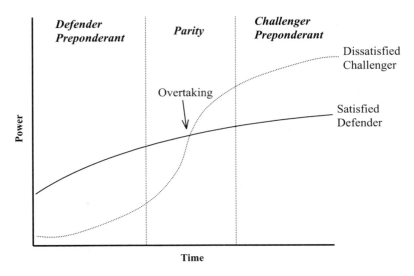

Figure 1.9 A Transition with a High Probability of War

rean peninsula would be short and would terminate with the imposition of South Korea's preferences over those of the North.

In figure 1.9 the challenger's high growth rate closes the relative power gap with the dominant power as they approach parity. While the dominant power remains superior, its ability to influence the challenger diminishes. In the zone of parity, both the challenger and the dominant power realize that an overtaking will take place. Here, Power Transition anticipates that war is likely to be waged when differences in perceptions about the status quo exist — that is, war will likely occur when the challenger is dissatisfied.

The classic condition for parity and overtaking may involve conflict. As figure 1.9 illustrates, war is the likely outcome when the challenger is dissatisfied and overtakes the defender. Recall that Germany and Great Britain fought long and bitterly in World Wars I and II precisely because Germany had overtaken Britain prior to each war and because Germany's leaders anticipated in each case that they had a fair chance of success due to a balance of forces. In general, overtakings provide the preconditions for conflict because the challenger anticipates a fair chance of winning. Yet mere parity, even accompanied by an overtaking, is not the direct cause of conflict. Parity and overtaking must be accompanied by a challenging state's determination to change the status quo and a willingness by its elite to incur significant risks in order to alter the rules of the existing hierarchy. From the defender's perspective, conditions for war are generated by the inability to persuade the challenger that its interests will be incorporated into the existing regime along with related changes in power structures.

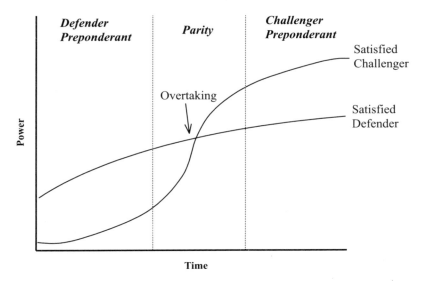

Figure 1.10   A Transition with a Low Probability of War

Parity and overtaking increase the probability that there will be an initiation of conflict. But, as illustrated in figure 1.10, the actual overtaking may be peaceful. This was the case of the United States and Great Britain at the end of the nineteenth century when both nations were satisfied. The United States' overtaking of Great Britain did not threaten the structure of the existing international order. It simply reinforced existing rules. Indeed, the reason that the dominant power does not preempt while it holds preponderance over a potential challenger is the hope for reconciliation of differences. If the dominant power and challenger were to realign preferences over time — as the United States and Great Britain did following the War of 1812 — a preemptive attack would not be necessary because satisfied challengers have a very low probability of initiating war with the dominant power.

This places Power Transition in accord with the proposition that democracies do not fight each other. For Power Transition, the important element is similarity of governments' foreign policy goals across time that fosters satisfaction with the status quo. Since the dominant power creates the global status quo in ways favorable to itself, it logically follows that similarly constituted states will also benefit from the status quo. Thus, states with economic and political institutions similar to those of the dominant power likely will be satisfied with the status quo. They will be peaceful with other satisfied and similar states. Democratic nations appear to generate and enjoy high degrees of satisfaction, arguably because the dominant

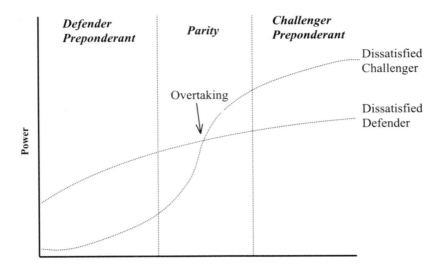

Figure 1.11   A Transition with a Very High Probability of War

power is a democracy. Political and economic similarity with the dominant state thus leads us to anticipate the existence of a democratic peace.[16]

Figure 1.11 illustrates the rare case of two equally matched dissatisfied powers at odds, a circumstance that has not occurred at the global level in modern times. Here both nations are at parity and face an impending overtaking, however neither is satisfied with the existing status quo and neither likes the status quo the other would establish. Such conditions may have been descriptive of relations between Egypt and Israel before the establishment of a regional status quo in their part of the Middle East. In such a case either side could initiate war because both are dissatisfied with the existing status quo. These rare conditions are the most dangerous in the international system. Wars are the expected outcome.

The Initiation of War

Power Transition is a powerful predictor of war in global and regional hierarchies because the specific confluence of parity and overtaking with at least one dissatisfied party are very rare events. At the global level following World War II, no nation has achieved parity with or threatened to overtake the United States. Consequently no great power wars have occurred. Between 1850 and 1950, on the other hand, Germany overtook the United Kingdom just prior to World War I and again just prior to World War II, thereby isolating this narrow period of opportunity for global conflict.[17]

A similar process takes place within regional hierarchies. For example, the conflict between Iran and Iraq was the result of Iraq's overtaking of Iran in the wake of the 1980 collapse of the Iranian political regime.[18]

Power relations are an important determinant of conflict when there are differences in the valuation of the status quo but not a material consideration when such differences are minimal. Nations can reduce the probability of war by reducing their differences. This is by no means easy. Dissatisfaction is based on perceived real differences between the populations in countries. A simple agreement will not nullify such effects. Populations have long memories. For example, it took time and major changes in government for European nations to accept that Germany was no longer a threat to their existence. Leaders are constrained by these enduring preferences of the populations because they have to respond to their desires of their public supporters to maintain political power. The acceptance of Germany as part of Europe has progressed far more among EU members than in the East European countries. Moreover, dramatic changes in the structure and behavior of the Russian leadership currently fall under persistent scrutiny in the United States. The important point here is that if differences between countries disappear, cooperation rather than confrontation becomes the rule.

Nations use two alternate means to ensure stability, deterrence, and satisfaction-building. In international interactions where confrontation is the rule, nations tend toward deterrence, which is a threat to respond in kind against anticipated challenges from an opponent. Clearly such nations also employ satisfaction-building measures, but they rely more heavily on their ability to increase costs to reduce probability of war. This is the story of the Cold War between the United States and the USSR, which ended not with reconciliation between these two opponents, but because of the collapse of the USSR. Ultimately, when a very dissatisfied nation cannot resolve its differences with the defender, they will resort to war. This was the case of Nazi Germany and England in 1939. When a power transition occurs, it takes a single *dissatisfied* challenger to initiate a conflict while it takes two *satisfied* nations to preserve peace.

In the nuclear environment, considered in further detail in chapter 4, the overall probability of war is attenuated because costs increase. Leaders will think far more carefully before initiating a conflict that has the potential for enormous casualties than in the case of a war with very limited consequences. Thus, when two satisfied nations acquire nuclear weapons, there is little potential for conflict regardless of power relations — as was the case between Britain and France after 1945. When a satisfied nation acquires nuclear weapons, as did the United States during the Cold War, the probability of war decreases and remains low until a dissatisfied challenger reaches parity. When a dissatisfied nation acquires nuclear weapons, as did the USSR after 1950, or when jointly dissatisfied nations do so, as is the

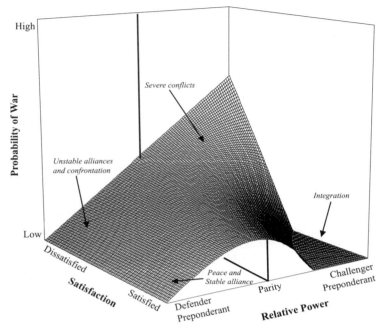

Figure 1.12   Relative Power, and Satisfaction, and the Probability of War

case for Pakistan and India today, the probability of war increases as they approach parity. Mutual assured destruction (MAD), therefore, from the power transition perspective is a tenuous condition that should be avoided rather than encouraged.

Power, Satisfaction, and Conflict

A summary of the arguments we have made thus far can best be visualized by displaying the relationship between relative power, degree of satisfaction, and the probability of conflict (see figure 1.12).[19] Note that as an overtaking occurs, if the challenger becomes satisfied, then the probability of war declines precipitously, sometimes leading to integration. The new preponderant power becomes a defender of the status quo under stable conditions, as we indicated was the case between England and the United States at the beginning of the twentieth century. In those cases where the defender fails to accommodate during the overtaking and the challenger continues to be dissatisfied, the probability of war is very high. Further, this probability increases after parity, leading to a very long period with a high probability of war. This was the case between Germany and the United Kingdom during the first half of the twentieth century. The choice now facing the United

States and China is to avoid the trap of dissatisfaction and transition, which greatly raises the probability of war.

Parity and overtaking set the timing conditions for conflict. But as we show above, even in tandem they cannot explain why some overtakings result in war and why others are peaceful. Satisfaction is the third variable critical to the calculation.

Great powers engage in conflict over preferences and policy differences and these stem from a country's sense of satisfaction. Satisfied nations are not expected to engage in conflict even if there is an overtaking among them. A peaceful transfer of responsibilities and leadership is anticipated due to the economic and security gains they derive from the international system. On the other hand, a dissatisfied challenger overtaking a dominant country calculates that its prospects for victory are increased by its rapid growth in power. Being dissatisfied with the international system, the leaders of these nations are conditioned to seek changes to the status quo. Parity, therefore, brings them opportunity. And they are likely to seize that opportunity at some point in the overtaking period. Dissatisfied challengers are disproportionately likely to initiate wars.

A challenger consumed with grievances may seek redress early in the parity period only to find its power and alliance system insufficient to achieve success. A more cautious challenger, having overtaken the dominant country, will aim for more than a redress of grievances. It will seek to establish an international system under its own rules and this will give rise to a war of great ferocity. It should be pointed out that statistically for wars among all states, initiators have won their wars far more frequently than defenders, but in major wars this trend is reversed as allies join the defender of the status quo to ensure their survival.[20]

One question that needs to be posed is, why doesn't a dominant power take advantage of its enormous power advantages, prior to parity, to initiate war against its real or potential enemies? The answer rests with the hierarchical system established by the dominant power. The dominant nation has created a system with standard rules and norms providing economic and security benefits. It has a supporting cast of satisfied nations. Under these conditions, initiating conflict is counterproductive since the dominant nation would abrogate the rules and cause uncertainty in the alliance of satisfied states, even possibly tearing it apart. Having set the international rules and norms, the dominant nation cannot disrupt them by its own actions without serious loss of support. Instead, by preserving the status quo, the dominant nation seeks to attract as many satisfied countries as possible to secure its preponderance. The formation of NATO demonstrates that the United States did not seek simply a balance of power with the USSR but rather a preponderance of power in order to minimize the risks of war. Most satisfied nations responded by bandwagoning[21] to create an overwhelming coalition against the Soviet Union.

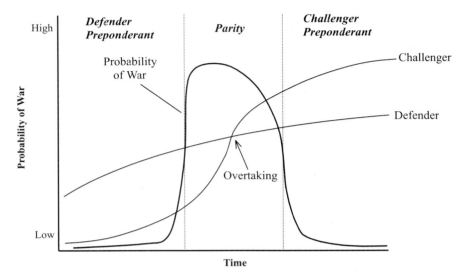

Figure 1.13 The Timing of War

Being reluctant to take on a potential challenger when it has clear supe-riority, the dominant power is even less likely to do so when that challenger becomes more powerful. Having passed up the opportunity to rid itself of an irritant early on, it now finds that the costs of war against a more power-ful challenger are increasingly high.[22] Once the dominant country sets the rules at the international level, its actions are inhibited by adherence to the status quo that it has devised.

The Timing of War

Understanding the logic of overtaking provides a perspective on the timing of war. Wars between great powers occur at specified times within the pe-riod of relative power parity. Examined from the other side of the coin, figure 1.13 shows that great power wars do not occur when there is a clearly superior dominant power. Imbalances of power preserve the peace. Conditions of relative equality or parity create the potential for conflict. Balances are warning signals of potential war.

The original presentation of Power Transition postulated that wars are initiated before the actual overtaking but after the challenger had entered the period of parity.[23] Follow-up research concluded that wars would occur after the overtaking.[24] Power Transition scholars continue to debate this question. The most recent research indicates that the probability of war in-creases prior to the overtaking but the severity of any war that does occur in this early parity period is diminished. After the overtaking, the probabil-

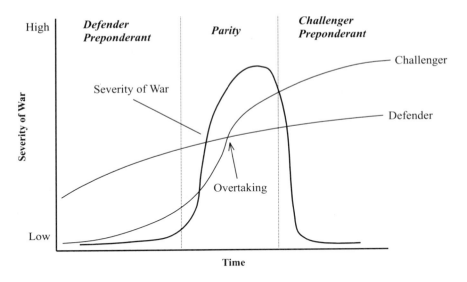

Figure 1.14 The Severity of War

ity of war decreases, but the severity of war increases. Thus, wars after an overtaking are rare but extraordinarily bloody (such as World Wars I and II), while more frequent confrontations of lesser magnitude occur before overtakings.[25]

The Severity of War

The severity of war depends on the timing of the outbreak of conflict during the parity period. As figure 1.14 shows, if a challenger miscalculates and initiates war early in the parity period, it faces significant risks. The dominant country has created a strong alliance structure and consequently has enormous resources to call upon to head off the challenge. In this situation, war will be expensive for the challenger but not as costly for the international system as under other scenarios. Later in the parity period, however, conditions have changed. First, the challenger has grown more powerful than the dominant country. Second, the dominant nation's alliance system will have weakened appreciably as some supporting great powers recognize the fundamental shift occurring in the international system and begin to decouple from the dominant power, if not realign completely with the challenger. The shift in these two conditions suggests that wars in the parity period following a transition will be intense and costly. World Wars I and II followed power transitions as anticipated while the Franco-Prussian War of 1870, for example, occurred at the time of overtaking.[26]

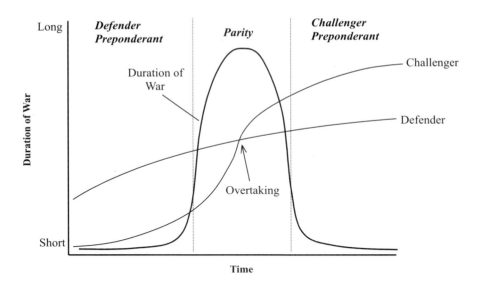

Figure 1.15 The Duration of War

The Duration of War

Power Transition also provides a guide to understanding the duration of war. Figure 1.15 shows that as a dissatisfied challenger approaches parity and overtaking with the dominant nation, the duration of any war that may occur increases dramatically. This reflects the relatively equal power that each nation brings to bear during a conflict. As neither the dominant nation nor the challenger possess a unilateral power advantage, both are likely to engage in a war of attrition. Hoping to wear the other side down, each side is fighting with an equal chance of winning due to their relatively equal power. World Wars I and II are testimony to the almost equal power of primary combatants and alliances in a costly and drawn-out war. The longer two rival nations are in relative parity, the longer the duration of any war they might fight. As either the challenger or dominant nation achieves a relative power advantage, the expected duration of war decreases. This is due to one side achieving an advantage over the other, increasing the likelihood of that side prevailing and the war therefore terminating.

Speed of Overtaking and War

There is some evidence linking the speed of the overtaking with the severity of war. Faster overtakings appear to lead to a lower probability of war and slower overtakings increase the probability of war. Integrating these empirical observations results in the conclusion that longer, slower transitions temporarily postpone conflict but may eventually result in the most severe wars. Shorter, faster transitions increase the likelihood but lower the severity of war.[27]

There is a policy logic to these conclusions. With fast overtakings, the two countries are in parity for a short period of time and there is relatively less opportunity for policy disputes to develop into war. But with slower transitions, these policy disputes have time to develop irreversible momentum leading to war.

Power Transition scholars agree that the period of parity remains as the zone of contention and probable war. The theory holds that conflict can occur anytime during the parity period but the probabilities and consequences vary with the specific conditions of that transition. The longer nations are in relative parity, the higher the probability of war and the longer the duration of any war they may fight.

The Consequences of War

When major war is waged, the relative resources among the great powers are redistributed. Contrary to expectations, nations recover relatively quickly from the consequences of war.[28] Dominant and other great powers can engage in war and return to their earlier position in the international system after one generation. For an advanced nation, the time necessary to catch up to its prewar growth pattern is less than twenty years. Power Transition theorists call this the *Phoenix Factor.*[29]

Because of the Phoenix Factor, the outcomes of great power wars do not change long-term growth rates. However, wars do have a dramatic effect on the distribution of satisfaction and dissatisfaction in the international system.[30] The lessons of devastating wars are that peace and stability is short-lived if dissatisfaction is allowed to flourish among the vanquished. A punitive peace, or a peace without efforts to reconstitute the vanquished state as a satisfied member, is likely to be a short peace. The restructuring of political systems in Germany and Japan and the provision of postwar assistance programs were designed to transform those nations from dissatisfied to satisfied societies.

The policy implications of Power Transition's Phoenix Factor are instructive. Following a conflict, the dominant nation must find ways to reconcile the norms and values of the defeated challenger (who will be in the position to challenge again within one generation) with its own. Otherwise, conflict will once more loom on the horizon. Thus, despite the fact that the power distributions following both world wars were very similar, the United States chose to transform the vanquished states after World War II and achieved a stable environment where power transitions among European great powers did not generate war due to widespread satisfaction. On the other hand, the French and English emphasized punishment of Germany following World War I, and reestablished great dissatisfaction among the vanquished Germans, who subsequently attempted once more to bid for dominance in the international system.

War in the Nuclear Age

Power Transition theory recognizes that the cost of war is not a perfect deterrent to the initiation of war. Nations are not universally nor uniformly deterred by the specter of massive costs. Rather, they are driven by dissatisfaction coupled with the opportunity for success presented by changes in relative power positions. This has distinct and important policy implications for the nuclear age. It also runs counter to the prevailing doctrine of the Cold War period.

The doctrine of mutual assured destruction declared that, despite whatever differences might divide them, nations with secure second-strike forces would be deterred from initiating nuclear war. Under these conditions, it was argued, nuclear war was rendered irrational and unthinkable. Thus "safety will be the sturdy child of terror, and survival the twin brother of annihilation,"[31] and the possibility of deliberate war was minimized if not eliminated.[32] Mutual assured destruction was the logical extension of balance of power theory into the nuclear age. It brought with it all the intellectual failings of the former and none of the promised security.

That there was no war between the United States and the USSR during this period is often cited as a confirmation of doctrinal success. Freed from the restraints of Cold War orthodoxy, this comfortable conclusion can now be debated. In retrospect, the degree of relative safety enjoyed by the United States was higher before the Cuban Missile Crisis than after. In our view, the period of MAD was by no means reassuring. Bounded by serious discussions on topics such as "launch on warning," post-attack survival capacities, national minimum and maximum death statistics, nuclear effects overlays on major cities, not to mention movies and television programs dealing with "day after" themes, it certainly did not "feel" like a safer period of time than today. Preponderance "feels" a good deal more secure.

The classic balance of power/mutual assured destruction logic suggested that the spread of nuclear deterrence ensured the peace. When a larger number of nations reached nuclear equality and entered the condition of mutual assured destruction, the theory argues, the likelihood of war among them decreased for the same reasons it did for the United States and the USSR during the Cold War. Pushing this argument to its logical extreme, the United States, Russia, and China should advocate the transfer of nuclear weapons to Iraq and Iran to diminish the probability of war between them and with Israel. Moreover, the nuclear tests undertaken by India and Pakistan should be viewed by classic MAD proponents as a welcome addition that brings stability to the region. And, in fact, some theorists take this position.[33]

Power Transition resolves this contradiction between proliferation and deterrence. The acquisition of nuclear weapons is not a remedy for conflict. The reconciliation of preferences, the attainment of satisfaction within the international order, is the remedy. Nuclear weapons in the hands of satisfied powers pose no threat. Nuclear weapons in the hands of dissatisfied powers, the risk takers of the international system, pose unusually severe threats. Power Transition does not hold that dissatisfied nuclear powers will be deterred from using those weapons by some nuclear counterbalance. Rather, the choice for war will relate to the twin pillars of power parity — determined by a nation's population, economic development, and political capacity — and opportunity for redress of grievance.[34] It is for this reason that the United States has invested so much to deny Iraq nuclear capability. Finally, Power Transition suggests that China not only must be watched at a global level when it overtakes the United States, but must be monitored within its regional hierarchy if India becomes a regional challenger in the mid- to late-twenty-first century. Overtakings, dissatisfaction, and nuclear weapons do not mix without serious consequences.

The Management of World Politics

Managing Alliances

Power Transition conceives of alliances as stable coalitions of states with similar evaluations of the status quo. Stable alliances are not agreements of convenience that can be altered easily or with few consequences. A case in point is the Allied coalition with the USSR during World War II, which was a temporary, unstable, and unreliable association that fell apart immediately after the end of the common conflict. In contrast, stable alliances in Power Transition are arrangements of persuasion where nations associate because of commonly held commitments to existing rules and the economic and security gains thus derived, as exemplified by U.S.-British relations and the larger NATO coalition. Such alliances tend to be long term with few defections. They are reliable because of the congruence of interest among the members.

Alliances created by the dominant power are designed to strengthen the stability of the system by creating a preponderance of satisfied countries. A successful dominant power attracts a large number of great and middle powers and some small powers in support of its leadership. Nations joining the dominant power become part of a status quo alliance system. U.S. foreign policy in the postwar era provides a clear example.

The objective of NATO is not and has not been simply the defense of the associated nations from an attack by the Warsaw Pact. Mutual security has been the dominating focus in public discourse and the vehicle used to justify the alliance within the capitals of NATO countries. But an equally important and perhaps even superior objective, according to Power Transition theory, is the maintenance of stability within Europe and the cementing of ties to the United States. NATO, under U.S. guidance, ensured that power overtakings among France, England, and Germany did not lead to the repetition of World Wars I and II. Satisfied alliance members do not fight one another.

Looking toward the future from the Power Transition perspective, the dominant power should attempt to integrate new members into the alliance as part of a larger effort of defending the status quo and converting states where necessary from dissatisfied to satisfied nations. The benefits for the dominant nation are obvious. It expands its pool of resources and supporters while transforming potential rivals into allies.

What then are the implications for NATO expansion? Power Transition justifies the expansion of NATO to Poland, Hungary, and the Czech Republic and to all others who now share the values (democracy and economic growth) and accept the rules (status quo) of the dominant power. This incorporation, however, does not substantially alter the distribution of power in the international system. The addition of small, newly satisfied countries is welcome but it does not change fundamental power relationships in the international system.

From the perspective of the current dominant power, the United States, the most important near-term adjustment it could make to the international alliance system is the integration of Russia into NATO. This would serve two purposes. First, it would accelerate the development of a satisfied nation out of one that retains the potential to revert to dissatisfied status. Second, it would significantly add to the pool of resources of the dominant country. The tight integration of Russia into the U.S.-led international system would be the largest single step to preserve the stability of the international system that can be taken in the near future.

Such an effort would certainly address complaints that current NATO expansion makes Russia feel isolated and threatened. To carry this argument to its next logical point, the subsequent foreign policy goal of the United States should be the creation of a satisfied China, either by direct integration into an alliance or by creating opportunities to socialize it into the existing international system whereby it accepts prevailing rules and norms. In both cases — Russia and China — the United States would be taking action to avoid a potential challenge by a dissatisfied power. In the case of China, an expansion of NATO to include this nation may help in creating the conditions for a peaceful overtaking, should that occur, thus reducing the possibility of global war.

Managing International Organizations

International organizations are institutional tools used by the dominant power and its supporting great powers to codify and/or adjust rules and norms.[35] International organizations also create conditions and arenas for resolving disputes that might foment conflict in dissatisfied nations. The permanent membership of the UN Security Council constitutes a useful vehicle for understanding the Power Transition perspective on managing international organizations.

The Power Transition perspective has important implications for international organizations. For example, permanent membership on the Security Council of the United Nations accurately represents a snapshot of the international power distribution immediately after World War II. The United States, Great Britain, France, and the Soviet Union were the great powers of that time. Since that time, however, the same economic modernization process that propelled these states to great power status has changed the power hierarchy. Great Britain and France have declined in power relative to Germany and Japan. The exclusion of Germany and Japan from permanent membership on the Security Council was logical at that time since they were defeated adversaries and did not hold substantial power. However, given their economic growth, their exclusion is no longer consistent with the current power hierarchy.

To enhance managerial ability and maintain satisfaction in the international system, permanent membership on the Security Council should reflect the current global power hierarchy. That translates into a permanent membership composed of the United States, China, Germany, Japan, Russia, and eventually India. Should that unlikely adjustment come to pass, the exclusion of the United Kingdom and France from the Security Council could be seen as weakening that body. But this would not necessarily be the result because both are satisfied members of the dominant coalition, and England is the most loyal ally of the United States. While this proposal may seem radical, it simply implies that the Security Council should not be static. In the future, India or some other viable candidate might emerge to replace Japan or Germany. Only by reflecting the current power reality can the Security Council play its critical role as a mediator of disputes, peacekeeper, and peacemaker.

Managing Satisfaction

To preserve the existing status quo, the principal objective of the dominant country and its closest allies is to expand satisfaction in the international system. The dominant country must be careful not to allow disputes or perceptions of inequitable treatment to metastasize into dissatisfaction with the system. This is particularly true among great powers that are or eventually could become challengers. This means that the dominant country must meet two foreign policy challenges: the creation of binding economic associations and the resolution of territorial disputes.

Power Transition theory suggests that the purpose of economic communities such as WTO, NAFTA, and the EU is to provide economic benefits that enhance satisfaction within the dominant country's coalition. The redistribution of benefits creates and maintains high levels of satisfaction in the dominant nation's alliance system and attracts energized members to the leading coalition while preventing conflict. If these economic communities stimulate growth, then this effort has the collateral benefit of adding to the power resources of the satisfied camp. This is an important consideration if a significant challenger appears. The record of NATO and the Warsaw Pact is a lasting testimony of how the United States used its economic and military preponderance to solidify its position over a potential challenge by the USSR. Support for the European Union provided the economic backbone, while the commitment to NATO yielded an enduring security arrangement that could not be challenged by a Soviet-led coalition.

Coalitions aside, territorial disputes remain important generators of conflict.[36] They have the potential to create long-lasting polarization often characterized by intractable positions colored by ideological or nationalist rhetoric. This is the breeding ground of national dissatisfaction. For this reason, the dominant country must go to great lengths to ensure that members of its own alliance do not enter into open conflict. The United States and NATO have been remarkably successful in managing internal conflict, with the arguable exception of Greece and Turkey's dispute over Cyprus. Although that conflict remains, clearly a cap has been imposed on the acceptable limits of Greek and Turkish policy actions. NATO efforts in the former Yugoslavia reflect the sensitivity of the alliance system to conflict. Despite some voices of disapproval in the Congress, U.S.-NATO leadership was imperative, not just for human rights purposes but to reduce the threats to national borders in an area of potential NATO expansion. That Russia, Turkey, Greece, and Iran have interests in the Balkans makes it even more critical that the United States managed the Kosovo crisis from the standpoint of its own international power interests.

Using the NATO alliance to limit territorial disputes among allies has distinct benefits for the United States. Within NATO, United States preeminence is an accepted value and its leadership role is virtually unchallenged. Within the United Nations, however, the U.S. role is circumscribed by the veto rights of the Security Council's permanent members and the disparate pressures of the broader international community. Thus the NATO alliance continues to serve its paramount purpose of unifying satisfied nations under the leadership of the dominant nation, and it remains the most efficient tool for the resolution of potentially conflictual situations.

Lastly, it should be noted that the Soviet Union was also successful in controlling territorial disputes within its coalition, the Warsaw Pact.

Unlike the United States in NATO, the Soviet Union resorted to limited conflict in order to retain Hungary, Poland, and Czechoslovakia in its sphere of influence. The strength of the USSR's conflict management can only be appreciated by comparison to current instabilities in the former Soviet Union.

Disruptive territorial disputes may occur outside the dominant country's coalition. Taiwan and China are relevant, if not potentially explosive, examples. The United States has moved to defuse this situation by the skillful application of the "One China" policy and the "Three Communiqués." Had China been part of the U.S. alliance system, this would be a much easier problem to address. Because China rests outside the U.S. system and because it has the potential to be a challenger, the Taiwan issue takes on significance well beyond its geographical context. The United States cannot afford to allow the China-Taiwan dispute to polarize U.S.-Chinese relations or poison the relationship to the extent that China becomes an aggressive, dissatisfied power (see chapter 7).

The situation on the Korean peninsula presents another potential application of Power Transition strategy. The potential for conflict has now passed as North Korea is no longer a viable regional contender vis-à-vis South Korea. Instability on the peninsula is driven by the isolation and dissatisfaction of North Korea but it no longer has the power to challenge the South. When parity existed between North and South Korea during the 1950s, the United States prevented an invasion by the dissatisfied North. Today with South Korea being predominant, the United States' role is to bring both nations into a relationship that resolves territorial issues and encourages the long-term prospects of a satisfied Korean peninsula.

As seen before, one of the most important insights derived from Power Transition is that peace is preserved when nations are satisfied with the international order. The capability of Russia to attack the United States with nuclear weapons has diminished but remains significant, even though its conventional capabilities have been reduced dramatically. However, the United States no longer considers such an attack to be likely. This represents a drastic change in expectations. The difference before and after 1991 is not so much the collapse of the Soviet Union, but the change in attitudes within that country toward cooperation with the West. The fundamental reforms of a democratic structure, an emerging market economy, and the extension of civil liberties to Russian citizens has contributed more to stability than the reduction of armaments.

Managing Power

With a mature economy growing at lower rates, a dominant country may find a fast-growing challenger arising from the ranks of the great powers. Being at different stages of economic development, it is impossible for the dominant country to accelerate its growth rate to compensate for a challenger located on the steep portion of its endogenous growth trajectory. How then does a dominant nation stay ahead and avoid an overtaking?

The dominant power faces two realities. Since substantial gains in relative power can no longer be generated internally, it must resort to adding external resources. It does so by expanding its alliance system, by expanding its economic reach, or both.[37] Over time the dominant power will attempt to bring new members into its alliance including, where possible, formerly dissatisfied powers. Each new acquisition adds to the power base of the alliance, the pool of resources that could be called upon in an emergency. This alliance system is not intended to "balance off" power with other systems and thus deter war. Its purpose is to acquire overwhelming preponderance of power and the resources sufficient to head off any fast-growing challenger. When looking to augment alliance resources, the dominant power could bring in many smaller countries, if available, or more efficiently find one large nation whose addition would make a sizable difference. If that nation was formerly dissatisfied so much the better. This is exactly the argument for why Russia should now be incorporated into NATO.

In some situations, formal alliance acquisitions may not be possible or even desired. Some acquisitions may be too costly for the dominant country or the other aligned great powers. With these constraints, the dominant power can then look to expanding economic alliances as an alternative device to increase the pool of resources available to the system.

Economic relationships are useful devices since they bypass the formal structures required of alliance association. Countries may, at least initially, disagree on some policy issues yet find common ground in the economic arena. The dominant country can reach out to a broader range of countries and pull them into its policy orbit through interlocking economic agreements. These agreements create reciprocal centers of self-interest in both countries, and by themselves, without other stimuli, may cause countries to resolve political differences. For this reason, economic agreements are the most subtle and least appreciated tools of the dominant power. The U.S. policy success in Europe following World War II is a classic example of effective power management by a dominant nation. Today, attempts to align Russia among market economy democracies could set the stage for an expanded European Union. Similarly, manipulation of economic incentives remains one of the most powerful policy tools the United States can wield in its relationship with China.

Globalization, which is the extension of internationally accepted rules and norms through non-state actors, also is a powerful asset of the dominant power. It is a subtle, indirect means of spreading satisfaction. Even if there is some erosion of nation-state power as a result of globalization, the overall interests of the dominant power are well served by extending the commercial and cultural systems it, in large measure, created. In some ways, globalization can be a more effective tool for influencing dissatisfied states, such as China, than direct U.S. initiatives.

In a similar fashion, information technology, with its ability to penetrate borders, open new markets, distribute information, create constituencies, and tie together common interests, serves the purposes of a status quo dominant power. While information dominance may increase the relative power of the leading nation for a time, its more useful purpose flows from the creation of subnational communities of interlocking self-interests. The information age may well be a principal vehicle for creating and distributing satisfaction.

Not all problems can be solved by the promise of mutually favorable economic relations. Intractable difficulties occur when neither the prospects for alliance nor economic association are attractive inducements for key nations. This can be seen in the Middle East, where the passions of ideology, religion, and culture outweigh the promises of alliance and economic integration. This is the reason that the Middle East always seems to be a "special case" in international politics.

Managing Nuclear Weapons

Nuclear weapons have changed the calculus of war. Unlike previous periods of time when dominant powers could defeat challengers while minimizing costs, nuclear weapons have raised the cost threshold dramatically, even for the winner. The costs or severity of war now are inversely related to the probability of war. Power Transition views nuclear proliferation as the single most dangerous element in the international system. Yet, that fact does not eliminate the possibility of very intense, if infrequent, war. When the conditions of overtaking and dissatisfaction are present, the probability of war is high, nuclear weapons *notwithstanding*. Nuclear deterrence is tenuous. The deterrent qualities of nuclear weapons are not absolute in the face of a rising dissatisfied challenger.

Nuclear proliferation increases the likely severity without eliminating the possibility of war. This is particularly threatening in the regional hierarchies where there could be numerous transitions in the relatively near future. From a Power Transition perspective, the proliferation of nuclear weapons to a given region, such as the Middle East, is particularly dangerous since transitions frequently occur there among dissatisfied, risk-taking states.

The Middle East is stable because Israel now is a preponderant nuclear power. If Iran or Iraq were to achieve nuclear parity, few doubt the region would remain stable. The proliferation of nuclear warheads to India and Pakistan offers a different perspective. Pakistan cannot hope to match the relative power potential of India over the long term. There will be no overtaking here. Thus a major war is not likely to occur, with or without nuclear arsenals. However, in the long term India's nuclear capability may increase that country's threat to China and an overtaking could occur between these two adversaries. This should give pause to those who assume that nuclear parity between rivals somehow makes the world a safer place.

Although proliferation of nuclear weapons has not been as widespread as technology permits, this could change over time. With proliferation and the multiplication of MAD-like conditions within hierarchies, deterrence becomes increasingly unstable. Assuming that few nations will give up nuclear weapons, as did South Africa, the Ukraine, and Kazakhstan, the challenge for a dominant power and its coalition is to guarantee that emerging nuclear weapons states are satisfied. Satisfied nations do not risk war.

Managing Local Crises

The United States cannot become the policeman of the world, even given its position as the dominant power and the leader of a great power coalition of historically unrivaled strength. The United States does not control and has only marginal influence over the fundamental growth rates of countries. The World Bank or International Monetary Fund (IMF) may influence China, India, or Indonesia but only marginally. The historical growth patterns of these countries are related to more fundamental pressures expressed domestically from their resource base.

Given rapid growth rates, overtakings, and dissatisfied challengers, conflict can be expected in many local hierarchies throughout the globe. The dominant power and its coalition will not see value in intervening in each case. The costs may be too high relative to the gains, there may not be a galvanizing rationale for intervention, or attention may be diverted to other issues. Whatever the reason, the dominant power must concentrate its attention on its key responsibilities, which are the maintenance and aggregation of its power at the global level, the satisfaction of its coalition member states, and the management of possible challengers. This means the United States should not attempt to intervene at will. It has more pressing responsibilities. It has to pick and choose which foreign policy crises deserve its attention, based upon the geostrategic vision that asks: *what actions, policy, and alliances can provide relative power preponderance or create satisfaction with the status quo within a regional hierarchy?*

Potential conflicts in local and regional hierarchies could be minimized with the suggestions offered in the discussion of managing international organizations. If local dominant and challenging powers in a local hierarchy are brought into the UN Security Council for deliberations on issues central to their regions, then the likelihood of a peaceful solution increases and the necessity for intervention by the dominant power decreases. For this reason, a successful dominant nation should adopt a globalist perspective and avoid the temptation to maximize short-term national sovereignty at the expense of long-term instability. The United States correctly focused on the USSR during the Cold War and should focus equal attention on China's territorial concerns over Taiwan and its internal economic development patterns. If these situations cannot be resolved so that the disputants accrue positive political and economic gains from the status quo — or any policy solution close to the status quo — it is in the dominant nation's interest to create unilateral power preponderance over the disputants.

Advance Warnings for Crisis Management

Power Transition is not only a useful description of the structure and dynamics of international politics, but more importantly it is a powerful tool for the policymaker. It provides a framework for understanding great power relationships as well as regional politics. As a dynamic theory, it constantly adjusts to the changing realities of power fluctuations and the resulting consequences for peace and war. It tells us which nations to watch for hostile intent, and when that intent may take the form of action. Specifically, it alerts policymakers in advance when conditions favor the outbreak of war.

Power Transition theory describes an international system under which dominant countries attempt to preserve world stability as well as regional stability within hierarchies. While it gives highly useful long-term guidance, it does not provide immediate policy advice on specific issues. It is, after all, a grand theory that identifies the preconditions for conflict. How to manipulate current policy to meet those conditions is beyond the scope of such systemic theory. However, Power Transition does identify general principles for how to manage foreign policy conduct, what positions to adopt, and which foreign policy interests are crucial.

For example, Power Transition theory shows that nuclear proliferation in the regional context is an especially dangerous prospect because of the likelihood of future regional overtakings and the concomitant risk of war among then nuclear states. But the theory does not give specific advice on policy implementation, nor on how to prevent the proliferation of nuclear or any other weapons of mass destruction in a specific case. This should not leave Power Transition practitioners with a feeling of helplessness. Widespread acceptance and use as one of the principles of international relations will foster the selection of appropriate policies that minimize the likelihood of conflict.

New tools are available to help the policymaker translate Power Transition theory into specific policy recommendations. The theory itself has a rich flow of general policy recommendations as discussed above. But for specific policy implementation and execution issues, and questions involving multiple actors with various intensities of influence and interests, we must turn to decision theory for assistance.[38]

The marriage between structural-dynamic theories such as Power Transition and decision-making approaches is powerful indeed. Structural-dynamic theories illuminate the conditions that are desirable to achieve in the international system, while decision theory provides the roadmap to specific ends. From the policy perspective, Power Transition provides the foreign policy goals and objectives while decision theory provides the means of execution. We do not intend to describe decision theory here since it is not the focus of this book. But we would be remiss not to highlight it as an extraordinary tool for the policymaker interested in manipulating complex political and economic variables.

Conclusions and Projections

The international system currently is composed of four large power centers: the United States, Europe, Russia, and China. India represents a fifth potential center. Beyond these five, no other large country or regional alliance currently appears to have the requisite resources, in terms of population-productivity-political capacity, to overtake the large power centers.

Under these circumstances, we forecast a limited number of future great power transitions. From today's vantage point, there are only two possibilities looming on the horizon. The first is China overtaking the United States, and the second, in the last half of the twenty-first century, is India overtaking either China or the United States. If China and India develop as satisfied great powers, then these transitions will occur under peaceful conditions. If they develop with significant grievances against the international system, then these transitions could result in war.

The timing of these possible transitions will depend, of course, on the relative growth rates, productivity, and political mobilization of the United States and the challengers. China will be the first to overtake the United States in terms of GDP but it will take many more years before that momentum can be channeled into actual power. Likewise, there are many pitfalls along this road. Chinese growth rates may slow; the central government may weaken or even collapse in the face of regional power bases; political mobilization may fragment with the dissolution of Communist Party controls. A Chinese challenge is by no means assured. Moreover, there is sufficient time for the United States to manage — through the extension of NATO to include Russia or India, for example — an emerging transition so as to avoid conflict. The transition with China could be either peaceful or dangerous. It is simply too early to tell. The development of India is much farther in the future and equally uncertain. The largest democracy in the world has just adopted a limited market economy and lags behind China in economic development. However, its population is expected to surpass that of China around 2040 and thus could pose both a regional and global threat.

Transitions will continue to occur within the local hierarchies, perhaps at even higher rates than now. There are a significant number of potential transitions lurking in Africa, the Middle East, and portions of Asia. This will give rise to preconditions for a continuing succession of conflicts at the regional level. The time and attention of the great powers will be greatly stressed by this eruption of conflict from below. Because they remain satisfied great powers, even if they come into policy conflict with one another, such as over supporting rival local hierarchical combatants, they will resolve these differences without resort to conflict at the international level. This will place a premium on the development and execution of peacekeeping and peacemaking skills, attributes we are just beginning to learn now.

While the prospect of war is unpleasant, the corollary is quite optimistic, perhaps even utopian. If great powers do not splinter like the USSR, if the European Union remains united, and if economic development patterns stay on course altering the power rankings among great powers as predicted, then the stage is set for a remarkable, even unique, period in history. If transitions involving China and India materialize and are resolved peacefully, then the top of the international system would no longer contain dissatisfied challengers. No new challengers would be likely to ascend from below. Therefore, the preconditions for great power conflict would be absent. We would enter a new age: *the age of great power peace.*

CHAPTER 2
Power Transition Theory Tested in the Nineteenth and Twentieth Centuries

More than an end to war, we want an end to the beginnings of all wars. — FRANKLIN DELANO ROOSEVELT

Since the dawn of the industrial revolution, population, economic productivity, and political organization have been the building blocks of national power. Since these variables change over time, there have been massive power shifts in the international system. As seen in chapter 1, great powers are the few nations at the apex of the global hierarchy capable of affecting the structure and distribution of power. Therefore, the story of the great powers is particularly important.

Historically, the great powers repeatedly lose ground relative to newly emerging nations. When this infrequent yet important power overtaking is underway, dissatisfied nations at the bottom of the great power hierarchy may rise to challenge the established leaders. Such challenges result in wars, which are very costly in terms of political, economic, and human resources. Successful challenges are followed by a major transference of power and privilege from the dominant nation and its supporting coalition to the challenger and its supporters. But not all challenges are successful. In the last century we have seen German ambitions thwarted twice by a British-American alliance. Likewise, in the last decade we have witnessed the Soviet threat to the U.S. international order run out of steam. Looking ahead, there are signs of another possible challenge, this time from China.

In order to answer the foreign policy threats that policymakers are likely to face in the next century, we must turn to the evolution of the international system over the past two hundred years for predictive models. There we see the history of great power competition and conflict written in the Power Transition process: a dissatisfied challenger — Germany or Russia — attempts to overtake the defender — the United Kingdom or the United States — and vie for the mantle of international leadership. Whether successful or not, the dynamics that propel great power competition can be traced though history, demonstrating that parity, overtaking, and the transition process frame the structural conditions for war.

Scholars and policy practitioners have learned a great deal about regularities and change in relations among the great powers. Among great powers that support the status quo, changes in the power structure do not lead to confrontations. Indeed the story of Europe following World War II is a peaceful one despite Germany's overtaking of the United Kingdom and France. In contrast, when changes in power structures involve rising opponents of the status quo, war becomes likely.

In order to capture these dynamics, we rely on extensive data series of gross domestic products, per-capita products, population, and satisfaction with the international status quo developed by political scientists, economists, and demographers over recent decades. To capture satisfaction and dissatisfaction with the rules of the international order, we turn to measures of economic and security policy alignment that reflect the swelling tensions between competing dyads as well as increasing cooperation.[1] The data offer foreign policy scholars and practitioners the opportunity to account for the dynamics and evolution of the international system, understanding the past from the Power Transition perspective with an eye toward managing the future.

Evolution of the International System since 1815

The dynamics established by great powers' relations not only generate the conditions essential to stability and peace, but also set forth the elements for change and conflict. The national power series in this chapter provides an evolutionary perspective of the great powers' system since 1815 using Power Transition theory. The GDP series provides a panoramic view of the explosive patterns of growth and collapse that have shaped the structure of the international system as well as the dynamics that may sculpt its future development. Figures 2.1 and 2.2 provide an overview of great power evolution. Using differences in rates of economic growth as a criterion, we can comfortably divide the data into three distinct periods.[2] The first stretches from the end of the Napoleonic Wars, when our series begins, to the end of the nineteenth century. The second period takes up the first half of the twentieth century. The third period begins with the Cold War and continues to the present day.

The International Power Distribution: An Overview

Figure 2.1 (p. 46) depicts the relative levels of economic performance and political power of the great powers from 1815 to 1995. The differences in growth across system members shape the dynamics of the international power distribution. While the broader discussion of comparing power between nations in chapter 1 considered the elements of political capacity and demographic base in addition to economic productivity, we will focus simply on the size of economies in this chapter. The data needed to compare these nations along political and demographic lines for the broad sweeps of

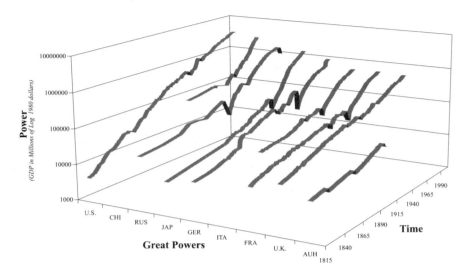

Figure 2.1   Great Power Shifts, 1815-2000

history we discuss in this chapter are simply not sufficient for the task. Since we are focusing on great powers, we expect that the comparisons we make here should closely approximate the actual notions of power this book suggests. The log GDPs, representing power, capture the percentage differences in constant rates over time. We have highlighted the three shorter periods that will be analyzed in detail later, but here we simply wish to provide an overview of the general power trends in the international system.

In the nineteenth century the economic expansion of all members of the system is relatively low, indicated by the flat GDP trajectories. All of the great powers are relatively close in terms of economic magnitudes. The United States is the only anomaly in the otherwise consistent pattern. The exceptional economic and demographic growth of the United States, reflected in the expansion of its domestic product toward the end of the century, signals the shape and direction of future system development. In this relatively peaceful period, the rise of Prussia and its overtaking of Austria-Hungary and then France stands out. Overall, however, systemic stability is guaranteed by the absence of major war between a dominant United Kingdom and any challengers on the continent. There are no significant shifts in the global power hierarchy.

During the second period, rates and levels of economic expansion begin to increase for the group of great powers as a whole. This process is rather uneven, however. Short periods of growth are interrupted by two world wars and a global depression. As suggested by Power Transition theory, massive international turmoil coupled with domestic political and economic difficulties limit economic gains and threaten system stability. Two German challenges to British leadership drastically alter the landscape of the global power distribution.

Finally, in the third period, economic growth accelerates rapidly. In the postwar period all members in our set experience major and sustained expansion of their economies. This increase in the relative performance of the great powers' economies radically transforms the nature of the system, yet does so without conflict. The creation of the European Community and the collapse of the Soviet Union occur in the absence of conflict despite multiple overtakings, producing the enigma of peace. Using the Power Transition perspective, however, we can explain system stability even in the presence of such large fluctuations in power.

Vast differences in the growth rates among great powers tell a large portion of the great powers competition story. The sharp spasms in growth caused by war and depression in the interwar period are apparent in our data. Even more visible is the remarkable explosion of growth after World War II and the differences in national power growth. This postwar phenomenon is the result of the Phoenix Factor effect. Germany, Japan, France, and Italy are not permanently damaged by the costs of war; the consequences of war are short-term. Within eighteen to twenty years, each of these nations returns to the growth trajectory anticipated by their prewar performance.

The stories of individual countries are compelling. The most distinctive and steady growth performance is that of the United States, which expands with only one major faltering — the Great Depression. Japan, on the other hand, experiences protracted economic growth, accelerating after World War II. This growth rate is sharper than that of the Soviet Union or Germany, though it decelerates toward the end of our series. Japan is now entering the maturation phase of lower growth rates on its endogenous growth trajectory.

Also notable is the profound growth of the Soviet Union for the decade and a half preceding World War II and the two and half decades after. This growth in power propelled the Soviets temporarily to the special power status of a potential challenger. Coupled with Soviet dissatisfaction, it created the Cold War. The deceleration of the Soviet economy in the mid-1970s is also apparent, including the free fall resulting from the implosion of the Soviet Union.

Toward the end of our series we find the important acceleration of Chinese growth, a harbinger of things to come. The rate of Chinese growth is rather flat until the interwar period. What is apparent, however, is China's position as an extremely large, yet undeveloped nation prior to beginning the modernization process. This signals its *potential* power. With a large population and high rate of growth, China eventually will accrue *actual* power and be guaranteed a predominant position in the international system. Already China can be seen as on the high growth portion of its endogenous growth trajectory. Let us now turn to the interactions among our power variables and conflict within each of the three periods.

The First Period: The Power Dynamics of Peace in the Nineteenth Century, 1815–99

In this period we explore the power dynamics following the Congress of Vienna and the evolution of great powers in the nineteenth century. The United Kingdom was predominant throughout the century until the U.S. overtaking near century's end. British dominance on the continent ensured the *Pax Britannica,* allowing the United Kingdom to impose rules and norms governing the European and global status quo.

In the global hierarchy, most other European powers are at similar levels of development and national power during these early stages of industrialization. Germany, France, and Austria-Hungary[3] all vie for the position to challenge the United Kingdom throughout the nineteenth century. In order to understand the structure and dynamics of this competition, we will concentrate on key dyads — the United States-United Kingdom and Germany-France — to ascertain whether overtakings are associated with major war and if power preponderance results in peace.

Figure 2.2 focuses on the global hierarchy by displaying the relative distribution of power among the United Kingdom, the United States, Germany, and France — the major actors during this period. First, consider the U.K. power trajectory throughout the nineteenth century. Our series indicate that the U.K. power advantage over every major European nation provides a favorable circumstance for Britain to establish stability on the Continent. British dominance is the first instance where the leader's power preponderance is derived from the modernization process. The new resources produced by an industrial economy are mobilized by a more effective government.[4] The British experienced accelerated growth up to 6 percent per annum compared to the 1.5 percent average for the rest of Europe.

The British power advantage over France, the largest and most powerful of its competitors, was the result of an overtaking most likely in the decades just before the Congress of Vienna.[5] The overtaking of France by the United Kingdom instigated an intense competition for control of the great power system. This competition was accompanied by a series of major power wars over twenty years. As figure 2.2 demonstrates, English international dominance over France became evident with the defeat of Napoleon in 1815.

Figure 2.2 shows the nature of power asymmetry between the United Kingdom and France throughout the nineteenth century. As expected by the Power Transition perspective, this period is devoid of war despite British foreign policy preoccupation with a potential French threat. In retrospect,

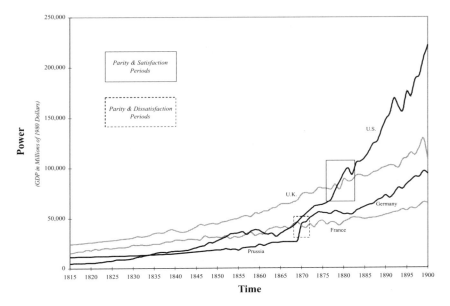

Figure 2.2 Great Power Competition, 1815-1900

this is similar to the Cold War between the United States and the USSR in terms of preponderance, dissatisfaction, and lack of war.

We now turn to the U.S.-U.K. dyad of great powers. In this period the growth of the United States is pronounced. The United States begins its modernization process during the 1840s, but progress is interrupted by the Civil War. After the war, the United States recovers quickly and returns to the high growth portion of its growth trajectory. Figure 2.2 displays the United States being propelled past the United Kingdom and all other great powers in less than fifty years. But the relationship between the United States and United Kingdom was peaceful because both nations supported the status quo established under the *Pax Britannica*.[6] The United States continued expanding its preponderance to the point that by the end of the nineteenth century, its power advantage was rarely less than twice that of Great Britain. The very large power asymmetry that the United States maintained throughout all of the twentieth century is rooted in its nineteenth-century growth performance.

The overtaking of the United Kingdom by the United States in 1879 could have been expected to induce system instabilities. Why then did the United Kingdom not resist the overtaking of the United States, as it was to do so bitterly, and at such cost, in the case of Germany thirty years later? Recall that parity and overtakings are strong but only probabilistic conditions for conflict initiation. A challenge to the status quo is also required. In the case of the U.S.-U.K. overtaking, there was no confluence between these two factors. Scholars do not identify these two countries as engaged in an arms buildup during this period, indicating they were both satisfied with the status quo.[7] This satisfaction probably derived from British leadership, a common institutional heritage, American political separation from European affairs, and a profitable market for British capital in America. All undoubtedly helped reduce British anxieties and suspicions of American growth.[8]

The issue of satisfaction has two parts. At the macro level, a national consensus over priorities and directions created a state of satisfaction in the United Kingdom and United States. The ruling political leadership forged a compromise of self-interest among the coalitions that comprised their political power base.[9] The reason why the United Kingdom declined to use or even threaten the use of force to head off the American overtaking was determined by its own economic self interest. A large and powerful sector of the British business community had a stake in the U.S. economy. British capital was critical in fueling the U.S. production machine. It was in the interest of the U.K. governing coalition that economic ties between the two nations be maintained.

An associated Power Transition question is, why did the United States accept the second spot for so long after it actually passed the United Kingdom in power? Why did the United States not insist on its right to the dominant position to which its power clearly entitled it?

Certainty is impossible, but we offer the following explanation. At the time of the overtaking of the United Kingdom, the United States was a decentralized political system. Business, labor, and regional interests had an enormous stake in maintaining that decentralization. They were not about to cede control of resources under their control to the central government. This domestic base of political and economic power had a dramatic impact on U.S. international relations. While resources were made available in cases of external attack, the story of the United States in the first half of the twentieth century is one of *imbalance* of domestic power. The reason why the United States did not press harder to obtain international leadership may have been that the central governmental elites were weak and could not command access to the vast societal resources necessary for translation of economic power into national power.[10]

Timing may also have been critical. The United States overtook all European powers before it initiated systematic involvement in European affairs. During this period the United Kingdom also had reason to be increasingly concerned with the more threatening prospect of German power growth.[11]

Using figure 2.2, let us now turn to the second overtaking, that of a dissatisfied Prussia and France. This was the greatest threat to system stability in nineteenth-century Europe. Prussia's growth propels it to come from behind to pass Austria in 1836 and France in 1870. Prussian and French progress paralleled each other until a sharp acceleration of Prussian growth immediately before the Franco-Prussian War. The struggle between Germany and France for preeminence among Continental powers results from this overtaking, coupled with Germany's desire to restructure the European status quo.[12] Figure 2.2 highlights the period of parity between these rivals during the late 1860s. The lack of cooperation and dissatisfaction between Germany and France is captured by the arms buildup that precedes the Franco-Prussian War of 1870.[13]

In summary, despite the German challenge, peace prevails among Germany, the United States, and the United Kingdom in the first period. The last decade of the nineteenth century shows Germany narrowing the power gap separating it from the United Kingdom, and, to a much lesser extent, that of the United States. The power asymmetry in the United Kingdom's favor preserves the stability in Europe and in the international system as a whole. With the narrowing gap between itself and the United Kingdom, German progress begins to appear menacing to European powers. Every advance heightened the realization of a future power alteration on the Continent.

The Second Period: Conflict Dynamics in the First Half of the Twentieth Century, 1900–1949

The race on the Continent dominates great power relations during the second period. It is a time characterized by German attempts to obtain systemic leadership in Europe. Concentrating on the main contenders, figure 2.3 (p. 52) illustrates the rise of Germany and the parity periods preceding war. Germany overtakes the United Kingdom in 1907 and again in 1936. The overtakings precipitated the most devastating wars in history, World Wars I and II. The prize of such conflict was control of the international system. Each case of German overtaking is consistent with expectations about conflict offered by the Power Transition perspective. That is, both parity and dissatisfaction were present. The German overtaking is an example of a more economically advanced society being passed in overall power by one less economically advanced but possessing a larger population. German population was a third larger than that of Great Britain whereas German per-capita product was roughly a third lower than that of the United Kingdom.[14]

The second condition conducive to conflict, dissatisfaction with the global status quo, also is present in this time period. Figure 2.4 (p. 53) depicts the changes in U.K. and German satisfaction and dissatisfaction. Up until 1910, although Germany was dissatisfied and the United Kingdom satisfied, their cooperative and noncooperative relations were approximately equal. The arms buildups that occurred between Germany and the

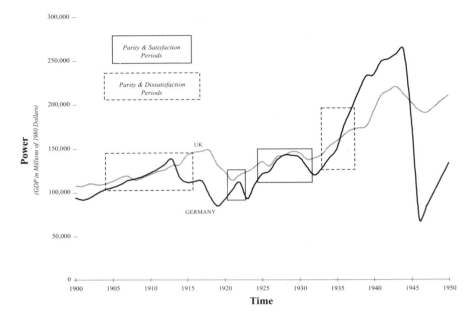

Figure 2.3   The German Challenge, 1900-1950

United Kingdom prior to both world wars, one starting in 1906 and the other in 1930, demonstrate the noncooperative nature of their relations.[15] Both world wars are classic examples of two great powers, at parity and with one dissatisfied, waging war for control of the international system. Notice that after World War II, both nations are satisfied with the status quo and pursue cooperative relations to maximize absolute gains.

As a result of these long periods of parity and dissatisfaction throughout the beginning of the twentieth century, the duration and severity of both world wars were high. Remember that Power Transition theory postulates that the longer a dissatisfied challenger and dominant nation are in parity, the higher the severity of war as well as the longer the duration of conflict. Figure 2.3 shows that the U.K.-Germany dyad was in relative parity for most of this period.

The dominant role of the U.K.-Germany dyad during this period accounts for the initiation of both world wars. Concurrently, there were a number of conflicts in regional hierarchies, including the Russo-Japanese War of 1905 and the invasion of China by Japan in 1932. These regional conflicts did not escalate to the global level because they did not pose a direct threat to the dominant power in the global hierarchy. Regional wars do not diffuse upward. Regional conflicts can, however, become part of world conflagration. Once war is waged at the global level, regional conflicts can

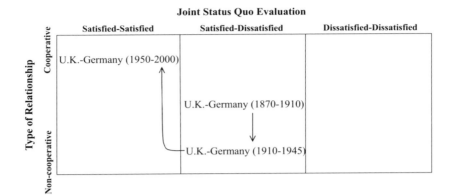

Figure 2.4   German-U.K. Status Quo Evaluation, 1870-2000

diffuse and escalate. The U.S.-Japanese Pacific theater of World War II is a perfect example. Despite the importance of the conflict with Japan, the resolution of the world war was dependent upon defeat of the major contender for global supremacy, Germany. Global wars diffuse downward.

In the first half of the twentieth century, two things are apparent from the Power Transition perspective. First, the United States had secured preponderance over all other great powers. Second, and more important, is the closing of the British power gap with a dissatisfied Germany and other nations. Whether the assassination of an archduke or the sinking of a ship ignited the conflict, the structural preconditions for war — parity and dissatisfaction — were present.[16] Europe truly was a "powder keg" at the time of both wars, as Power Transition anticipates.

The consequences of World War I, though massive, varied by nation. The price of war for Austria-Hungary was severe, leading to the dissolution of the Hapsburg Empire in 1918 and Austria's disappearance from the roster of great powers. Russia emerged from this conflict torn by the Bolshevik Revolution of 1917, compounding the enormous losses suffered during the war. At the global level, fluctuations of GDP in the late 1920s and early 1930s show the effects of the worldwide depression on all the great powers. The United States, even though spared the direct burden of war, experienced a sharp decline in growth rates followed by a slow recovery. After World War I, French power and economic performance suffered greatly, and did so again after World War II.

Violent, protracted world wars should have long-term costs. Counterintuitively that is not the case. From the ashes of destruction great powers rise anew. After World War I, German power declined substantially. Combined with territorial losses and the burden of reparations, Germany's devastation demonstrated exactly the high costs of war. Nonetheless, German recovery began as early as 1924 and continued in a sustained fashion after 1932 due to the Phoenix Factor. With Hitler's accession, German power rapidly increased from 1932–39 so that by the outbreak of World War II Germany overtook the United Kingdom for the second time.

Figure 2.3 demonstrates how victory or defeat in war does not permanently alter the long-run evolution of power. Germany after World War I and Germany, Japan, and Italy after World War II shrugged off the heavy losses suffered as a result of their defeats.[17] Note that German growth reached pre–World War I levels just prior to the outbreak of World War II. After German GDP was reduced by one-third in World War II, it regained prewar levels in less than ten years. In retrospect, the losers have done much better than the winners. The performance of combatants before the war was a predictor of how nations would perform after the war. It was a better predictor than the actual outcome of the war.

Whether a nation chooses peace or war, it cannot manipulate its underlying power dynamics or those of its competitors. Nations may lose great power wars and rise to even higher levels in the international system. Great powers who win and hold on to their relative power preponderance do not have to fight.[18] These observations have major implications for policymakers and scholars alike by highlighting the constraints and opportunities that the international power distribution places on national foreign policy goals.

The Third Period: The Dynamics of System Transformation and Peace, 1950–95

The postwar era is characterized by the lack of major conflict among the great powers. This period of peace is the result of the power preponderance of the United States. Despite the challenge of a dissatisfied USSR during the Cold War, peace was maintained because there was no overtaking. Figure 2.5 shows the asymmetric power difference between the United States and the Soviet Union throughout the Cold War period, culminating with the 1990 Soviet economic collapse. The logic of Power Transition suggests that the conditions associated with the successful maintenance of peace were present throughout the postwar period. The vast power asymmetry between the United States and the Soviet Union prevented an overt challenge to U.S. dominance.[19]

This asymmetrical distribution of power was known to both sides, and that fact gave the United States useful leverage. When tensions erupted between the United States and the Soviet Union in disputes like the Cuban Missile Crisis, the Soviet Union backed down. The United States chose not to interfere with Soviet control in Eastern Europe, allowing Soviet intervention in Hungary, Czechoslovakia, East Germany, and Poland because it did not threaten the stability of the international order. With the buildup of NATO in the 1970s, the U.S.-led coalition developed overwhelming superiority over an increasingly weak and divided Warsaw Pact coalition.

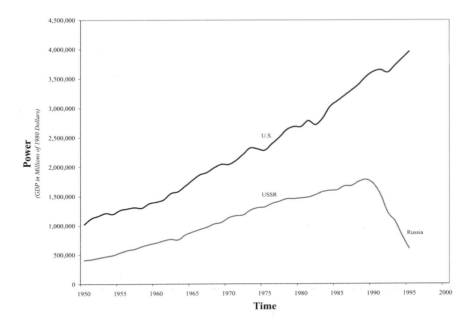

Figure 2.5 Superpower Competition, 1950-2000

The dynamic period of Soviet power growth began with the communist revolution in 1917 and lasted into the early 1970s, at which point the Soviet economy began to stagnate. Even at the height of Soviet power, however, there never was parity between the United States and the USSR. In the second half of that period, the possession of nuclear weapons masked the Soviet's fundamental inferiority. But these weapons were powerless to compensate for Soviet deficiencies in political, economic, and social resources. From the perspective of Power Transition theory, it was this imbalance of power with the United States that created the structural conditions for peace.

Given this imbalance of power, why did both the U.S. and the Soviet leadership believe explicitly and implicitly in a rough balance of power?[20] Why did many political analysts suggest that American "hegemony" was coming to an end?

It is a fascinating puzzle that the leaders of both the Soviet Union and the United States maintained that there was power parity between the two countries. As seen in figure 2.5, the power ratio between the United States and the Soviet Union hovered always around two to one in favor of the United States, and indeed, the interval between them actually increased as the Cold War went on. The claim to the contrary by both governments contains, in our view, the key to understanding the dynamics of the Cold War.

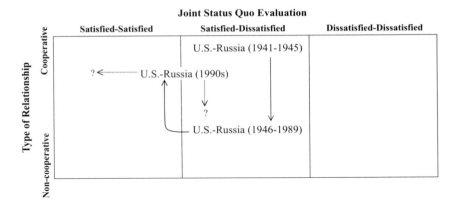

Figure 2.6   Superpower Status Quo Evaluation, 1941-2000

We hypothesize that such a claim served the purposes of the subsets of elites leading the two nations. The assertion of power parity rendered credible the leadership claim that the adversary endangered its society. The power of that claim made it possible to obtain the resources needed to buttress their country's position and, concomitantly, their own.

Without their claim of encirclement and the threat of aggression by the United States, the Soviet leadership would have found it very difficult, if not impossible, to extract and allocate sufficient resources from its society to support its huge national security apparatus — the party, the secret police, the military, the governmental bureaucracy, and the heavy-industry sector. On the U.S. side, without a claim that the nation was in mortal danger from Soviet military expansion, deterred only by U.S. military power, it would have been impossible for the political leadership to obtain the resources required to fight off isolationist forces and meet international challenges. The belief that both nations were equal in power had its uses.

Figure 2.6 depicts the evolution of U.S. and USSR relations since 1941. During World War II, the cooperative Allied relationship was necessitated by German and Axis aggression. With the emergence of the Cold War and Russian dissatisfaction with American leadership of the international system, both the Soviets and the Americans pursued noncooperative and competitive policies across most issues. In the aftermath of the Cold War, the U.S.-Russian relationship could move in either direction. If the United States allows Russia to slip away into a state of dissatisfaction in the future, it will be a strategic miscalculation of historic proportions.

Although serving domestic elites' interests, the Cold War was grounded equally in traditional "power politics" of foreign policy competition. The Soviet Union headed a substantial international order of eleven nations comprising roughly one-third of the people of the world while at the same time leading an international communist movement. Had the Soviets actually overtaken the United States, their foreign policy goal of a Soviet-led international system would have greatly increased the probability of global war. Being a dissatisfied challenger, the Soviet Union would have sought to dismantle the existing international order and substitute one of its own.

The U.S. policy of meeting the Soviet challenge around the world under the containment doctrine was consistent with Power Transition theory. Given U.S. strategic concerns regionally — in the Middle East, Asia, and Latin America — the United States was willing to expend significant military and economic resources in order to maintain or create a preponderance of satisfied minor powers in a regional hierarchy that would support the U.S. global status quo. Since the Soviets could not overtly challenge the United States at the global level due to American preponderance, they attempted to destabilize the American-led status quo in various regions. Moreover, by changing regional hierarchies around the globe from supporting the United States to a more pro-Soviet alignment, the Soviets might ultimately abet an open challenge to the United States at the global level.

The Soviet-American confrontation officially came to an end with the disintegration of the Soviet empire, costing the newly reconstructed Russia a loss of 100 million citizens and an economic collapse as seen in figure 2.5. The consequence for the global power distribution is Russia's decline from the number-two spot in the great power hierarchy to the middle of the pack. Whether it can survive as a great power in this century will depend on its government facilitating economic recovery and renewed growth.

Having dealt with the U.S.-Soviet competition, let us now turn to regional hierarchical relationships during the third period. European and Japanese satisfaction with the status quo maintained the peace in regions supervised by these states. Overtakings occurred throughout the postwar era as most European nations were at similar levels of national power. Germany passed France and the United Kingdom again, emerging once more as a predominant power in Europe. This time however, the passage was entirely peaceful. The European powers no longer competed for leadership of the international order because they approved of the status quo. Within the region they created the European Union, ensuring the distribution of satisfaction and the resulting peace.

A telltale sign of the differences between the first two periods and the postwar era is the total absence of arms buildups among key competitors in Europe.[21] Germany, the United Kingdom, and France no longer direct their military establishments against each other. For the first time since the Congress of Vienna, all of the European great powers are members of the same security alliance, NATO, while forging common economic ground in the European Union. This major system transformation takes place as a consequence of the emergence of the *Pax Americana*.

Cumulative restructuring of the global hierarchy occurs in this last period. The shift from a European to a global hierarchical structure was linked to the ascendancy of the United States and Soviet Union over the relatively smaller nations. Indeed, the Western European nations that had been the great powers in the nineteenth century were at the bottom of the great powers' roster by the middle of the Cold War.

Coupled with the decline of the European great powers, the *Pax Americana* took form when the United States claimed the leadership position after World War II. This was not only a turnover in dominance, but a systemic restructuring as well. The American international order differs in important respects from its predecessor. Most prominently, great power control over the developing world has changed radically. The rigid and increasingly costly structures of political colonialism were dismantled, and American dominance was exercised through a more flexible and far less invasive form of political and economic controls.

U.S. elite decisions to claim leadership and the Soviet collapse allowed for realities and perceptions about international rule to coincide at last. We have witnessed the passing of the first American century, with the second already underway. U.S. leadership and order is based on a long-standing, stable, and large power advantage over all other great powers. The overwhelming stability of the American power asymmetry can be seen in the following statistics: The United States possessed approximately 40 percent of the power of the entire great power system in the years 1913, 1938, and 1985. Its advantage over the main contenders in the twentieth century, Germany and Russia, remained unvaried over this long period of time at a ratio of almost two-to-one. American isolationist policies masked the reality of American power preponderance at the start of this period.[22] The great difference after World War II was the U.S. decision to move to an internationalist posture, dedicating enormous resources to enforcing its leadership position.

Conclusions and Projections

The major argument of this chapter focuses on differences in the size of the resource pools that nations possess, consequently establishing not only the distributions of international power, but moreover the structural conditions for war and conflict. These pools are a function of three components: population size, productivity, and political capacity. Combined they define the size of a nation's resource potential available for exercising power. Only when the dominant nation has a power advantage is system stability ensured. Differences in rates of economic change among national resource potentials drive shifts in the rankings of great powers and contain the dynamics associated with conflict. In the Power Transition perspective, the overtaking challenger's satisfaction with the global status quo strongly affects the prospects for war or peace. These are the constraints of the international power dynamic. The aggregate measures of economic performance and the Power Transition perspective allow social scientists and policymakers alike to identify and explain these important phenomena.

Our overview of the development of the international system since 1815 leads us to pose several essential questions. First, what is the potential for future overtakings? Second, how peaceful will such passages be? Finally, what can be done to enhance the probability of peace? The rest of this book is dedicated to answering these questions, but some summary policy conclusions can be foreshadowed here.

In the next few decades, China will overtake the United States. The potential for an arms buildup between these two cannot be dismissed. If such an event occurs, past experience is mixed. Recall that British and German elites chose war repeatedly before opting for cooperation and peace. On the other hand, the United States overtook England without conflict and accepted the mantle of leadership when its leadership was assured. The central question then becomes what can be done to ensure that China follows the latter path rather than the former.

It is incorrect to compare the potential overtaking by China with the Soviet challenge during the Cold War. There are critical differences between theses two challenges. The power asymmetry that secured U.S. hegemony from Soviet threats was based both on productivity and population. China has the potential to overtake the United States because it only requires a level of productivity one-fifth that of the United States due to its tremendous population advantage. Short of a catastrophic nuclear war or domestic disintegration, one cannot but anticipate the emergence of China as the largest and most productive nation in the international system.

The historical experiences we have evaluated suggest that overtakings by themselves are not sufficient conditions for conflict. China might readily accept international rules and accommodate its interests within that framework. If such changes do occur, we do not anticipate the buildup of arms between the challenger and dominant nation. There would be no alternation in the status quo, and the result would be a peaceful overtaking. If China does not modify its current resentment toward the rules established under the *Pax Americana,* the prospects of conflict increase. Needless to say, in the nuclear era such a confrontation has systemic implications. Chapter 7 deals with the potential China challenge in depth.

Knowledge of history does not leave us helpless. The resolution of long-term conflicts in Europe suggests possible changes likely to help peace prevail. The creation of the European Union should not be seen only as an exercise in economic integration. It must also be viewed as the creation of a peaceful environment that has replaced long-standing confrontations. Following the collapse of the Soviet Union, the United States and the European powers face very similar challenges to international stability. If NATO is expanded to include not only Eastern Europe but Russia as well, the security threat that dominated the Cold War will be a distant memory. The expansion of the European Community into Eastern Europe, the former Soviet republics, and eventually Russia, would restructure that community as much as the original EEC restructured Western Europe. Moreover, the possibility of a broader coalition, including the United States, greater Europe, and Japan, could become a bloc of such magnitude that the power asymmetries that ensures international stability could be preserved for a significant period. This "superbloc" would stave off the imminent dominance of China, maintain system stability, and guarantee the peace irrespective of Chinese dissatisfaction with the status quo. Chapter 6 addresses the foreign policy implications of alliance formation and management with a specific focus on NATO and Russia.

Our analysis has strategic implications for future international distributions of power. China, India, or perhaps other members of the successful developing world eventually must be invited to the company of the great powers. Maintaining power asymmetry provides breathing space for the international community to reconcile differences and forge acceptable rules that all members can support. China and other populous developing nations cannot be excluded from the set of satisfied nations if we hope to maintain peace and stability in the twenty-first century. For surely the same modernization and power dynamics that propel the current great powers will also thrust the developing world to preeminence.

Part II

Applications

Regional Applications: Multiple Hierarchies

> *A general theory of international politics is necessarily based on the great powers. The theory once written also applies to lesser states that interact insofar as their interactions are insulated from the intervention of the great powers of a system, whether by the relative indifference of the latter or by the difficulties of communication and transportation.*
> — KENNETH WALTZ

The discussion thus far generally has focused on interactions among the great powers. This is a time-honored tradition in international politics research. Nonetheless, power transitions between the very strongest states are rare phenomena, while most of the conflict in the international system occurs in regional interactions among less powerful states. This fact has a powerful political imperative. In the absence of a great power challenger, U.S. policymakers focus on regional conflicts, be it warfare in Iraq and Kosovo or the potential of conflict in North Korea. As is often the case in international politics, the immediate displaces the long-term. For Power Transition theory, this change of venue is not a handicap.

The wealth of empirical support for Power Transition theory has created a preliminary consensus among many international relations researchers that the probability of conflict increases dramatically when two countries are roughly equal and decreases comparably when would-be adversaries are vastly different in power.[1] Since many of the findings upon which this consensus is based evaluate power relationships and conflict for all pairs of states, there is a logical extension that the relationship between parity and war is applicable to minor powers as well as great powers, to regional subsystems as well as to the overall system.

Power Transition theory posits that preponderance by the dominant power is pacifying, while parity between the dominant power and a dissatisfied challenger greatly increases the probability of war. If the conflicts described by Power Transition theory were boxing matches instead of interstate wars, only heavyweight title fights would be pertinent to the theory. In this chapter we argue that, provided the great powers do not intervene,

Power Transition theory applies to all divisions, from flyweight to heavy-weight. The purpose of this chapter is to establish the existence of a general relevance for Power Transition theory beyond the great powers.

A generalization of Power Transition theory to regional conflicts in-creases confidence in the accuracy of the overall theory in international relations. This increased confidence justifies using Power Transition theory to offer guidelines to formulate foreign policy strategies.

Multiple Hierarchies in World Politics

The multiple hierarchy model asserts that the international system is com-posed of regional hierarchies with parallel functions.[2] Power Transition theory has focused on the overall global hierarchy, which is dominated by the great powers. Wars fought for control of the global hierarchy are fought for control of the global system. Such conflicts involve the very strongest of states and are devastatingly destructive. This overall global hierarchy is what most refer to as *the* global system.

The multiple hierarchy model extends this approach to smaller powers around the globe. Their regional hierarchies function identically to the over-all global hierarchy. In the regional hierarchies there is a regional dominant state that establishes and maintains a regional status quo. Other states in the regional hierarchy either are advantaged by and satisfied with this re-gional status quo or disadvantaged by and dissatisfied with it. Should one of these regionally dissatisfied states achieve power parity with the regional dominant state, a war within the regional hierarchy is likely. Thus, power parity and negative evaluations of the status quo are associated with war in regional hierarchies, just as they are in Power Transition theory's overall global hierarchy. Great powers atop the global hierarchy probably could upset the outcome of any confrontation at the regional level, but they seldom do so.

Figure 1.1 (p. 7) diagrammatically represents the global international hierarchy as a triangle where height represents greater power and width re-flects the fact that there are more states at lower levels of power than at higher levels. The strong are few while the weak are many. It might be easiest to conceive of the multiple hierarchy model's addition to Power Transition theory by visualizing the triangular international system as a three-dimensional cone within which smaller cones are nested. Each cone represents a power hierarchy. The largest cone is the overall global hi-erarchy, exactly the same power hierarchy as that represented by Power Transition theory's original triangle. The smaller cones within the overall cone are the regional hierarchies.

This reconfiguration of the triangle as a cone adds a third dimension of geographic distance. Brazil and India, for example, may be similarly powerful and would thus be placed at approximately the same height in

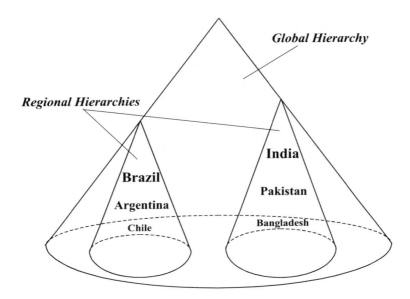

Figure 3.1 Regional Hierarchies in the International System

the triangle, but they do not interact within the same regional hierarchy. They are separated by many thousands of miles of oceans and continents. Therefore, India is an important actor in a regional hierarchy in South Asia, Brazil in a regional hierarchy in South America. They would consequently be found in separate smaller cones nested within the overall cone. Figure 3.1 depicts this emendation to the original figure 1.1.

Regional hierarchies function just like the overall global hierarchy, but there is at least one important difference. The regional hierarchies are necessarily subordinate to the overall global hierarchy. It is as though the regional hierarchies are international arenas over which external and more powerful actors spectate. Should the great powers wish to interfere with relations among regional hierarchy members, they can do so. International history offers many examples of great power interference in minor power affairs. Thus, when conceptualizing the world as a series of functionally similar power hierarchies, one must bear in mind that the regional hierarchies are subject to external intervention, while the relations between great powers at the peak of the overall global hierarchy are not. Consequently, some caution is required when determining the impact of great power behavior on relations within regional hierarchies. At the same time, it is important to bear this distinction in mind when conceptualizing to what the status quo of a given regional hierarchy might refer. We refer to these concerns in more detail below.

The Multiple Hierarchy Model

First we must have an operational definition of regional hierarchies. A wealth of scholarly effort has been dedicated to the identification of "regions," "subordinate state systems," "subordinate international systems," "international subsystems," "geographic zones," "regimes," "regional subsystems," "politically relevant neighborhoods," or "clusters of nations."[3] A wide range of empirical concerns and data sources have been associated with these various efforts to define meaningful subsets of the international system. The criteria by which the various subunits have been constructed have included cultural similarities, trade patterns, common membership in international organizations, alliance patterns, and demographic similarities. Distilling this complexity reveals that two common characteristics are disproportionately used to define regions: proximity and patterns of interaction.

Proximity

Studies have shown that the presence of international borders plays an important role in subsequent wars between countries.[4] It is not the borders per se that cause wars, but rather that borders are symptomatic of proximity. Proximity increases interactions between countries, forces countries to take each other seriously, and increases the potential for disputes.[5] Some scholars, noting that territoriality is an important characteristic of virtually all animals, argue that territoriality makes people sensitive regarding the space they inhabit and threats to it.[6] Since proximity increases interactions, and people are sensitive about interactions involving territory, the potential for conflict increases with proximity.

Such considerations are important for evaluating the multiple hierarchy model because in order to determine whether minor powers fight wars under the same circumstances as the great powers, we first have to know which minor powers to consider. Anyone would know not to evaluate the international relations of Paraguay with Thailand because the two countries lie so far apart there is virtually no chance they will go to war with each other. We need to remove from consideration all pairs of states such as Paraguay and Thailand and focus instead on states that consider each other when assessing potential threats to their security. Sets of minor power states that could plausibly assess each other as potential security threats comprise a regional hierarchy.

With such variables in mind, regional hierarchies have been defined as existing where minor powers' "politically relevant neighborhoods" overlap. The politically relevant neighborhood of any state is that part of the earth's surface with which the state concerns itself. More powerful states will have larger areas of concern. Less powerful states will be, necessarily, constrained to think of international affairs in more regional terms since they do not have the resources to affect matters far from their borders. The procedure by which regional hierarchies have been operationally defined explicitly assumes that states pay more attention to that part of the globe within which they can exert military influence. This is not to say that the leader of a minor power state would ignore the superpowers, but rather that when formulating his or her state's foreign policies and making strategic plans, these will remain primarily regional.

Given that a state's politically relevant neighborhood is defined as the area within which it can exert military influence, it is possible to measure this area by consideration of the logistics of military transit. One way to do this is to begin with a country's power resources (measured in ways described below), and then give consideration to how far these can be dispatched. In calculating this, a "loss-of-strength" formula is developed that takes into account the actual terrain that would be faced in any effort to move military resources from point A to point B. This formula adjusts national power by degrading it for the distance to be covered.[7] Adjusted power is thus the amount of original power left over when the impact of distance is taken into consideration.[8]

The innovation in the use of this formula for multiple hierarchy model purposes concerns the "miles-per-day" component of the exponent. This component is supposed to represent the possible transit range allowed by available technology. Previous uses of the exponent had assigned a transit range of 250 miles from 1816 to 1918, 375 miles from 1919 to 1945, and 500 miles per day after 1945.[9] While it is true that advances in transportation have dramatically increased the transit ranges of military forces, 500 miles per day is especially overoptimistic for the military forces of minor powers.[10] Consequently, the version of the formula used here takes into account obstacles that lie between potential minor power adversaries such as mountains, jungles, or rivers; as well as how fast these obstacles can be overcome.

Adjusted power is designed to determine which minor powers are able to interact militarily. It defines a state's politically relevant neighborhood as comprising all those other states to which it can move 50 percent or more of its power into the other's national capital. This 50-percent threshold is justified by the assumption that if most of a state's capabilities are spent in transit, the distance is probably too great to warrant the expenditure of resources. In defining regional hierarchies, this formula is applied to each state's capability share over the distances to each other state to determine the politically relevant neighborhood for each minor power state. When two or more states' politically relevant neighborhoods overlap, those states very likely think of each other when formulating foreign policy or considering military activity. Politically relevant neighborhoods are the central element of regional hierarchies.

Patterns of Interaction

Regional hierarchies are functionally similar to the overall global hierarchy. While the dominant global power establishes a global status quo that benefits itself, regional dominant states establish regional status quos. What aspects of international interactions can the regional leaders "carve out" as their own? Although no definitive answer exists, the regional status quo concerns issues primarily of regional concern. Access to strategic or otherwise valuable territory must play an important part. Many, if not most, minor power wars have been fought for territorial gain. Who was to have access to the mineral riches of the Atacama Desert justified the War of the Pacific pitting Chile versus Peru and Bolivia in the 1870s. Who will control the religious sites of Judaism and Islam undergirds much of the Arab-Israeli conflict. India and Pakistan are unable to agree about control of Kashmir.

The overall dominant power is little concerned with who specifically controls these various parts of the globe, so long as the mineral riches are exported and the global status quo undisturbed. Thus, access to various territories must be an important part of the regional status quos. By territory we should probably think broadly in terms of navigable waterways, defensible borders, access to holy or culturally important sites, as well as arable lands and mineral deposits. Thus, the territorial focus of regional status quos may also have important components aside from the intrinsic value of the land.

That regional status quos are primarily territorial does not predetermine that they will be exclusively concerned with the possession of territory. It is quite possible that regional status quos will be characterized by ethnic, military, economic, or ideological disagreements between regional dominant powers and regional challengers. For example, one of the regional hierarchies identified in Africa comprises the central African states of Rwanda and Burundi. Any regional status quo between these two states will have a heavy ethnic quality. Although the horrific violence in these countries has been largely domestic rather than cross-border, there are substantial connections between Rwandan and Burundian Hutus and between Rwandan and Burundian Tutsis that indicate the leaders of either state would prefer that their ethnic confreres be dominant in the other.

An ideological regional status quo example can be drawn from a regional hierarchy in Southeast Asia. With its victory over and absorption of South Vietnam in 1975, the Democratic Republic of Vietnam became the strongest state in Southeast Asia and thus the regional dominant power. For some time, North Vietnam's leaders had been encouraging a communist insurgency in Laos, and in 1975 they invaded Cambodia and instituted a similar regime in Phnom Penh. It seems clear that the Vietnamese status quo in Southeast Asia, though limited in time, was primarily ideological.

The character of the regional status quo gives strong indications about potential great power interference within regional hierarchies. A regional status quo concerned with the distribution of territory is unlikely to be of interest to external great powers for the simple reason that so long as the resources of that territory are made available for export, who specifically controls the territory is inconsequential to the great powers. However, when the regional status quo concerns a matter of interest to the great power, as was the case in Southeast Asia in the 1960s and 1970s, interference is much more likely. Of course this does not mean that great powers will be totally uninterested in regional hierarchies where the regional status quo is primarily territorial, rather it simply means that there is a greater likelihood of great power interest and interference when the regional status quo is more salient externally.

Such concerns are not trivial. A monkey wrench can be thrown into regional hierarchy interactions if great powers interfere. In contrast, leaders of regional hierarchies cannot interfere with the hierarchy of the great powers. There is no clear-cut answer to questions of how much this inequality of interference affects world politics. But it seems clear that the less interference from above, the more the regional hierarchies parallel the overall global hierarchy. In fact, the basic hypothesis of the multiple hierarchy model extension of Power Transition theory is that *absent* such interference, regional hierarchies will function in the same way as does the global power hierarchy. Thus the main hypothesis of the multiple hierarchy model extension is operative only absent great power interference.

This raises an interesting question of how often and to what degree great powers actually do intervene in minor power relations. Here the surprising conclusion is that great powers rarely involve themselves overtly in minor power interstate relations.[11] To be sure, there are dramatic examples to the contrary offered by the cases of wars in Vietnam, Korea, and Afghanistan. Great powers such as the United States or Soviet Union are more involved in minor power relations than are smaller members of the global hierarchy. But when one considers the number of minor power interactions and the potential opportunities for interference compared to the actual number of interventions, the startling conclusion is that the great powers by and large ignore the weaker states of the world.

There is dramatic evidence for this claim. The Militarized Interstate Dispute data set[12] lists all instances in which one state threatened, displayed, or used force against another between the years 1816 and 1992. In total, there are more than 2,000 such militarized interstate disputes in the data set. If we consider only disputes that begin between minor powers and treat each minor power militarized interstate dispute as a potential intervention opportunity for each of the great powers,[13] there were more than 5,800 such opportunities. Of these nearly 6,000 opportunities for each of the great powers to intervene, there are fewer than seventy total instances of overt military participation and this includes threats, displays, and use of force by the great powers. The great powers have intervened in minor power interstate conflicts in just over 1 percent of all opportunities to do so. Great powers usually ignore the minor powers.[14]

The previous two paragraphs are not offered as proof that regional hierarchies are free of great power interference. Instead, they are offered as suggestive evidence that there is more independence of minor power relations from great power interference than an impressionistic perusal of current events might convey. Again, the hypothesis of the multiple hierarchy model is that the regional hierarchies operate parallel to the overall hierarchy, absent external interference. The results below suggest the parallel operation is accurate. The validity of the results is enhanced by consideration of the plausibility of the independence of regional relations from great power interference.

A final point we would make along these lines is that logically there still are implications from Power Transition theory about when such rare interventions/interference might occur and how great powers might intervene effectively. Readers should not assume great powers never intervene in minor power affairs or that great powers ought not intervene in such affairs. The observation above of limited great power interference is most likely the consequence of a strategic interaction between great power expectations and behavior with minor power expectations and behavior.

Specifically, whenever the stakes (the regional status quo) involved in a minor power dispute are consequential to great powers we should anticipate great power interference. The leaders of minor power states, however, should expect this interference too. Consequently, they will probably be less likely to get involved in conflicts they expect to provoke great power interference because doing so would largely remove control of their affairs from their own hands. Leaders of minor power states are thus probably disproportionately likely to construct their relations such that their disputes do not involve stakes consequential to great powers or to resolve disagreements about such stakes in such a way as to avoid great power interference.

All of this suggests that great powers do interfere with minor power relations, but either at the margins or via expectations before conflicts actually erupt. Knowledge of the likely nature of great power interference offers suggestions for productive ways in which great powers, like the United States, might achieve objectives in regional hierarchies. Making it known ahead of time that the United States will involve itself if some regional status quos become challenged (for example, there appears to be a reasonably strong precedent to this effect with respect to the territorial integrity of

Kuwait), might be an intervention that would prevent such a challenge in the first place. Such policy relevant applications are raised in the concluding section of this chapter and in chapter 8.

Regional Analyses of the Multiple Hierarchy Model

In regional hierarchies, the relations between each regional dominant power and each regional challenger are studied to determine whether or not power parity and dissatisfaction with the regional status quo are associated with war within the regional hierarchies.[15] Simply put, we discern whether periods in which a dissatisfied regional challenger is roughly equal to the regional dominant power coincide with periods in which wars occurred within regional hierarchies.

To apply the multiple hierarchy model, regional hierarchies are defined for South America, the Middle East, Africa, and the Far East.[16] Empirically, Power Transition theory's expectations about parity and status quo evaluations are sustained. South America experienced two wars[17] during this time frame, the War of the Pacific and the Chaco War. Both occurred under conditions of power parity and status quo dissatisfaction by the challenger. In the Middle East there were four wars during the covered years (Six Day War, Yom Kippur War, Israeli-Syrian 1982 War in southern Lebanon, and the Iran-Iraq War), all but one of which (Israeli-Syrian) occurring under conditions anticipated by the theory. East Asia's five relevant wars (India-Pakistan 1965, India-Pakistan 1971, North-South Korea 1950, North-South Vietnam 1965, and Vietnam-Cambodia 1975) were all fought under conditions of status quo dissatisfaction, but only two of them (Korea and Vietnam) were fought while the principal belligerents were at relative parity.[18] The two wars in Africa since 1960 (Ethiopia-Somalia 1977 and Uganda-Tanzania 1978) did not occur as anticipated by the theory, neither power parity nor dissatisfaction were observed (although, power parity and status quo dissatisfaction do have important impacts in Africa because they increase the probability of disputes and wars, as described below).

The studies summarized in figure 3.2 (p. 72) evaluate the probability of observing a war within a regional hierarchy given variation in the presence of power parity and/or status quo dissatisfaction on the part of the regional challenger.[19] Figure 3.2 can be interpreted intuitively. It represents the probability of war occurring under varying combinations of power distributions and satisfaction. For example, the probability of a war occurring within African regional hierarchies is far less likely when neither parity nor dissatisfaction is present. Figure 3.2 makes such comparisons possible by providing the conditional probability of observing a war given different combinations of power parity and/or status quo dissatisfaction.[20]

For all five regions, the probability of war increases dramatically as parity and dissatisfaction obtain. Indeed, war is five to ten times more likely

Conditional Probability of War by Regions
(in percentage)

		Great Powers	Africa	Far East	Middle East	South America
Parity and Satisfaction	*No parity, satisfaction*	7.9	0.8	2.2	1.4	1.2
	Parity, satisfaction	14.8	1.5	4.2	2.7	2.3
	No parity, dissatisfaction	32.0	4.0	10.7	7.1	6.1
	Parity, dissatisfaction	48.6	7.8	19.4	13.3	11.6

Figure 3.2   Probability of Regional Wars

when parity and dissatisfaction are jointly present. The relatively low probabilities of war in minor power regions (7.8 to 19.4 percent) still indicates that power parity and dissatisfaction are dangerous. War is such a ghastly business that even seemingly minor increases in its probability are dangerous. A conditional probability of war of 19.4 percent might seem low, but this still means that one in five Far Eastern dyads characterized by parity and dissatisfaction go to war. From our perspective, this is substantial.[21]

The cell entries of figure 3.2 are conditional probabilities of war based on logistic regression analyses. To see how much going from preponderance to parity increases the probability of war for a given great power dyad, one would compare the second row of the first column (14.8 percent) to the first row of the first column (7.9 percent). Doing so provides the change in the probability of war for the average great power dyad as it varies from a situation of preponderance to one of parity. What we learn by making this comparison is that the average great power dyad under parity is twice as likely to go to war as is a great power dyad not characterized by parity. Similar comparisons can be made within each of the other regional contexts; all lead to the conclusion that parity and dissatisfaction make war much more likely.

In the case of the great powers we observe that as we go from neither parity nor dissatisfaction to situations in which there is parity alone or dissatisfaction alone to situations in which there is both parity and dissatisfaction, the estimated probability of war increases from about 8 percent to about 15 percent, then to 32 percent, and finally reaches its peak at almost 49 percent. These are enormous substantive changes. Parity and dissatisfaction make war six times more likely than is the case when these two belligerent conditions are not present. This is impressive support for Power Transition theory, but it is support we already anticipated based on the discussion of Power Transition's empirical validity in chapter 1 and the graphic support adduced in chapter 2. What is perhaps much more interesting, and certainly unique to this chapter, is that the same sorts of increases are observed within minor power regional settings as well.

When we make comparisons across the cells of figure 3.2 for the minor power regions, we find that the probability of war in African regional hierarchies increases almost tenfold (from 0.8 percent in the first row to 7.8 percent in the bottom row). Similarly, in Far Eastern regional hierarchies the probability of war when the conditions Power Transition theory suggests are the causes of war increase almost ninefold (from 2.2 percent in the first row to 19.4 percent in the bottom row). In the Middle East the probability of war in regional hierarchies increases almost tenfold (from 1.4 to 13.3 percent), and the same is true in South American regional hierarchies (where the corresponding increase as we go from neither parity nor dissatisfaction to the joint presence of these two dangerous conditions is from 1.2 to 11.6 percent). Parity and dissatisfaction make war, on average, ten times more likely in minor power regional settings. This is strong empirical validation of the multiple hierarchy model's expectations.

Why should this be a surprise to anyone? Why should we care about this finding? The answers to both questions are related. Over the years there has been a tendency in academic circles and in foreign policy organizations to focus on what is unique or specific to a given country or place. The U.S. Department of State is organized by "country desks," units specific to each foreign country with which the United States carries on diplomatic relations. In academic circles it is very common to train "area specialists" who become experts in the politics and history of a given country or region.

While country desks and area specialists are important, even essential repositories for detailed descriptive information, their very existence suggests the assumption that there is something unique about the place in which they specialize. Similarly, popular opinion holds that there is "something different" about Africans compared to Europeans, or about Middle Eastern interstate relations compared to relations between Canada and the United States. We hear of intractable disagreements, irrational attachments to holy war, to tribe or caste affecting relations between minor powers. In contrast, the states of the developed world are presumed, if only implicitly, to be more rational, more calculating, and thus less emotional in their interstate interactions.

The findings reported in figure 3.2 suggest that the factors associated with the occurrence of war are similar enough across minor power regions and across the minor-major power divide that we can use one theoretical structure to explain and thus anticipate when wars will occur around the world. There may still be important differences between Arab-Israeli relations compared to British-German relations, but those differences are of degree, not kind. Regardless of culture, level of development, or whatever other variable allegedly makes some part of the world "different" from the rest, the presence of power parity and dissatisfaction with the status quo has a substantial and consistently positive impact on the probability of war. This means that we can have great confidence in using Power Transition theory to guide our expectations about future international interactions within minor power regions as well as among the great powers.

Dynamics of Regional Transitions

An additional and perhaps more intuitive way to demonstrate the importance of Power Transition arguments for analysis of minor power interactions and their relationship with major powers can be achieved by considering the dynamics of transitions in important regional conflicts. Two cases were selected based on their high visibility and impact in the twentieth century.

North and South Vietnam

Figure 3.3 shows the relative power shares of North and South Vietnam.[22] When this ratio is above parity, the challenging North is more powerful than the defending South. The countries face prolonged parity from 1954 until the defeat of South Vietnam in 1975. These are the classic conditions for a serious and prolonged war, specified by Power Transition theory. Figure 3.2 is divided into two periods. The early war period refers to the initial conflict between North and South Vietnam, rooted in the regional hierarchy. Interference by the foreign actors is minimal during this period. The French withdrew from North Vietnam following their defeat at Dien Bien Phu and were only minor participants during this period. The United States involvement was increasing but still limited prior to the Gulf of Tonkin incident. During the U.S.-supported war period, which begins in 1964, the conflict shifts from a regionally focused war to a conflict involving global powers, who were critical in determining the final outcome.

Following the overtaking in 1955, short of external intervention, one would anticipate that North Vietnam would have defeated the South and unified the country. The extension of the war beyond 1964 is clearly the result of American intervention, which shifted the balance of forces in favor of the South. Despite massive U.S. support, parity is maintained throughout the conflict.[23]

The regional dynamics of power and status quo evaluations account for the initiation of this conflict. Both countries were dissatisfied with the existing distribution of territory, which was the result of the French defeat. From the perspective of the United States and other major powers, this was a war of limited scope. While U.S. fatalities exceeded fifty thousand, the magnitude of loss was not as substantial as in World Wars I and II.

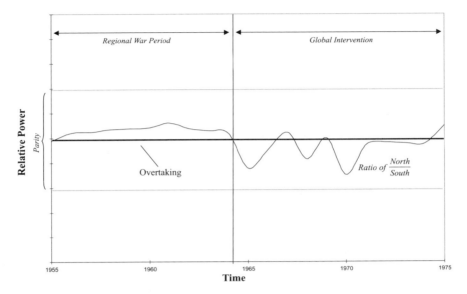

Figure 3.3   Relative Power of North and South Vietnam, 1955-75

For the Vietnamese, this was the regional equivalent of the most dramatic wars at the global level. Indeed, as Power Transition anticipates, the most severe wars occur at times of parity, both at the regional and global level. Severe regional wars can be affected by the intervention of great powers, which will not accept losses of the same magnitude as with a global war. This is the difference between the global hierarchy, where war outcomes are unaffected by the involvement of other actors, and the regional hierarchies, where anticipated outcomes can be reversed by great power involvement. Indeed, to fully understand regional wars, one must consider the pattern of interventions and influence in the global hierarchy — enhancing the levels of uncertainty.

Iran and Iraq

The case of Iran and Iraq illustrates different dynamics in the regional transition process. Figure 3.4 (p. 76) demonstrates that Iran was stronger than Iraq consistently from 1962 through the 1973 oil crisis. This major disturbance of the Middle East region did not cause a conflict. Iran soon recovered from the economic dislocation this engendered and returned to a position of superiority over Iraq. However, in the late 1970s Iran's power share declined precipitously because of the Iranian Revolution of 1978. This domestic strife gutted Iran's share of power within the regional hierarchy. After the installation of the Ayatollah Khomeini, Iran experienced

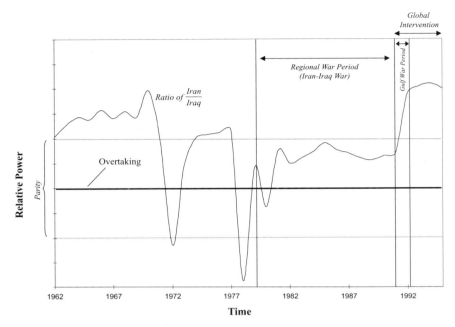

Figure 3.4   Relative Power of Iran and Iraq, 1962-95

a swift recovery. Faced with a narrow window of opportunity, Iraq took advantage of this new Iranian weakness and initiated the Iran-Iraq War. Figure 3.4 reveals that Iran and Iraq remained in the parity region for the duration of this very bloody conflict. This is the likely reason the war endured so long.

The Gulf War, pitting United Nations forces against the Iraqi military establishment, may have precipitated a settlement of the Iran-Iraq War. That earlier conflict had dragged on without clear resolution of the underlying claims. Although overt fighting had stopped, its renewal was seen as likely by many. However, the war over Kuwait brought in the United States and other international powers, which dramatically shifted power relations within this regional hierarchy. This limited war destroyed the relative balance in the region. Iraq can no longer hope to challenge Iran in the near future. Although Iraq clearly remains dissatisfied with regional relations, Power Transition theory does not anticipate a resumption of the conflict unless Iraq somehow regains parity with Iran. Given continuing sanctions against Iraq, such a recovery is not anticipated anytime soon.

These figures are only illustrative, but they demonstrate how Power Transition theory anticipates when minor powers wage war against one another. Discussion above about the various regions and a comparison between the third and second rows of figure 3.2 (p. 72) suggests that dissatisfaction with the regional status quo has a larger impact on the probability of war than does parity. These figures demonstrate the plausibility of the extension of Power Transition theory to analysis of minor power relations and substantiate the importance of parity not only on war onset, but also on war's likely severity and duration.

In sum, evaluation of minor power interactions within regional hierarchies in South America, the Middle East, the Far East, and Africa demonstrates that minor powers fight wars when expected to, based on the multiple hierarchy model of Power Transition theory. Thus, Power Transition theory provides a powerful explanation of most minor power conflicts, as well as of the traditional major power wars.

The Diffusion of War

Nothing within Power Transition precludes the diffusion of a global war into regional hierarchies. In fact, one might anticipate such diffusion based on Power Transition theory. Since the global wars between the dominant power and dissatisfied challenger are fought for control of the international system, they are expected to be very large, very widespread conflicts. Only the great powers have the ability to project power outside of their region. Great powers thus might decide whether a conflict should remain confined or be expanded. Power Transition suggests that direct challenges to the status quo are the foundation of serious wars. The original conceptualization of these wars involved direct threats to the territorial integrity of the belligerents.[24]

The great powers can threaten the territorial integrity of the small powers. The reverse is not true. For example, World War II diffused from the original conflict between Germany and the United Kingdom to encompass virtually every hierarchy in the international system with the exception of South America. Even that exception is debatable since several South American states were successfully induced to join the Allies by declaring war on Germany, and there were naval skirmishes in South American waters, as when the German battleship *Graf Spee* was cornered in Uruguay by the British navy.

As Germany failed in its bid to overcome the United Kingdom in the Battle of Britain, Hitler chose to expand the scope of the conflict to include Russia. The war between Japan and China, which had been waged in a regional context since 1936, escalated to an attack on the British. World War II rose to global proportions when Japan challenged the United States for control of the Pacific. The United States placed primary emphasis on the international challenge by supporting the United Kingdom in its war against Germany. Later it reallocated forces for the Pacific theater. The United States chose this order of priority because it understood that the European effort was for control of the international system. Wars in the global hierarchy that diffuse to the regional level generate serious conflicts because of this underlying imperative.

Regional conflicts, on the other hand, are waged over regional concerns. When minor powers initiate such conflicts, their goal is to establish prominence within the regional hierarchy. Such conflicts do not diffuse upward to the global hierarchy because the nations involved in such challenges lack the power to make credible threats against great powers. And yet, the severity of conflict within regions can be heightened by the intervention, even by the limited interventions, of the great powers.

Despite fears to the contrary, the Vietnam War did not escalate outside of Southeast Asia because none of the minor power countries involved could challenge the interests of the great powers. The same argument holds for the conflict in Korea, which was internationalized but never escalated beyond that restricted region. In Korea the threat of escalation to other regions involved the potential conflict between China and the United States following the crossing of the Yalu River. However, the conflict did not escalate since the United States could not be challenged outside of Northeast Asia. Similar arguments apply to the conflict in Afghanistan and the recent sequence of wars in the Middle East.

In contrast, an apparently regional conflict can escalate when great powers are directly involved and their interests are at stake. World War I started because of the minor conflict between Austria-Hungary and Serbia. Serbia's Russian support provided a context for seething conflict between Germany and England to express itself, thus sparking the broader war. More recently, a similar conflict in the Balkans did not escalate because no great power's interests were at stake — their goals were to limit the conflict. In order to initiate war in the global hierarchy, a direct challenge to the dominant power must exist.

Analysts frequently worry that a conflict in any part of the globe can escalate to a serious global conflagration. The multiple hierarchy perspective suggests that such perceptions are incorrect. Major wars start because of parity conditions in the global hierarchy and their related challenges to the status quo. Minor wars start because of similar conditions within regional hierarchies. Diffusion from the global to the regional hierarchy is possible because the countries involved can make such choices without directly affecting the primary threats they face. Members of the regional hierarchy are dependent in this sense, because escalation is limited without great power involvement. Such involvement is unlikely, since the great powers generally do not face direct challenges from regional actors.

The multiple hierarchy model offers an extension of Power Transition theory that can be used to analyze minor power international interactions. Preliminary empirical evaluations suggest the basic premise of the model — that minor powers fight wars when power parity exists between a regional dominant power and a dissatisfied regional challenger — is supported by

the evidence. This is good news for those who would base policy prescriptions on Power Transition theory, because it suggests that in addition
to being internally logical and consistent, the theory also offers an accurate description and persuasive explanation of a wide range of interstate
relations.

Conclusions and Policy Implications

A number of policy implications follow directly from the multiple hierarchy
model of Power Transition theory. The first is that it may well be possible to anticipate when regional minor power wars will occur. Power parity
between a regional dominant power and a dissatisfied regional challenger
dramatically increase the probability of war between minor powers. If a
contentious pair of minor powers are not roughly equal, or if neither seems
dissatisfied with the regional status quo, war is unlikely to occur between
them. This knowledge could well help policymakers predict how serious
conflicts might become in various "trouble spots."

For example, North Korea has drawn a great deal of American attention in the last few years through its efforts to develop a nuclear arsenal,
as well as its repeated claims that the Korean peninsula should be united
under North Korean leadership. Whether North Korea would act on such
claims has been an important question. The multiple hierarchy model of
Power Transition theory and the evidence summarized above suggest that
any attack by North Korea against South Korea is very unlikely indeed.
Figure 3.2 (p. 72) suggests that a dyad such as North and South Korea has
only a 10-percent chance of war (since North Korea is clearly dissatisfied
but is not at parity with South Korea). By gathering data on status quo
evaluations and relative power within minor power regional systems, any
analyst could generate similar predictions about the potential for war in
whatever area of the world in which they might be interested. Such predictions do not mean that no conflict will occur, but they will indicate how
likely it is that crises and/or disputes will escalate to the serious level of
open warfare.

Acting upon such knowledge, American foreign policy leaders could
take steps to render wars even less likely in various minor power regions.
For example, faced with a persistent conflictual relationship between adversaries such as Egypt and Israel, two different steps could be taken. First, the
United States could ensure that one side (presumably the one with which it
had more common interests) remained preponderant over the other. Such a
policy would likely be very expensive since it would entail massive resource
transfers from the United States to the recipient state, but, if carried out
to the point where clear preponderance was achieved, it should pacify the
relationship.

Such efforts arguably were undertaken by the United States and Soviet

Union with respect to the Egyptian-Israeli dyad during the Cold War. However, in this case the two superpowers may have only offset each other's contributions.[25] In an effort to make their favored minor power belligerent stronger, they may have succeeded in making them equal, and thus prolonging the conflictual period of parity. A much better way to pacify minor power relations is to help the minor powers come to an accommodation with each other over the regional status quo.

A second area in which the multiple hierarchy model of Power Transition theory can offer policy implications concerns the conditions likely to favor intervention into ongoing minor power conflicts. First, if there is a dispute or crisis between two unequal minor power states, that dispute or crisis is unlikely to escalate to war. In such circumstances the United States need not necessarily fear that war will follow if it does not act quickly. Two roughly equal minor powers involved in a dispute or crisis have a much greater probability of escalating their hostilities to war, and thus the sense of urgency would necessarily be greater. Faced with a number of crises simultaneously, the United States could literally prioritize them based on their probability of escalating to war and then deal with them sequentially.

Building on these minor power interstate crises, there is a final policy implication of the multiple hierarchy model. The characteristic of the regional status quo likely determines whether or not a peaceful resolution of minor power conflicts can be achieved. If the regional status quo can be easily divided, then a peaceful solution to minor power conflict will be much more likely.

We mentioned above the minor power competition between Chile, Peru, and Bolivia over the Atacama region along the Pacific Coast of South America. We might also have drawn attention to the similar Paraguayan-Bolivian competition over the Chaco Boreal in the 1920s and 1930s. Aside from the material value of the nitrate deposits in the Atacama (and the access to the sea it granted Bolivia) and suspected oil riches in the Chaco, there was nothing about either territory that could not have been divided. These cases of regional war might well have been averted had the United States or another actor managed to serve as mediators. Were the maintenance of peace in western South America in the 1870s and 1880s, or in central South America in the 1920s and 1930s important enough, the United States may have even been able to provide sufficient financial incentives of its own to forestall these tragic wars.[26]

Such territory-based regional status quos may be more amenable to negotiated settlements than others. By contrast, many would argue that the territorial dispute between India and Pakistan over Kashmir is of a different nature than that between Bolivia and Paraguay over the Chaco. This may well be true, but the fact that accommodation between Egypt and Israel was found strongly suggests that efforts could and should be made toward a similar goal in the subcontinent. Given that India and Pakistan are now both nuclear states, the incentive to find a way to keep both satisfied with their regional status quo has never been greater.

This chapter has described a transformation of Power Transition theory into a general theory of war initiation. The ability to identify the conditions under which wars are most likely to occur is critical for the optimal construction of foreign policy. An understanding of regional hierarchies should play an important role in the foreign policy of the dominant world power, for these miniature international systems comprise a substantial part of the international system within which the preponderant country establishes interstate relations.

CHAPTER 4
Security Applications: Deterrence and Proliferation

> *The splitting of the atom has changed everything save man's mode of thinking: thus, we drift towards unparalleled catastrophe.* — ALBERT EINSTEIN

This chapter explores the policy implications derived from the Power Transition perspective for the nuclear era. Focusing on distributions of power as well as the spread of nuclear capabilities, the Power Transition research program challenges some aspects of existing policy on nuclear deterrence but generally supports current policy on proliferation.

Unlike the classical model of deterrence, in which mutual assured destruction (MAD) associates stability with nuclear parity, Power Transition suggests that nuclear parity can generate *instability*.[1] The theory accepts the proposition that nuclear weapons diminish the likelihood of war by raising the costs associated with conflict. Increasing the size of nuclear arsenals unquestionably magnifies the potential severity of war. But Power Transition tells us that deterrence is not an absolute. The deterrence offered by nuclear weapons will not guarantee the peace under all circumstances. Power transitions in the nuclear era remain dangerous events that can result in war, nuclear weapons notwithstanding. Under nuclear parity the probability of conflict is lower than in a conventional parity environment, but it is still higher than at nuclear preponderance.

These insights on deterrence fundamentally challenge some aspects of existing beliefs and doctrine. This chapter contends that nuclear deterrence is structurally unstable and therefore unreliable, particularly when nuclear parity is achieved. These conclusions are at odds with the long-held tenets of U.S. arms control policy that it is in the United States' interest to maintain nuclear equality among potential contenders and that security is ensured by reducing nuclear arsenals simultaneously. We find that nuclear preponderance in the hands of a defender who is satisfied with the status quo ensures peace. Nuclear parity or preponderance by a dissatisfied challenger can lead to nuclear war. That distinction alone distinguishes Power Transition from current theories on deterrence.

With regard to proliferation, Power Transition argues that the spread of nuclear weapons is particularly dangerous. When relatively dissatisfied nations such as India or Iran join the nuclear club and there are regional or global transitions, the probability of nuclear war rises. Thus, Power Transition's insights on proliferation are consistent with current U.S. policy, although the underlying rationale may be different.

Deterrence and arms control are the twin pillars upon which the U.S. security policy was based throughout the Cold War. While deterrence has faded in importance, proliferation, long a secondary threat, now has become a central focus of U.S. policy. More than a decade after the end of the Cold War, neither of these concepts has been systematically challenged.[2] This lapse of interest could have grave consequences. We intend to address some of the fundamental issues here.[3]

The Costs of Nuclear War

Nuclear weapons significantly raise the stakes of interstate conflict. Recognizing that there are many techniques and controversies about calculating the costs of nuclear war, we offer figure 4.1 (p. 84) as one design. It is based on calculations for the United States and the USSR. The vertical axis of this figure represents the likely percentage of population that would be destroyed sixty days after a nuclear exchange. The horizontal axis represents the total number of megatons launched during a war.

Since we have observed the effects of a nuclear war only once at low magnitude, we must rely on estimates of the likely costs of such a dispute. The lowest estimate considers only the effects of the impact per megaton from the blast radius.[4] This estimate suggests that at least 500 equivalent megatons are necessary to destroy more than 20 percent of the total populations of the two combatants. A less conservative estimate considers the effects of radiation, implying that 1,000 equivalent megatons will destroy closer to 40 percent of the population of the target country.[5] Finally, the grimmest estimate suggests that the impact of nuclear devices will cause a nuclear winter due to the dust and debris that will be forced into the lower atmosphere. This ancillary destruction, it is argued, will raise the level of destruction to nearly the entire population with just over 1,000 nuclear warheads. It would destroy well over 40 percent of the population with approximately 500 equivalent megatons.[6]

Arms agreements reached at the time of this writing still permit the United States and Russia each to maintain an arsenal easily capable of destroying the other country. Such arsenals also would destroy China and the European Union because of the higher geographic concentration of the population and urban centers. Regional hierarchies pose a much different picture. In the Middle East, for example, weapons delivering the equivalent of 10 megatons would more than suffice to destroy any society in that region. Likewise, on the Korean peninsula, the ability to deliver 5 equivalent megatons would destroy most life there.

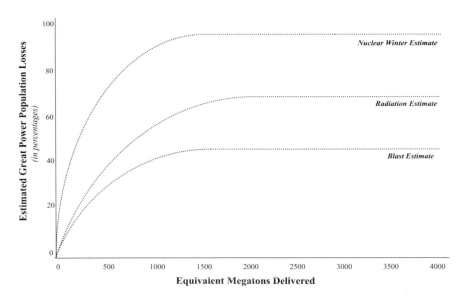

Figure 4.1   Nuclear War Population Losses for Great Powers

There can be no doubt about the destructive nature of nuclear weapons. Contrast these estimates with those achieved by conventional conflict. Conventional conflicts at the magnitude of World Wars I and II destroyed, at their height, up to 15 percent of the total population among combatants. In World War II, the highest casualties as a percentage of the nation's population were suffered by Poland at 19.6 percent, Yugoslavia at 10.6 percent, and Russia at 10.1 percent, while Germany endured losses of about 9 percent, France 1.5 percent, the United Kingdom less than .07 percent, and the United States less than .02 percent.[7] Such losses pale in comparison with the 40 percent or greater estimated for serious nuclear exchanges, or the specter of a nuclear winter that could decimate most life on the planet.

Nuclear weapons are as destructive as advocates of deterrence contend. They increase the cost of war. But do they offer the permanent security of peace through deterrence? Do the horrible costs make war obsolete? We think not. Power Transition warns policymakers not to put ultimate faith in nuclear deterrence. We will present our conclusions on this theoretically and then in policy terms.

The Structure of Deterrence

Let us review the main theoretical perspectives on deterrence and the policies that follow from them. Classical nuclear deterrence, our base case

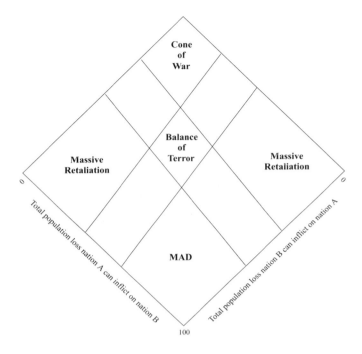

Figure 4.2 The Structure of Deterrence

for comparative purposes, is a derivative of the balance of power theory.[8] We choose the classic deterrence position, rather than one of its variants, because it offers the most unambiguously clear contrasts with Power Transition theory. Obviously there are many clarifications and extensions of classic deterrence theory that would modify the comparisons in the following three sections. But the stark contrasts serve our purpose of encouraging others to challenge dogma. We examine the structure of deterrence as defined by the interaction between two competitors.[9]

Based on the casualty estimates implied in figure 4.1, figure 4.2 matches the expectations of cost to theoretical arguments about deterrence. In figure 4.2, the right axis portrays the total population loss the challenger can inflict on the defender in the event of an all-out nuclear conflict, while the left axis represents the total population loss that the defender can inflict on the challenger. Each of these axes diminishes in intensity. At the bottom of the figure, mutual assured destruction represents the almost complete eradication of each population in an all-out nuclear exchange. This portrays the nuclear relationship between the United States and the Soviet Union toward the end of the Cold War. Mutual assured destruction assumes that both countries hold a secure second-strike capability and posses massive nuclear arsenals. Classical deterrence postulates that MAD is ultrastable. Power Transition challenges this conclusion.

As the challenger is less able to inflict damage on the defender we move to the right and left side of the figure into the massive retaliation regions. This represents a relationship of extreme asymmetry in nuclear capacity. This condition currently exists between Israel and its Arab neighbors, where the defender easily can destroy any challenger without fear of nuclear reprisal. The left side of the figure shows a relationship where the defender dominates the challenger, as was the case during the early Cold War. The right side of the figure shows a condition where the challenger dominates the defender in terms of nuclear capability. Thus far, we have no empirical experience with this condition. In classical deterrence theory, these outcomes are identical, but we will show that from the perspective of Power Transition these are very different conditions. As the historical record indicates, massive retaliation in the hands of a satisfied defender preserves peace. Massive retaliation in the challenger's hands is far less stable.

In the center of this figure is a region called balance of terror, which reimposes symmetry to a nuclear relationship. This represents "vulnerable parity" in the nuclear capability between the two countries because neither side can assure that it is capable of destroying its opponent after a preemptive first strike. India and Pakistan coexist in this tenuous condition today. The absence of a secure second-strike capability distinguishes the balance of terror from MAD. In the former, a preemptive war is anticipated as each side wishes to strike first in case of a confrontation. In the latter, neither side wishes to wage a nuclear conflict since the consequences of such a decision are unthinkable. Both classical deterrence and Power Transition anticipate that balance of terror is a temporary condition, resolved by the buildup of nuclear arsenals.

The cone of war, located at the top of figure 4.2 represents two countries with only conventional or very limited nuclear capabilities. Deterrence, in the sense of reducing the probability of war, may apply here, but deterrence in the sense of prevention of war does not. Since neither side can inflict costs on the opponent that are sufficient to deter action, the use of war to resolve disputes is prevalent. The historical record discussed in the previous chapter attests to the validity of this claim.

Both classical deterrence and Power Transition can be structured within the parameters established by figure 4.2, but each perspective produces very different implications. The following sections describe and then evaluate the differences emerging from these theoretical approaches to nuclear weapons and their derived policy prescriptions.

The Classical Deterrence Perspective

Classical deterrence argues that a first strike is unacceptable because the only use for nuclear weapons is the implicit threat of retaliation. It is undesirable to use such weapons to advance nondeterrent policies. Classical deterrence posits that the reason for a first-strike ban is that the high anticipated costs of war deters aggression and thereby ensures peace. Figure 4.3 (p. 88) demonstrates the implications of this perspective in terms of the probability of war.

The logic of classical deterrence states that a balance of power (that is, parity) does not by itself assure peace. A nuclear balance that increases costs to unacceptable levels assures peace.[10] The cone of war is unstable because conventional arsenals produce relatively low casualties.[11] That is, they do not deter, and therefore nations choose war over peace as they did in World Wars I and II. Classical deterrence, following Carl von Clausewitz, argues that in conventional environments war is the continuation of policy by other means, and it can be waged under any power configuration.

Nuclear arsenals are limited under balance of terror, as neither side has achieved a secure second strike. A balance-of-terror condition prevailed between the United States and the USSR in the 1950s and early 1960s. This is the condition that exists today among India, China, and Pakistan. Here classical deterrence anticipates conflict because the uncertainty about opponents' intentions can motivate war, and a preemptive strike can avert retaliation. The potential for winning and concurrently averting defeat by preemption makes this region even more unstable than the cone of war.

Under MAD, the costs of war become prohibitive. Neither opponent will initiate or retaliate. Classical deterrence argues that the guarantee of overwhelming destruction is the reason for lasting peace. MAD is ultrastable and peaceful because each side is terrified by the potential consequences of a nuclear exchange. In practice, advocates of MAD argue that the Cold War did not heat up because nuclear weapons were present. The USSR and the United States did not fight because of the fear of retaliation that would ensure mutual destruction. Such statements have face validity: nuclear weapons have not been used, thus far, between nations with equivalent arsenals. The question raised here is whether we can entrust future peace to the nuclear balance.

Massive retaliation also is stable, but some instability can emerge during the period of transition to MAD. Classical deterrence postulates that a preponderant nation does not initiate war. The nuclear attack by the United States against Japan, however, presents a consistency problem. One can argue that the United States was not in a position to impose massive retaliation, or that the decision essentially was a "conventional" one in the context of the war. Whatever the interpretation, the record shows that war is possible under nuclear preponderance.

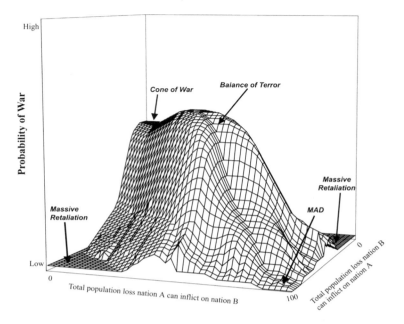

Figure 4.3   Classical Deterrence and the Probability of Nuclear War

One counterintuitive addition proposed by classical deterrence is that any nuclear nation in anarchy will not strike first, giving up its temporary advantage. Once nuclear parity is achieved, nuclear contenders will only assure opponents that any aggression will lead to nuclear retaliation. To achieve consistency in these policy prescriptions, classical deterrence creates a serious logical inconsistency by rejecting the assumption of anarchy under massive retaliation but reincorporating that assumption under MAD. Recall that anarchy is defined as the absence of government rules and norms. That is, they do not deter and therefore nations choose war over peace as they did in World Wars I and II.[12] Yet under nuclear preponderance anarchy is abandoned since war will not be waged, as nuclear weapons have no use other than to deter war.[13] On the other hand, anarchy is reintroduced as each side is secured by the threat of mutual retaliation, and arsenals must be maintained to ensure this capability.

Under nuclear preponderance, therefore, classical deterrence rejects anarchy and accepts the assumption that a nuclear nation prefers the status quo to war since it will retaliate only when challenged. It attributes such behavior only to nuclear nations and not to all nations. Thus, classical deterrence introduces an assumption that holds only for the nuclear nations and not for conventional powers. When classical deterrence considers

MAD, however, the argument shifts back to anarchy. Now classical deterrence argues that peace is preserved only through retaliatory threats. Advocates are concerned, for example, that the deployment of defensive weapon systems will lead to the loss of a retaliatory capability by one side, and thus produce a preemptive war initiated by the side without a nuclear shield. Yet if a nation does not initiate war when it holds nuclear preponderance, then why should the reintroduction of massive retaliation be a danger that is worth the nuclear war?

The practical implications of this logic are unexpected. Extending the classical deterrence argument to its logical conclusion, one expects that had the Soviet Union, China, Iran, or Iraq developed nuclear weapons first in their respective hierarchies, they would have been as self-deterred as the United States, Britain, or Israel. To date, we have so little relevant data that the argument cannot be tested. Yet if a dissatisfied nation faces high costs or even defeat in a conventional conflict, is it plausible to argue that it would not utilize a first-strike option against an opponent?

Specifically, had Iraq acquired nuclear weapons prior to the Gulf War, would such weapons not have been used, even if the government of Iraq were directly in danger of losing a conventional conflict? Much of the policy community overlooks these very troublesome aspects of classical deterrence by neatly separating regional from global affairs. The development of nuclear weapons by India and Pakistan is universally seen as causing instability. Yet, the development of nuclear weapons by the United States and Soviet Union presumably ensured stability during the Cold War. With the buildup of nuclear arsenals across multiple actors, we no longer have the luxury of preserving such inconsistencies.

Let us now consider the dynamics generated by changes in the size of nuclear arsenals. The transitions from massive retaliation to MAD produce uncertainty and instability. From the classical deterrence perspective, nuclear preponderance under massive retaliation is superior to nuclear symmetry because no retaliation is possible, and the first nation has no intention to preempt while preponderant. As a potential opponent builds its own nuclear arsenal, however, a transition from massive retaliation to MAD is generated. Under such circumstances, the still preponderant nation has every incentive to preempt.

One would expect preemptive strikes to prevent such transitions. There is a limited record of such events. Of the states that have weapons-grade nuclear capabilities, only Israel attempted to thwart Iraqi nuclear development by force. Others did not. The United States subsidized British nuclear development. France's efforts received tacit support.[14] The United States allowed the Soviet nuclear program to grow without challenge. Further, China developed nuclear weapons with neither of the two superpowers using preemptive strikes to slow down or prevent that effort. Israel, South Africa, Pakistan, and India received only minor, if any, sanctions for their nuclear programs. Nuclear arsenal buildups do not automatically lead to external intervention.

Turning one more time to figure 4.3 (p. 88), note that once MAD is achieved, a credible deterrent shield emerges for both parties. This point becomes ultrastable when all parties achieve second-strike capabilities against potential opponents. Classical deterrence implies that once in MAD, there is no reason to exit. As discussed later, the Strategic Defense Initiative is opposed by some because a reverse transition from MAD to massive retaliation would threaten the secure second-strike capability and prompt preemption. Some strategists argued the USSR would attempt a preemptive nuclear strike before full deployment of a U.S. defensive shield.

The important point is that shifts in the relative retaliatory capability of one nation are destabilizing. Only MAD is ultimately stable. If this is so, why do nuclear nations seek to prevent proliferation so selectively? Why is the United States, for example, making major efforts to prevent the acquisition of nuclear technology by North Korea, Iraq, and Iran while it winks at larger deployments by Israel or France? Given the size of nuclear arsenals held by these nations, only the latter two have the potential to threaten the United States directly. Yet U.S. preventive actions are directed only at the dissatisfied nations. Classical deterrence is mute on this issue.

Classical deterrence advocates imply that to ensure stability, nations should choose nuclear parity over nuclear preponderance. As we will see, to enhance MAD, classical purists argue that (1) nuclear proliferation be accelerated to achieve nuclear parity throughout the entire international system, (2) second-strike technology be shared, and (3) one-sided technological breakthroughs be avoided.

Finally, classical deterrence views the elimination of nuclear weapons as dangerous. This is not only due to the transitions required but also the realization that returning to a conventional world places competitors once more in the cone of war. Without nuclear weapons, the world would face the very conditions that generated World Wars I and II. According to classical deterrence, nuclear weapons protect peace. In a nuclear world, nations should seek a nuclear parity that ensures stability. Change is destabilizing.

The Power Transition Perspective

The Power Transition perspective postulates that parity is associated with war, while preponderance is associated with peace. Figure 4.4 demonstrates the implications of this conclusion in terms of the probability of war across various conditions.

Power Transition stipulates that world politics is played in a hierarchical rather than an anarchic environment. Within the global hierarchy, preponderance leads to stability. The satisfied dominant nation and its allies seek to preserve the status quo. While they maintain an interest in expand-

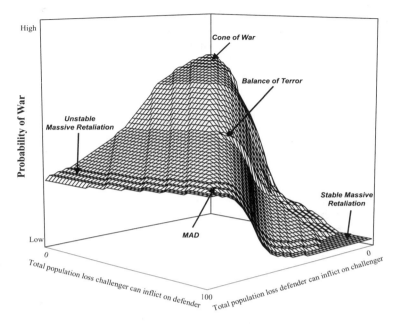

Figure 4.4 Power Transition and the Probability of Nuclear War

ing their power and security, they do not find it necessary to exercise all their coercive options to do so.

As in the case of conventional weapons, in the nuclear era the danger of major war is maximized under parity. The driving force remains a power transition, resulting from convergence generated by differential patterns of economic growth among nations. The effects of nuclear weapons, therefore, are different from those anticipated by the classical perspective. Nuclear preponderance in the hands of a satisfied defender produces stability, while in the hands of a dissatisfied challenger the outcome is unstable. In direct contradiction to classical deterrence, the probability of nuclear war is high at nuclear parity (MAD) if at least one of the nuclear powers remains dissatisfied.

We recognize that the potential for massive casualties reduces the probability of war. Figure 4.4 shows that the probability of war consistently declines as nuclear arsenals grow. Leaders must contemplate the far more serious costs of a nuclear as opposed to a conventional confrontation, thus the probability of war is higher in the cone of war than in the period of MAD. At this point asymmetries emerge. Under MAD, the probability of nuclear war is much higher than under massive retaliation when the dominant power enjoys nuclear preponderance. Yet, the high probability of war under MAD is similar to that under massive retaliation when the challenger is preponderant, though this is an unlikely event. Finally, war under MAD is likely to escalate to massive levels while war under massive retaliation led by the challenger is likely to remain limited because of the defender's inability to respond in kind.

Unlike classical deterrence, Power Transition anticipates that increased costs reduce the probability of conflict but are insufficient to prevent conflict or avert escalation. Increased costs make nuclear conflict under parity less likely, but if waged, far more severe. Nuclear arsenals do not, therefore, offer the cold comfort of stability through fear promised by mutual assured destruction. Instead, if war breaks out under parity the large nuclear arsenals held by nuclear contenders allow them to escalate the costs of war to levels as yet unseen.

Consider first the MAD conditions broken down along adherence and opposition to the status quo. The effects of dissatisfaction are disturbing. A dissatisfied nation that matches the nuclear capacity of the defender is expected to use its capability to advance demands for a new status quo. From this perspective, the Cold War remained cold because the United States was preponderant, and the USSR could not credibly challenge the United States or its NATO allies. The only questionable case is the absence of nuclear war between China and Russia immediately following the collapse of the USSR. To act during this overtaking, China had to have nuclear parity, which it did not. Still, conditions close to those described by Power Transition were present for a very short period, and a conflict did not take place.[15]

When conventional parity is present along with dissatisfaction, the probability that disputes will be resolved with a nuclear attack rises sharply. For this reason, the future relations between the United States and China are seen as far more dangerous than the previous relations between the United States and the USSR. When China reaches conventional parity and threatens to overtake the United States sometime in this century, the possibility of a nuclear war should rise unless these two nations reconcile their differences.

Nuclear conflicts in regional hierarchies also are possible. In the Middle East, for example, several nations are attempting to challenge the Israeli nuclear monopoly that has ensured the peace. As the economies of dissatisfied Arab nations grow, the potential for nuclear war is expected to increase since peace will no longer be ensured by the nuclear preponderance of the relatively satisfied Israel. Several of these nations are attempting to develop nuclear weapons, and there is a realistic potential for a power transition with Israel. It is worth noting that the nuclear capability required for these nations to achieve nuclear parity with Israel is far less demanding than that achieved by the major powers. Regional nuclear wars of devastating magnitude are possible even when nuclear arsenals are very small. Less than a dozen one-megaton warheads or their equivalent, mounted on short-range missiles or airframes are sufficient to assure the destruction of any nation

in the Middle East, and even fewer would be required to destroy
rean peninsula. For this reason, attempts by Iran, Iraq, and others in the
region to acquire limited nuclear arsenals could produce regional nuclear
parity almost overnight.[16] All the preconditions conducive to nuclear conflict (power transition, dissatisfaction, and nuclear parity) are emerging in
this region. Several dyads are at risk, including the most obvious of Israel/
Iraq and Iraq/Iran. If Power Transition theory is correct, the stability of deterrence will be sorely tested over the next two decades in these regional
hierarchies. These Middle East scenarios squarely challenge the logic of
classical deterrence.[17]

Similar distinctions appear with regard to the effects of nuclear proliferation. Power Transition posits that stability is assured under parity
when both sides approve of the status quo, but not otherwise. Selective
proliferation is the policy of nuclear nations. For this reason the United
States encouraged British acquisition of nuclear weapons, probably covertly
assisted the Israelis, and offered only token resistance to the indigenous development of nuclear capabilities by France. These countries all supported
the global status quo.

The United States opposed the acquisition of nuclear capabilities by
Russia and China because both were dissatisfied with the global status quo.
It also objected to the acquisition of weapons by India and Pakistan. So
did China, albeit somewhat after the fact. The United States is working
very hard to prevent nuclear proliferation to Iran, Iraq, and North Korea. Consistent with Power Transition, variations in response to nuclear
proliferation generally are directly related to the degree of dissatisfaction
among nations. They are not direct responses to the acquisition of nuclear
weapons per se.

Let us next consider massive retaliation. When the balance of nuclear
arsenals favors the dominant and satisfied power in a hierarchy, Power
Transition and classical deterrence contend that the likelihood of conflict is
minimal. The United States did not initiate World War III against the USSR
following such events as the Berlin Crisis or the Hungarian Revolution because its goal was to preserve the status quo. The United States did not use
nuclear weapons against China to resolve the war in Korea for precisely the
same reasons. The Soviet Union did not use nuclear weapons against China
during the Sino-Soviet split because China could not challenge the USSR's
conventional capability at the time.

Power Transition differs fundamentally from classical deterrence regarding the implications of massive retaliation when nuclear preponderance
favors the challenger. A preponderant challenger would initiate probes to
alter the status quo. Facing a preponderant, dissatisfied nation, the non-
nuclear defender would most likely give in, but might fight a short defensive
war. This condition is very unlikely and has not materialized thus far. A dissatisfied nation is most likely to score low on technology and productivity,

thus it is unlikely that this nation would lead in the deployment of nuclear weapons within its hierarchy. Yet if such conditions do emerge, then the dissatisfied nation should attempt to challenge the status quo because it is disadvantaged by it. Unlike classical deterrence, the Power Transition perspective postulates that massive retaliation in the hands of a dissatisfied challenger is very dangerous to peace. Had Hitler, Stalin, or Hussein acquired nuclear weapons first, they surely would have used them to advance a new status quo for the globe or region.

The policy implications offered by classical deterrence and Power Transition could not be more different. Given the likely consequences of a failure, knowing which perspective is more accurate becomes extremely important. As discussed later in this chapter, there is indirect evidence, both logical and empirical, to suggest that the implications drawn from Power Transition theory are more consistent with reality than are those from classical deterrence.

The Dynamics of Deterrence

Extensions of Power Transition suggest, in their newest formal models, that specific dynamics underlie deterrence.[18] So far, studies of war initiation have resembled a static photograph. The new Power Transition dynamic models, in contrast, resemble an animated movie where situations evolve and decisions develop over time. Our theoretical argument, which is consistent with policy insights, states that leadership preferences and national power change over time and that such changes affect the timing of war. The introduction of time produces important insights.

From Power Transition's perspective, the relative strength of one nation to that of its opponent increases over time during the transition. During the transition, anticipated gains increase as time passes, and a leader waits until the chances of victory are maximized before initiating a fight. At the same time, leaders discount the value for victory over time.[19] The decision to fight under Power Transition occurs because of the combination of an increase in power and a reduction in utility for conflict over time. The optimal point is reached when the initiator anticipates that there will be no more relative gains in power, and concurrently, the anticipated gains from conflict are expected to decline.

During a power transition, a nation is expected to wait before waging war until the gains it foresees from a conflict are maximized. Similar arguments can be made about classical deterrence in a more static context, because balance is the condition for peace and growth patterns do not affect the expected outcomes. Figure 4.5 shows the different derivations obtained from these competing perspectives.

Figure 4.5 charts the sequence of choices facing a leader.[20] In the Power Transition dynamic, leaders of dissatisfied nations will refrain from making

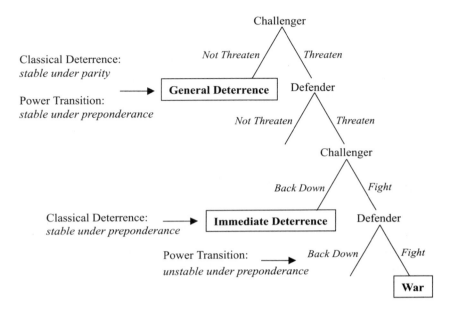

Figure 4.5   The Dynamics of Deterrence

a threat when the dominant power is overwhelmingly preponderant because the probability of success is minimal. Such conditions are overcome during a power transition. Then war initiation is reached after two stages.

In the first stage, threats are made, and in the second stage, these threats are executed. In other words, a nation first threatens to fight, and then, if its opponent resists, it decides whether or not to go to war.[21] Peace is preserved when *general deterrence* is successful, which is the condition when no threats are made. Peace is also preserved when *immediate deterrence* is successful, which is the condition when the challenger threatens to fight, sending a hostile signal, but then backs down.

General deterrence is hard to illustrate because when it succeeds nothing happens. The absence of war in Europe illustrates this condition, but it is very difficult to attribute it to the existence of nuclear weapons since other prospective "causes" of peace coincidentally have been present. Immediate deterrence, on the other hand, can be illustrated easily. U.S. actions in Berlin, in Korea, and most notably in Cuba illustrate serious crises that were resolved, or not resolved, by the explicit threat to use nuclear weapons. In this context, classical deterrence and Power Transition draw very different conclusions regarding the stability of these two stages of deterrence.

From the classical deterrence perspective, when two nations are equal in power, general deterrence is more likely to succeed because the challenger makes trivial demands that do not require war to settle. General deterrence fails (that is, the challenger makes a threat and succeeds) only when the challenger is sure before making such a threat that escalation will not occur. Immediate deterrence is rarely stable since it becomes relevant only once the challenger has anticipated its failure. This perspective explains the stability since World War II. The crises over Berlin, Hungary, and Cuba that could have involved the United States and the USSR in a major nuclear war were defused when one or the other side yielded. Both sides understood that they had the potential to escalate to World War III.

On the other hand, in the Korean, Vietnamese, and Afghani crises, neither side yielded because both sides understood that there would be no escalation to nuclear warfare. The question is what will happen in the next crisis? Will a crisis escalate to nuclear proportions between India and Pakistan? Would a crisis between Iran and Iraq, if both were to obtain nuclear weapons, escalate to war? We cannot answer such questions now with a static approach that recognizes a sequence of decisions but places leaders in a time vacuum and does not contemplate their past, present, and future calculations. Adding a time dimension to the calculation of payoffs in such a context, as proposed by the dynamic perspective of Power Transition, reverses these results.

From the Power Transition perspective, general deterrence is stable under preponderance. As the challenger's power rises, however, general deterrence is increasingly likely to fail. A critical moment is reached when the challenger believes it cannot gain more, but the defender is still willing to resist. On the other hand, immediate deterrence is more likely to succeed under parity before the critical moment is reached and is more likely to fail under preponderance. Here, the implication is that a satisfied nation like Israel is not likely to use its weapons first even against threats. If Iraq, a dissatisfied nation, held such an advantage, it likely would use it.

Using the dynamic approach, the most critical policy implications extracted from the analysis of deterrence steps are reversed. First, whereas classical deterrence suggests that the success of general deterrence prevents nuclear war and immediate deterrence does not, Power Transition postulates that general deterrence can fail as the challenger approaches parity, but immediate deterrence may still prevent a conflict. Stability in classical deterrence depends on the size of arsenals. Stability under Power Transition requires arsenals but depends on successful implementation of immediate deterrence — decision makers count. When structural conditions are aligned in favor of war, the choices made by leaders make the difference between war and peace.[22] Effective diplomacy, not the sheer size of arsenals, prevents nuclear war. As before, if the status quo is made favorable to the challenger, stability is maintained. If dissatisfaction rises and the conditions are ripe, nuclear weapons ensure a more devastating war.

The Middle East is an excellent illustration of this argument. Classical deterrence suggests that as long as Israel is preponderant, general deterrence is tenuous because only the unwillingness to strike first prevents Israel from attacking its neighbors. Under nuclear parity and MAD both sides would be deterred. On the other hand, the Power Transition perspective argues that as long as Israel is preponderant and supports the status quo, general deterrence is likely to succeed. If dissatisfied nations surrounding Israel grow in power and approach parity — which is likely given their populations — the addition of nuclear weapons increases the danger of a regional nuclear war. Under these circumstances, general deterrence by Israel is likely to fail against potentially nuclear countries like Iran or Iraq that wish to revise the regional status quo. Skilled diplomats can defuse conflict during the period of immediate deterrence, but the potential for a conflict escalating to a nuclear war in such an environment will rise with the proliferation of nuclear arsenals.

Nuclear Proliferation and the Likelihood of War

Given the arguments above, it is important to know when nations are likely to proliferate and how dangerous these decisions are for world and regional stability. Remember that the Power Transition perspective suggests that dissatisfied nations will seek nuclear weapons in order to challenge the existing status quo. The most dangerous nation in a hierarchy is the fast-growth dissatisfied challenger that acquires nuclear weapons. A supporter of the status quo under equivalent conditions will seek peace. In other words, the defender would allow proliferation by an ally, but would oppose acquisition of nuclear weapons by an adversary.

Decisions by dissatisfied nations to acquire nuclear weapons increase the probability of a conflictual outcome, whereas the decision to acquire nuclear weapons by satisfied nations reinforces peace.[23] To place this argument in context, figure 4.6 (p. 98) traces the evolution of proliferation since 1990.[24]

The propensity of countries to build nuclear weapons is unrelated to the amount of time necessary to develop an effective nuclear device. Note in figure 4.6, the horizontal axis indicates the time required to develop nuclear weapons given technical capabilities available to the nation. The vertical axis estimates the willingness of national government to expend resources to acquire such capabilities. The dotted vertical line represents the point of nuclear acquisition. On the right-hand side we find the few nations that have acquired nuclear weapons. Within this nuclear club, the United States and Russia have a secure second-strike capability. France and the United Kingdom have appreciable arsenals but not a secure second strike. The remaining members of the nuclear club have only a limited number of nuclear devices sufficient for a preemptive strike. The arrows in figure 4.6 roughly track changes in the nuclear capacity of countries during the last few years.

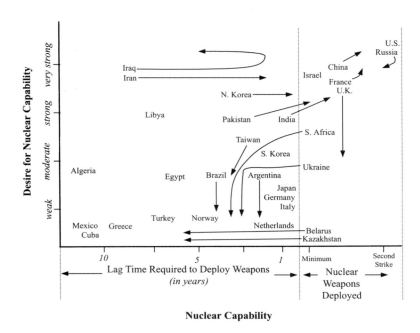

Figure 4.6 Shifts in Nuclear Capabilities, 1990-2000

To show the most immediate dynamics of the proliferation process, we center on the limited number of nations that underwent major changes during this decade. Four nations have given up their nuclear devices during this time period: the Ukraine, South Africa, Belarus, and Kazakhstan. India has enhanced its capability. Pakistan matched this development. North Korea and Iran have nuclear research programs underway. Iraq's efforts continue but have suffered a major setback because of sanctions and bombing that followed the Gulf War.

Figure 4.6 shows that the vast majority of countries capable of producing nuclear weapons have chosen not to do so. Classical deterrence implies that, driven by anarchy and seeking security, most if not all technically capable nations should try to acquire nuclear capabilities. Yet this figure clearly illustrates that technological capability is not the determinant of nuclear proliferation. The claim that proliferation is inevitable is false. Only a few nations choose to proliferate. A larger set has chosen to bypass this capability. This is a key consideration since in the near future the technology now readily available to developed nations will become more accessible to developing nations.

Classical deterrence anticipates wide-ranging nuclear proliferation. Power Transition, in contrast, argues that nuclear proliferation will be

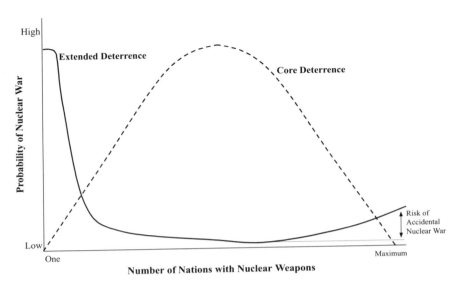

Figure 4.7 Classical Deterrence, Proliferation, and Nuclear War

limited mainly to the dissatisfied nations. The dominant nation develops, enhances, and expands its nuclear arsenal when it sees a challenger on the horizon. This was the case in the global hierarchy with the competition between the United States and the USSR during the Cold War. Despite U.S. satisfaction, the potential Chinese challenge continues to drive nuclear modernization. The few satisfied nations that choose this option are dissatisfied within their region. Israel, for example, supports the global status quo but developed nuclear weapons to ensure regional preponderance. Brazil and Argentina, which now support the status quo, gave up nuclear programs at the regional and global level when regional competition diminished. The French acquired nuclear weapons following the Cuban Missile Crisis because they feared the USSR, and perhaps the United States, and could act unilaterally in Europe. Such weapons may eventually be transferred to the EU. Most members of NATO are able to develop such weapons but have not yet taken this step.

The most important policy inconsistency between classical deterrence and Power Transition is whether stability is enhanced or diminished by nuclear proliferation. Consider first the arguments from classical deterrence, represented in figure 4.7.

Classical deterrence suggests that nuclear proliferation enhances peace because the costs of war rise, and consequently the probability of war declines. Two major variants emerge: The extended deterrence argument proposes that if only one nation has nuclear weapons, nuclear war is likely.[25] When two or more nations acquire this ability, they deter the original nuclear nation and provide a nuclear umbrella to their allies. Thus the probability of war drops dramatically. This argument was made frequently during the Cold War; both the United States and the Soviet Union were expected to defend their respective allies against nuclear attack. Note that there is a rise in the probability of war as the number of nations becomes very large due to the possibility of accidental nuclear war.

The core deterrence argument is similar, proposing that nuclear nations only defend themselves against nuclear attack. The probability of nuclear war initially rises with the acquisition of nuclear weapons since each new competitor can attack with impunity all others. When the number of nations with the potential to hold nuclear arsenals exceeds one-half of the maximum, the probability of nuclear war declines. When all nations with this potential have nuclear weapons and assured second-strike capabilities, the likelihood of nuclear war reaches its lowest levels.[26]

Power Transition suggests a very different dynamic resulting from nuclear proliferation. The probability of nuclear war is associated not with the level of destruction but with the level of dissatisfaction (see figure 4.8). As the number of dissatisfied nuclear nations increases, the probability of nuclear war also increases. The proliferation of nuclear weapons is not as dangerous if they are held by satisfied nations, as the probability of nuclear war will not be changed. However, satisfaction with the status quo may change as the dominant power changes, threatening the stability of the international system.

Of most concern are those nations that are very dissatisfied with the status quo. Given nuclear capability, these nations will risk conflict even if the costs are enormous. Nuclear weapons reduce the likelihood of great war given the enormous casualties involved, but they do not by their mere presence deter war. As the number of nuclear nations increases, the probability of nuclear war also rises. Terror creates fear but is not sufficient to prevent war among nations that desperately wish to change the status quo. Indeed, few doubt that if Israel were to face the possibility of losing conventional war, nuclear weapons would be used to deflect the enemy. The most dangerous situation occurs when such weapons are introduced into highly contested arenas. Thus, if Iran and Iraq had had access to nuclear weapons during their conflict in the 1980s, Power Transition anticipates that such weapons would have been used to resolve the conflict (see figure 3.4, p. 76). If Hitler had had nuclear weapons, they likely would have been used even if the United States had disclosed similar capabilities.

The difference between the classical view and the Power Transition view of deterrence can best be seen under conditions of mutual assured destruction. If this structural condition is ultrastable, as classical deterrence and balance of power contend, then proliferation across regional hierarchies should result in stability. As a matter of policy, nuclear proliferation

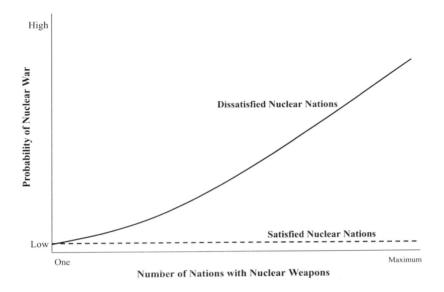

High

Probability of Nuclear War

Dissatisfied Nuclear Nations

Satisfied Nuclear Nations

Low

One

Maximum

Number of Nations with Nuclear Weapons

Figure 4.8   Power Transition, Proliferation, and Nuclear War

should proceed quickly — augmented by technological transfers — to assure that a secure second strike is achieved promptly and universally. Speedy action would avoid the instability associated with the balance of terror and the transitions from massive retaliation to mutual assured destruction and conversely. If one accepts the argument of classical deterrence, one must also logically accept universal proliferation of nuclear weapons to achieve ultrastability.[27] Few policymakers find this agreeable. We believe there are good theoretical reasons for their skepticism.

In striking contrast, Power Transition sees the proliferation of nuclear weapons as a potential danger under all circumstances, and as an actual danger when dissatisfied nations acquire such capabilities and threaten to overtake a satisfied rival. Power Transition argues that nuclear deterrence is at best tenuous. Under nuclear asymmetry, stability can be maintained by a status quo nation. Under nuclear parity, conventional overtaking by a dissatisfied challenger can lead to war.[28]

Unlike the classical deterrence argument that connects peace with a secure second-strike capability, Power Transition asserts that nuclear weapons symmetry, combined with parity of conventional weapons, greatly increases the probability of war. Proliferation by dissatisfied states is extremely dangerous. In fact, all proliferation is destabilizing. Even advocacy for selective proliferation to satisfied states — such as Britain, France, or Israel — must be tempered by the realization that those states could one day become dissatisfied. And if they remain satisfied with the global hierarchy, in a regional context they may be dissatisfied. This would allow conventional conflict to escalate into a regional nuclear war. Nuclear proliferation, in sum, increases the probability of nuclear war.

How effective are nuclear weapons as an instrument of national policy? The record shows that in a surprisingly large proportion of crises pitting a non-nuclear state against a nuclear opponent, the non-nuclear state prevailed.[29] Vietnam, Afghanistan, and Korea are the most visible exemplars of a well-established pattern. Moreover, the outcome of conflicts since 1945 can be accounted for accurately without considering nuclear weapons. This is attested by consistent evaluations of initiation, escalation, and termination that consider only conventional capabilities. Even when the nuclear state made an overt threat to employ its nuclear capacity, the proportion of accurately predicted outcomes was not altered nor was victory or defeat assured.[30] Initiation was not averted because one side was nuclear. Escalation was not prevented because one side was nuclear. Termination was not imposed because one side was nuclear. Nuclear weapons clearly increase the costs of conflict, but it is not clear that nuclear exclusivity alters the calculus of war.

This lesson may have already been learned by small nuclear nations that face a far larger foe. Power distributions account in part for choices to abandon nuclear arsenals. Power Transition implies that the rejection of nuclear arsenals by the Ukraine, Belarus, or Kazakhstan illustrated in figure 4.6 (see p. 98) resulted from the massive conventional asymmetry between these countries and their neighbors. These three relatively small nations were no doubt aware that their nuclear arsenals could not stop — without self-immolation — a conventional invasion by Russia. Indeed, holding on to their nuclear arsenals could provide an excuse for invasion. From the Power Transition perspective, a smaller nation confronted by a potential foe with an insurmountable conventional preponderance should opt to give up nuclear weapons. In a conflict they only assure a more disastrous defeat. Power preponderance, in sum, continues to preserve the hierarchical relationships even in a nuclear world.

Policymakers intuitively understand that a world full of nuclear weapons is dangerous. Most accept the proposition that nuclear asymmetry in the hands of satisfied nations can ensure peace in the global and regional hierarchies. Many accept the proposition that nuclear asymmetry does not prevent conventional war. A dissatisfied nation, such as Iraq, may be willing to risk nuclear war to advance its objectives. The challenge to the policymaker is to develop strategies to reduce the number of dissatisfied fast-growth countries that can challenge at the global or regional level. If that strategy fails, and if nonproliferation rules are not strictly enforced, the likelihood of nuclear war looms large on the horizon.

The Case of Ballistic Missile Defense

Since the 1960s, U.S. strategic thinking has wrestled with the development of ballistic missile defense systems. Classical deterrence proposes that, once MAD is achieved, the addition of antiballistic missile systems is dangerous because the other side then loses the capacity to deter. Such deployment forces a transition back from the ultrastable condition of mutual assured destruction to the less stable condition of massive retaliation.[31] For this reason, the classical deterrence community opposed President Ronald Reagan's proposal for the Strategic Defense Initiative.

To overcome the instability problem, proponents of the Strategic Defense Initiative — including President Reagan — suggested that once a shield was deployed over the United States, the technology would be transferred to the USSR. However, this transfer was also dangerous according to the logic of classical deterrence because both nations would be forced back into the cone of war where conventional weapons would once more dominate battlefield planning. By the logic of classic deterrence, the solution would generate the structural conditions for war. The transfer idea was dropped almost immediately.

From the Power Transition perspective, preponderance by a status quo nation is the key to peace. The Reagan administration intuitively understood that a balance of nuclear capabilities was dangerous, as the defender could not hold off challenges from a dissatisfied nation willing to endure larger casualties.[32] The logic was consistent with that of Power Transition. The current debate centers on whether a defensive shield can accomplish its goal. Can it defend against a large dissatisfied opponent? Preliminary indications are that while the idea is attractive, technical obstacles are overwhelming and their cost prohibitive. For this reason, proposals are now limited to defending against accidental and low intensity attacks. If we assume that a universal or a limited shield can be built, the logic for deployment is clear: it is far less dangerous to have nuclear preponderance than to face nuclear parity. Controlling for technical considerations, Power Transition implies that maintaining peace requires a preponderance of power and nuclear capabilities in the hands of the dominant status quo nation.[33] Credible defensive deployments by the defender increase stability.

Power Transition logic also supports the deployment of a limited defensive shield to protect status quo nations. Such a shield decreases the risk of war initiation by a dissatisfied challenger by further reducing the effectiveness of the challenger's military threat. The United States has acted consistently with this postulate by providing theater defense capabilities to Israel and is considering the same for Japan.

These conclusions do not generalize to the challenger. If a challenger deploys a defensive shield, instability increases. A preponderant nuclear challenger could use its capabilities to advance its goals to restructure the

... It could also risk a major nuclear war under parity if it believes ...at its population could survive. For this reason, the argument that a defense shield should be transferred to a challenger makes little sense in a global or regional context.

Conclusions and Policy Implications

It is naive to anticipate that the specter of serious regional war, including nuclear conflict, can be eradicated by the buildup of nuclear arsenals. Choices for war and peace remain in the hands of decision makers. Power Transition postulates that anarchy does not rule world politics. Rather, the power hierarchy supports a status quo that is recognized and respected. A dominant nation can be proactive in setting the status quo conditions firmly in place prior to relinquishing its position. The United States has the opportunity to ensure global stability during the next half-century. Based on structural conditions anticipated for the first half of this century, a number of policy prescriptions can be postulated.

Most important, the probability of global war appears to be waning in the near term. Global nuclear wars can be waged only among the great powers. Small nuclear nations, like Israel, cannot challenge at the global level. Given this inference, the only danger period is during the anticipated overtaking of the United States by China, or perhaps India far into the future. If these obstacles are passed, a long period of peace at the global level should follow. For this reason, the United States can take steps now to minimize the likelihood of global conflict later. Arms races cannot add to stability, but increasing the commitment to the status quo from Russia, China and India would reduce the probability of war. The United States accomplished a similar objective after World War II and helped create the EU. Reconciling differences among the remaining dissatisfied major powers now is the prescription for peace.

The story is much more grim at the regional level. Given the extension of nuclear weapons into the Middle East and other hierarchies where regional power transitions loom, nuclear proliferation has a high potential to generate regional nuclear war. Nuclear weapons in the hands of dissatisfied nations can lead to nuclear war. Note that Iran, Iraq, Libya, and North Korea are precisely the actors seeking nuclear weapons. Under conventional parity, interstate war is not deterred by the size of nuclear arsenals. Instead, it is deterred by the ability of decision makers to support a status quo.

In the Power Transition dynamic, nuclear proliferation is not an innocuous decision. Rather, nuclear proliferation is intimately related to the choice between war and peace made by a dissatisfied elite willing to challenge the status quo. When a dissatisfied challenger can credibly threaten another nation with the prospect of conventional defeat, war is likely. As stability is achieved at the global level, nuclear proliferation at the regional level enhances the prospect of nuclear war. The prescription for war remains the same: conventional parity and dissatisfaction are the triggers for war. The fear of destruction is insufficient to deter war. Nuclear proliferation can lead to war in regional hierarchies where dissatisfied nations approach the point of overtaking.

The implications drawn from both the static and dynamic Power Transition perspectives are consistent with common sense. The likelihood of nuclear war increases, and its timing is determined by conventional plus nuclear parity when the new nuclear nation is dissatisfied (for example, the USSR, China, North Korea, Iran, or Iraq). The likelihood of war is unaffected when a satisfied nation that supports the status quo acquires nuclear weapons (for example, the United States, the United Kingdom, or France).

Power Transition policy prescriptions related to the proliferation of nuclear weapons are at odds with classical theory, but generally agree with current policy. The choice to acquire or develop nuclear weapons rests with individual nations. More than two dozen nations have the capacity to build substantial nuclear arsenals from existing stockpiles, but continue to choose not to do so. Another large set of states could develop them within ten years, and still a third set could acquire such weapons from foreign sources. Yet only a fraction of nations with the capacity to deploy nuclear weapons have exercised this option. The nuclear club includes Russia, China, and the United States (which dominate the world nuclear arena); Britain and France (which are small nations by conventional measures); Israel (a minuscule actor in the global context); and India and Pakistan.

Structural constraints account in part for choices to abandon nuclear arsenals. Power Transition implies that the rejection of nuclear arsenals by the Ukraine or Kazakhstan resulted from the massive conventional asymmetry between these countries and their neighbors. These small conventional nations are aware that nuclear weapons could not stop a conventional invasion by Russia, their most likely opponent.[34] From the Power Transition perspective, a smaller nation confronted with an insurmountable deficiency in conventional capabilities should opt to give up nuclear arsenals because in case of conflict, they only assure a more disastrous defeat. Power preponderance continues to ensure hierarchical stability even in a nuclear world.

In sum, the dominant nation can help prevent the repetition of global war but cannot ensure regional peace. During this period of U.S. preponderance, therefore, American decision makers can help solidify the tenuous stability we now enjoy by acting, where possible, to manage nuclear arsenals and to prevent the proliferation of nuclear weapons to regions where challenges are anticipated. Nuclear arsenals cannot be eliminated but they can be managed cooperatively by satisfied nuclear nations. Given the real prospects of regional nuclear war, we urge policymakers to consider counterproliferation measures far more active, definitive, and if need be, preemptive then presently the case. To meet the challenges of deterrence and proliferation, the United States should systematically initiate foreign policy programs to reduce dissatisfaction in fast-growing countries likely to challenge the United States or regional dominant powers. If this fails, the danger of limited proliferation can be moderated by securing regional power asymmetries that favor satisfied states.

We remind readers that this period of peace should not be seen as a permanent condition derived simply from the presence of nuclear arsenals. For American decision makers, this is a time for action. Inaction will set the preconditions for instability, uncertainty, and possibly war.

CHAPTER 5

Economic Applications: Growth, Trade, and Democracy

In the new era, our first foreign policy priority and our first domestic priority are one and the same: reviving our economy.
— BILL CLINTON

The Politics of Security and Economics

Power Transition bridges the gulf between traditional national security practitioners, who view economic factors as of secondary importance, and economic theorists, who concentrate on economic trends to the exclusion of political dynamics.[1] Power Transition recognizes no distinction between security and economics. The status quo is defined by the dominant nation's assertion of its preferences regarding security and economic relations with the rest of the world. For both the security and economic dimensions, the dominant power and challengers will approach each other cooperatively or noncooperatively, depending on their degree of satisfaction with the status quo and the relative distribution of power in the international system.

Power Transition posits that international economic relationships are inextricably tied to power relationships. One cannot be explained without the other. The political interaction between competitors can only be understood by appreciating the basic power relations conditioned by the dynamics of growth and their interrelated assessments of the status quo. Economic relations cannot be understood without consideration of the power hierarchy.

From a policy perspective, cooperative and competitive dyadic relations guide both economic and political interactions. If the competitors support the status quo, then disputes are resolved with the dominant nation generally following a cooperative strategy. If opponents challenge the status quo, then the dominant nation follows a competitive strategy, frequently producing confrontational situations that may lead to war. The political and economic arenas are interconnected — not two different worlds that must be described by alternate theories.

Traditional policy analysts argue that economic interactions that concentrate on maximizing cooperative relations are fundamentally distinct from political interactions that emphasize competitive relations.[2] The classic illustration of the cooperative relations principle is profit. Businesses, seeking to maximize their net present value, often pursue cooperative relations. Every dollar added to the bottom line increases profit. Year-end sales of cars illustrate this principle. Since so much economic analysis concentrates on profit, there is a mistaken belief that cooperative relations are the sole objective of all economic phenomena.[3]

Business relations also are competitive. When two firms compete over market share, their purpose is to dominate an existing market. Profit in the short term takes a backseat to market share. The Boeing-Airbus competition, for example, is not centered on profits but control of a market. Likewise, the Microsoft-Netscape competition is focused on control of the emerging Internet market as much as on immediate profits. Depending on circumstances, business leaders select either a cooperative or competitive strategy.[4]

From the perspective of a policymaker, the international system may appear to be framed by an ever-expanding list of crises. No sooner is one resolved then another erupts. Simultaneous crises create severe strains on resources, both human and material. Despite this feeling about the conflictual nature of world politics, peaceful interactions are the norm rather than the exception. Confrontations are infrequent, and within this small set, few escalate to crisis. Among crises, only a fraction metamorphose to limited war. Even fewer limited wars explode into global war.

Interactions in world politics are dominated by transactions where the objective is to cooperate. Diplomatic exchanges, transfers of goods and services, and most negotiations are resolved cooperatively. Examples include educational and cultural transfers, tourism, international contracts and investments, international banking activities, and space collaboration. Like their economic counterparts, political leaders can select either a cooperative or a competitive strategy depending on circumstances. Our point here is that policymakers can use Power Transition to more effectively manage the choice between conflict and cooperation. Cooperation may be the norm, but conflict is defining.

Power Transition recognizes that bargaining postures reflect the degree of satisfaction and dissatisfaction within a dyad. Economic and security interactions are not distinct and alternate states of the international system.[5] There is a distinction of degree rather than kind between economic interdependence (as exemplified by relations between Canada and the United States, or among European Union [EU] members) and confrontational interactions (as characterized by Soviet-American relations during the Cold War or current Arab-Israeli relations). These are examples of cooperative relations where conflict is rare, and noncooperative interactions where conflict is frequent. Either strategy can characterize political or economic bargaining. Power Transition provides clues about the nature of both.

The Status Quo and
International Political Economy

Power Transition argues that supporters of the status quo disproportionately will use cooperative strategies with one another. The rules of the international system closely reflect the preferences of satisfied nations, which in turn select strategies to strengthen their national goals and objectives. Direct challenges to the status quo from such actors are rare and war among them is unlikely.

Dissatisfied nations, on the other hand, wish to change the status quo and, when provided the opportunity, will aggressively seek to modify the structure of relations in the international arena. They will rely on a noncooperative strategy to weaken opponents. A noncooperative strategy combined with an overtaking can lead to war.

Figure 5.1 (p. 110) illustrates the relationship between the joint satisfaction of two countries and the degree of cooperation. The horizontal axis reflects the degree of joint satisfaction of a challenger and defender, where the defender is always satisfied with the status quo, while the challenger's satisfaction varies.[6] The vertical axis reflects the degree of cooperation present in their relations, ranging from extreme non-cooperation to perfect cooperation. The curve illustrates the relationship between these factors as suggested by Power Transition theory.

Economic interactions among satisfied nations, including such issues as trade and capital flows, generally are resolved cooperatively.[7] Note in figure 5.1 that Canada and the United States are depicted as a jointly satisfied dyad exhibiting an extremely cooperative relationship. The European Union's interaction with the United States is only slightly less satisfied, and thus relations are slightly less cooperative. The overriding goal of nations attempting to cooperate is to reach agreements that strengthen their partnerships without losses to the individual nations.

By contrast, noncooperative strategies take on a different form. In figure 5.1, the Arab-Israeli example is considered noncooperative, reflecting the Israeli satisfaction with the regional status quo compared with Arab dissatisfaction. U.S.-USSR Cold War relations are an even more dramatic example. Soviet dissatisfaction and U.S. support for the status quo created a pervasive noncooperative climate. The main goal of competing nations is to reach agreements that strengthen them individually, regardless of the costs or benefits accrued by the other nations.

Let us complicate this picture somewhat by jointly considering security and economic concerns. Modern mercantilists treat competitive relations as the goal of all foreign policy elites. They argue that the need to defend international primacy and maximize gains dominates all policymaking concerns.[8] An alternative view suggests that foreign policy practitioners follow a mixed strategy that combines conflictual and cooperative inter-

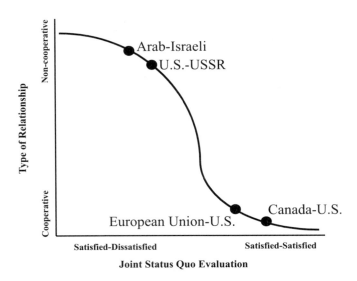

Figure 5.1   Maximizing Cooperative and Competitive Dyadic Relations

actions. Power Transition suggests that the unified view of these differing motivations is an effective representation of policy choices.

While figure 5.1 focuses on economic interactions, figure 5.2 illustrates how security interactions also follow these alternative paths. The vertical axis again places the degree of cooperation along a continuum. At one end are extremely noncooperative policies, when nations select strategies that provide maximum benefits for themselves not considering and even minimizing the benefits accrued by opponents. Thus they will enter into absolute gain agreements that provide proportionally more to them than to opponents. As generally anticipated, challengers will avoid agreements when the defender gains more.[9] At the other end of the continuum, cooperative relations describe a foreign policy stance where the nation seeks to cooperate, producing relative gains for both and the largest joint benefits. Under cooperation, agreements are possible even if one side gains more relative to the other. Nations will not enter into agreements that result in absolute losses.

The horizontal axis again places the joint evaluation of the status quo along a continuum where at one end there is a mixture of satisfied and dissatisfied states, and at the other end jointly satisfied nations. The relationship between the degree of cooperation and satisfaction differs for security and economics concerns. In general, satisfied nations cooperate with satisfied opponents because they are less concerned with improving their relative position than in accruing individual gains. They maximize ab-

Figure 5.2   Economic versus Security Concerns

solute gains. Relations between dissatisfied nations and satisfied nations are dominated by attempts to maximize relative gains. Using noncooperative policies, each side attempts to augment its position through security and economic exchanges.

As discussed in chapter 1, jointly satisfied nations tend to cooperate as there are no issues to generate dispute. A satisfied-dissatisfied dyad, on other hand, is defined by noncooperation, as the goals of these two nations are in conflict. For example, interactions among members of NATO generally are cooperative. In order to maintain stability in the Western world during the Cold War, for example, the United States subsidized the military preparedness of Europe. This created a "free ride" situation where allies could take advantage of each other in the short term.[10] The net result was a strategic success of significant magnitude as NATO's resolve contributed to the collapse of the Warsaw Pact and the subsequent incorporation of some of its key members into NATO. The United States adopted similar principles toward nuclear proliferation. Nuclear weapons were given to England and technological transfers helped France and Israel to develop nuclear programs.[11] Status quo nations are cooperative in both economic and security interactions.

Equivalent actions by challengers of the status quo are competitive. The United States and the USSR engaged in a significant arms race during the Cold War. Despite overwhelming superiority, the United States kept military expenditures high — as an attempt to secure changes in Soviet policies and modifications in the Soviet system of government. Restrictions were placed on technological transfers. Military assistance was provided to countries not only on the basis of commonly held values, but also in reaction to or anticipation of confrontational moves by the USSR. These events characterize the competitive conditions in a challenger-defender relationship.

Figure 5.2 displays how security shifts among economic and security considerations reflect the difference in interactions among cooperating and noncooperating nations. Security is a primary concern among opponents, while economics dominates interactions between allies. Note that the *security shifts* differ along the joint satisfaction dimension. Economic concerns are less critical than security concerns for nations that are dissatisfied. Cold War relations between the United States and USSR were volatile in the security dimension, but trade interactions generally were not as hostile. The reason is that threats to the political existence of a nation are more highly regarded than their economic well being.

When security threats diminish, economic considerations take over. Note in figure 5.2 that Russia's relationship with the United States changed following the collapse of the USSR. The gap between security and economic concerns widened. Economic interactions became mildly cooperative while security considerations remained noncooperative, but at a much less intense level. If Russia's satisfaction with the status quo improves, then even more cooperation should be forthcoming. U.S. policymakers have recognized the importance of this phenomenon by allocating resources and supporting international efforts to reinforce Russian cooperation. The ultimate outcome will not depend so much on the outside world as on the ability of Russian leaders to resolve their economic difficulties internally.

The relationship is reversed among satisfied nations. The security relations between the EU and the United States are firmly anchored by NATO, but economic disputes may become more competitive. Already there are some trade frictions. Conflict in other areas can emerge, for example, if the value of the euro is kept artificially low compared to the dollar. Once security concerns are resolved, economic concerns remain conflictual within an overall cooperative environment. Power Transition argues that economic disagreements among satisfied nations can generate confrontations but these do not escalate to war. For example, disputes may emerge within Europe over the euro, but the overall relations among these nations are anchored by security collaboration. The difference between economic and security concerns is driven by attitudes toward the status quo. There are no high or low politics, just politics.

We hold the view that a dominant nation, such as the United States, should not assess satisfied nations as potential security risks.[12] Following the collapse of the USSR, many academics and some policymakers argued that Japan would challenge the United States for international hegemony. Similar concerns preceded and followed German unification.[13] Power Transition argues that this is a dangerous misunderstanding of the power dynamics in world politics. Given demographic change and the pattern of economic growth, Japan can no longer challenge the United States The same is true for Germany. Even though a unified Germany is the dominant power within the EU, it cannot become the preeminent power of the twenty-first century. A similar argument applies to Russia. Challenges to American dominance, given current alliances, can only come from Asia.

The economic implications of Power Transition have been explored far less than its security implications. The rest of this chapter concentrates on areas where Power Transition offers insights that frequently challenge current policy. We will discuss the implications for integration as well as international trade, foreign aid, monetary policy, labor policy, and technological transfers. The intent is to motivate policy attention and additional research in this important interaction between politics and economics.

Power Transition and Economic Policies

The Power Transition perspective suggests that the degree of cooperation in economic policies — in particular trade, aid, monetary policy, labc policies, and technology transfers — is related to the level of satisfactior between a challenger and dominant country. Nations that support the status quo generally will follow a cooperative strategy when their partners also are status quo nations. They will assume a competitive strategy or even total exclusion when the recipients challenge the status quo. The argument is not that trade, aid, and technology follow the flag, but that the status quo, geostrategic circumstances, and the potential impact of such interactions on the dynamics of growth drives these decisions.

Trade

Political analysts repeatedly note that the dominant nation invests political capital to create and encourage a free trade regime. Yet such actions do not necessarily maximize the competitive economic advantage of dominant and large nations.[14] Dominant nations sometimes engage in aid transfers that strengthen potential competitors or with nations that do not share common values. Such actions run contrary to the notion of anarchy, where the objective would be to utilize competition in the international system to ensure national sovereignty. Power Transition accounts for both competitive and cooperative strategies, providing a framework that helps sort out the political motivations of actors that pursue seemingly inconsistent policies in their trading relations.

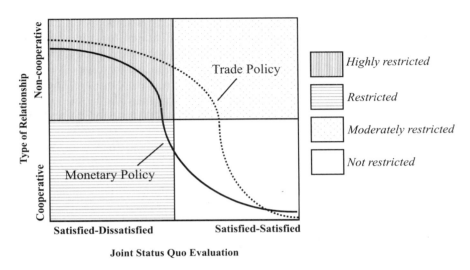

Figure 5.3   The Dynamics of Trade and Monetary Policies

Figure 5.3 compares the relationship between trade policies and monetary policies within the Power Transition framework. Between jointly satisfied nations, complete satisfaction implies free trade, yet trade is restricted much sooner than monetary policy. For example, even though Japan and the United States were both satisfied in the 1980s, they adopted a restrictive trade policy. Monetary policies, on the other hand, tend not to be as overtly competitive. As the challenger becomes more dissatisfied in each case, a noncooperative strategy is adopted resulting in more restrictions (as suggested by the shading of the figure). Note, however, that trade policy rarely becomes so competitive that complete restriction of trade is imposed.

When competing nations are threatened by the proximity of great power parity, they will adopt a cooperative attitude toward trade with their allies. As the Cold War between the United States and the Soviet Union intensified, trade between both superpowers and nonaligned countries increased.[15] The defender offers generous trade policies to consolidate its political position with nations wavering between satisfaction and dissatisfaction with the status quo.

As nations are farther from parity, the immediacy of the security threat decreases and the defender can shift more toward a competitive strategy. The Soviet Union's actions in the Middle East during the Cold War are consistent with this logic. During the Cold War, trade subsidies and foreign assistance were provided in response to geopolitical necessities. With the reduction of systemic tensions, foreign assistance declined and reciprocal trade increased.[16]

Unlike the classical benevolent view that advocates free trade, neoclassical economic research shows that large nations have incentives to use optimal tariffs to restrict trade. While small nations benefit from specialization to gain competitive advantage in a free trade environment, specialization provides no trade advantage to large economies. Economies as large as those of the United States or the EU begin to approximate the resilience of world market[17] and can impose tariffs as part of a competitive strategy. On the other hand, since small countries lack market diversification, they compete best under free trade when they specialize in areas where they hold a comparative advantage. These nations cannot afford to impose tariffs on imports and must rely on the world market.

In world politics, large dominant nations advocate free trade while small ones frequently resist such advances.[18] Utilizing a competitive strategy, large nations should restrict trade through optimal tariffs. Empirically, the opposite prevails, particularly in the case of dominant nations. The United States in the latter half of the twentieth century and Britain in the first half of the nineteenth century generally supported free trade.[19] After World War II, the United States encouraged the creation of the International Monetary Fund (IMF), the purpose of which is to provide a loan and credit system to facilitate international trade by stabilizing exchange rates. The Word Trade Organization (WTO), the successor to the General Agreement on Trade and Tariffs (GATT), is an institution devoted to minimizing trade barriers and standardizing trade transactions. Participation in such organizations and encouragement of their regulatory role deprives great powers in general, and the dominant nation in particular, of the ability to utilize superior political and military capabilities to advance trade objectives.

This unexpected economic behavior of great powers is consistent with expectations from Power Transition. The United States accepts cooperation in trade transactions with allies because such policies foster support for the status quo. The United States accepted trade restrictions imposed by Germany and Japan — the largest global exporters — during the Cold War in order to strengthen the security coalition pitted against the USSR. After the collapse of the USSR, security needs declined and cooperation was abandoned in favor of a more mixed strategy, but the United States still did not revert to pure competition.[20]

Political considerations directly affect the willingness of nations to subsidize others. Despite meek attempts to do so in the past, after 1989 the United States actively sought to restructure trade agreements with Japan because there was no longer the need to accommodate in order to maintain a strong anti-Soviet alliance. Policy negotiators during the Bush and Clinton administrations advocated an even playing field with the intent of reducing and eventually eliminating trade deficits. U.S. policymakers did not advance the notion of recuperating past losses or generating trade surpluses similar to those of Japan. Instead, the objective became "evening the terms of trade."

The dominant nation uses trade and aid to incorporate potential competitors into the status quo. From the Power Transition perspective, it is critically important to engage China in economic cooperation. This stance, started under President Richard Nixon, extended under President George Bush, and further emphasized by Bill Clinton's administration, is an appropriate choice. Its aim is to encourage China not to be a hostile security competitor down the road. Trade policy is one tool that can be used to shift the preferences of dissatisfied nations from confrontation toward cooperation.

If the United States is able to co-opt China into satisfaction with the global status quo by waiving the annual vote on most favored nation (or normal trade relations) status, by supporting its entry into the WTO, and by creating incentives to expand market forces, then it may head off a major challenger within the power hierarchy. In a similar way, the financial support provided Russia following the collapse of communism is motivated by the attempt to accelerate the movement from security competition to relative cooperation.

Sanctions

Power Transition theory does not suggest that positive incentives are the only means to achieve compliance. In interactions with dissatisfied great powers, economic sanctions can have useful short-term consequences. Heavy reliance on sanctions, however, is dangerous, as long-term readjustments tend to nullify short-term advantages. There is an explicit policy tradeoff in imposing trade restrictions on nations as they move toward the status quo. Sanctions could delay the evolution of lasting partnerships. Encouraging open trade could accelerate cooperation.

It is not surprising that the policy debate between those who stress international consequences and those who concentrate on domestic concerns can be summarized by the degree to which each side *trusts* the policy preferences of the stipulated foreign elite. In the United States, the imposition of technical trade restrictions on Britain, Germany, or Japan usually only has the support of parties directly affected by the economic implications. Imposing similar constraints on Cuba and China attracts immediate support far beyond those directly impacted by the economic consequences. Failure to impose restrictions on Iran or Libya would be equivalent to political suicide. The domestic motivations for each situation vary.

Power Transition recognizes the risks involved in policies that attempt to move nations toward the status quo, yet risks must be taken to advance the cause of peace. The effective long-term policy toward nations that support the status quo is an open trade policy. Liberal trade policies have the potential to diminish opposition to the status quo. In the long-term, a free trade policy has the potential to reinforce the *Pax Americana*.

Trade sanctions should not be allowed to undermine the stability of the status quo. Such action can easily be counterproductive, as when critical members of the status quo — such as the EU or Japan — refuse compliance with sanctions. Attempts by the United States to impose comprehensive sanctions on Cuba and Iraq have failed thus far to produce the desired results and have generated serious dissension within the status quo coalition. The reason is that successful economic sanctions require unanimity. Such agreement is difficult to achieve among satisfied nations that are not directly challenged on the security dimension.

Figure 5.3 (p. 114) indicates that collaboration on trade never completely ceases because of the self-interest generated by this exchange. Nor is trade completely unrestricted, because of domestic concerns. President Jimmy Carter, for example, levied broad economic sanctions on Russia following its intervention in Afghanistan. These were ineffective when Europe and Japan filled the trade vacuum left by the United States. These sanctions were abandoned after intense pressure by the agricultural lobby. Moreover, despite their short-term political appeal, sanctions in the wake of the Tiananmen Square massacre had little effect on events in China, as other satisfied nations demurred. From a Power Transition perspective, the effectiveness of trade sanctions is very limited. It is encouraging, therefore, that despite political rhetoric during the 1996 election campaign, President Clinton did not follow up on promised restrictions to force China's hand. The limited restrictions imposed on India following its nuclear tests again indicate that the United States realizes that sanctions and confrontation cannot resolve disputes among great powers. Power Transition suggests that trade satisfaction is the key to successful relations with nations that have enormous growth potential and may challenge in the future. This is the underlying reason that sanctions are used so sparingly and that, despite economic drawbacks, free trade is advanced.

Monetary Policy

A major objective of the dominant nation is to preserve stability. To maintain an effective flow of trade, the status quo must include an effective exchange-rate system. From a geopolitical perspective the defender's objective is not to dominate currency exchanges, but to assure members that key currencies are stable. In figure 5.3 we see that a cooperative monetary policy is chosen even when the challenger becomes slightly dissatisfied.

Following World War II, the United States pegged the dollar to gold in the Bretton Woods Agreement. The United States took on significant responsibility for helping to stabilize world currencies and control global inflation through a guarantee that the dollar could be converted to gold on demand by the central banks of other countries. This created what was known as a dollar-gold equivalence standard. It provided a means to control inflation and stabilize money supplies by making the U.S. dollar the world's reserve currency. Currencies had fixed exchange rates pegged to the value of the dollar. One ounce of gold was set at $35, so that anyone trading in an ounce of gold could demand $35 from the U.S. government. This guarantee facilitated international transactions as dollar holdings could be exchanged for gold.

President Nixon ended this practice in August 1971. He did so because the United States was no longer the world's largest exporter and could not unilaterally maintain the fixed exchange-rate system since gold was being withdrawn beyond the limits of the United States' replacement capabilities. As gold reserves dwindled, the United States, facing pressure from the British and French to convert even more dollars into gold, reneged on the agreement reached at Bretton Woods. This ended the fixed exchange rate system. The replacement system allows exchange rates to float. Now currencies respond to market forces and are not supported by the United States.[21] One consequence was a rapid devaluation of the dollar against gold. Before August 1971, gold sold for $35 per ounce. Afterwards, it soared to about $400 an ounce. A sustained outbreak of global inflation followed.

So dramatic were these changes that some scholars argued that the termination of Bretton Woods and its aftermath marked the end of American economic dominance. This perception had only surface validity. Because of the collapse of European economies following World War II, the United States emerged as the largest exporter and producer in the international community. For a short period of time, the United States produced more than half of the world's total output. It was a hegemon.[22]

By U.S. design, this economic preponderance was short-lived. As recovery in Europe proceeded, the relative product of the United States declined to its prewar share of the world product. While the United States no longer could maintain a fixed exchange rate, it could maintain satisfaction by sharing this responsibility with other *satisfied* nations. Today the G-7 plus 1 (Russia) allows markets to determine the exchange rates. These nations periodically intervene to stabilize the exchange rates for currencies under pressure. Such actions have a limited effect since market forces dominate. Interventions are designed to assure status quo members that unwanted currency instability will be averted whenever possible.

Currency devaluation is a critical element in monetary relations. It is used to increase exports as domestic goods become cheaper and to decrease imports as foreign goods are rendered more expensive. Nations choose devaluation when they face large trade imbalances. A number of Asian and Latin American countries have used such policy instruments. Generally, dominant nations hold currencies constant even under economic duress. The United States, the global dominant power, has not monetized its debt, despite long-term trade deficits with Japan and, more recently, China. The USSR maintained an artificially high ruble before 1989 when it was the dominant regional power. Despite the Asian crisis of 1998, China, also a dominant regional power, resisted devaluing the yuan.

Power Transition theory suggests that dominant nations avoid monetizing debt and exporting their problems because they want to satisfy the members of their regional or global hierarchies. They strive to maintain monetary stability within their hierarchies and avoid fostering expectations of deflationary policies among member countries of the status quo coalition. This minimizes the chances of a challenge to their leadership. The dominant nation holds the key to international trade. The dollar, like the British pound before it, is the global trade currency. The euro, with the backing of the European Union, has the potential to provide a dual-currency stability standard for global trade.

Power Transition also suggests that distributing the burden of status quo support across satisfied nations is beneficial as it enhances commitment to and investment in the status quo. While supporting the euro may sacrifice some of the strength of the dollar, the overall gains in promoting a strong status quo are far preferable. The United States will not be the dominant nation in the world system as the twenty-first century progresses unless it can increase the number and strength of status quo powers. Thus the dollar will not be the single monetary standard. The question is whether the Chinese or the European currency will act in this capacity. Clearly, it is in the interest of the United States to ensure that the European currency assists in setting the standard in addition to the dollar and the yuan.

Labor Mobility and Technology Transfers

Policies affecting the mobility of labor and restrictions on the transfer of technology vary in similar ways to trade and aid. Figure 5.4 (p. 120) compares the degree of cooperation given different distributions of satisfaction in labor policies and technology transfer policies. As illustrated in figure 5.4, the mobility of labor is mildly restricted even between jointly satisfied countries. For example, immigration policies in the United States apply broadly to both satisfied allies and dissatisfied opponents.

Most nations try to keep their own high-skilled labor at home while excluding other nations' low-skilled labor. The EU is unique because it allows labor to move freely across borders, but domestic restrictions apply as labor migration is minimal compared to that within the United States. Simply put, political restrictions are applied far more to labor than any other economic factor.

Technological transfers have a similar relationship among the satisfied

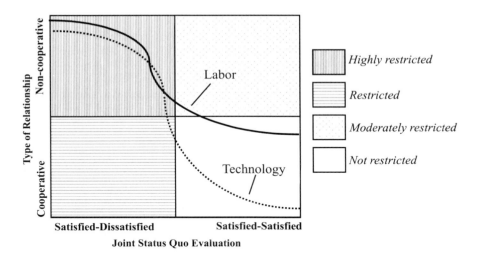

Figure 5.4   The Dynamics of Labor Mobility and Technology Transfers

and dissatisfied powers. Extreme dissatisfaction leads to acute noncooperation. Technology is shared quite freely between friends and even mild competitors. Any nation with sophisticated technology can transfer some of that knowledge to enhance the rate of development in other countries. High technology transfers frequently generate security externalities.[23] Even when no direct security issues can be identified, transfers of technology can accelerate the potential growth of the recipient. When the transfers are made from a high technology nation such as the United States to low technology nations such as China, this effect is magnified. In figure 5.4, we see that satisfied countries are expected to share technology freely. Minimal restrictions persist even when the challenger is slightly dissatisfied, but once this dissatisfaction becomes more pronounced, the restrictions on technology increase quickly.

As in the case of trade, the choice of how to approach technological transfers depends on the perception of elites regarding the degree of cooperation between potential recipients. If elites conclude that leaders of the recipient nation are satisfied, a cooperative relationship should emerge and restrictions will be limited by commercial competition. If they conclude that recipients may eventually challenge, then a competitive relationship should emerge. The United States imposed severe restrictions on the export of technology to the USSR and other Eastern bloc countries during the Cold War to avoid the transfer of dual-use technology. Evidence suggests that such actions delayed the technological advancements in the restricted areas, but did not thwart them.[24]

Applying technological sanctions to dissatisfied nations is reasonable.[25] However, such sanctions are contrary to the interests of individual firms within one's own nation. Absent a consensus among domestic coalitions within status quo nations, preservation of technological restrictions is problematic. Restrictions on technology were relatively successful during the Cold War when members of the dominant coalition concurred — including Germany, France, Italy, Britain, and Japan. After the thaw in relations during the détente period, Europe and Japan no longer consistently complied. As a result, the effectiveness of sanctions diminished.[26] Coordination problems escalate when there is no agreement among status quo nations about the future. Effective policies to co-opt the dissatisfied are doomed if some members of the Western coalition believe that Russia and China will never willingly join the satisfied coalition while others contend they will.

A case in point is the provision of missile guidance technology to China. Both sides agree that such transfers improve the launch reliability of communication satellites. The same technology can be adopted to improve warhead-delivery vehicles. If one accepts the view that China is moving toward the status quo, a cooperative strategy is preferable. If the technology had been denied, launch failure would persist — reducing gains for both parties. The provision of improved guidance systems diminishes the costs for American telecommunication groups, increases their competitiveness in the global information market, and ensures that U.S. technology will be utilized in future launches. Furthermore, to prevent failure, China would no doubt seek similar technology elsewhere. Russia or Sweden are likely targets because they can provide an effective guidance systems at low cost.

If one anticipates that China is not moving toward the status quo, the answer is to adopt a competitive strategy. From this viewpoint the provision of guidance technology is a serious problem. First, guidance transfers improve the commercial viability of China's low-priced launchers and reduce U.S. opportunities to compete effectively in this area. Second, the security danger to the United States and regional stability is intensified, as effective guidance systems can easily be adapted to improve intercontinental ballistic missile (ICBM) accuracy.

These positive and negative assessments are derived from similar geostrategic considerations but each varies in movement along the status quo dimension. Policymakers should base strategies not on technical grounds but on political assessments about expectations of future behavior along the status quo dimension. The shadow of the future should drive current policy not the fears of the past.

From the Power Transition perspective, policies that affect technical transfers involve risk. Outcomes are preconditioned by geostrategic conditions, but final decisions are made by decision makers who evaluate the future of economic dynamics and changes in the status quo. If a risk is to be taken, we believe it should be taken in favor of creating stability.

Confronting China or Russia is unlikely to produce a stable international system. Co-opting these nations may produce a lasting peace. Since the United States and China will approach parity in the future, a policy that builds trust in the status quo is the best bet to achieve peace. The alternative is a policy that leads to the collapse or fragmentation of China. The second option was successful during the Cold War but there is no assurance that the outcome with China will be the same.[27] If the U.S. banks only on a collapse strategy and that option fails to materialize, the result could be conflict.

Economic Growth and Regime Change

Economic growth frames the political dynamics that lead to war. Peace is ensured when cooperation persists despite power transitions. In world politics, then, the dynamics of economic change lead to challenges against the status quo only if nations are dissatisfied. The dominant nation and key members of the international system have an overriding interest in ensuring that long-term economic growth persists at the regional and global level and that the international status quo is preserved.[28]

The policy objective is to encourage economic and political congruence.[29] Economic growth by itself is not the sole policy goal. World Bank stabilization programs reinforce market economies and encourage political structures congruent with those adopted by the dominant nation. The international status quo set up by the United States supports market competition, encourages the adoption of strong property rights, fosters the application of consistent patent rules, and insists on repatriation of profits. In addition, the United States advances democratic principles and human rights. The evolution of democratic principles goes hand in hand with the preservation of international fiscal and trade regimes. Political and economic convergence is desirable to preserve systemic stability.

Let us consider first the economic dynamics that underpin challenges to stability. Despite its desire to ensure growth for status quo members, the dominant nation cannot maintain prosperity for all. Nevertheless, the resources and policy instruments of the international status quo are used to encourage growth where possible. A stable economic environment can go a long way toward accomplishing this goal. Following World War II, the Marshall Plan was instituted to help Western Europe and Japan recover from war, avoiding the repetition of fiscal failures that followed in the wake of World War I. Economic growth is particularly desirable among nations supporting the status quo since it helps to ensure stability.

Power Transition provides a unique perspective on growth. In chapter 2 we saw that the hierarchy of power is altered by dynamic changes in economic performance. The international status quo can only be preserved in the long term if other nations agree to its structure and, in turn, preserve it. The reason the United States overtook Britain without bloodshed in the nineteenth century is that both nations shared similar principles and had close economic ties. As one democratic system overtook the other, the leaders in these nations chose not to fight and instead forged a special relationship that still persists.

The relative size of a dominant nation imposes natural limits on the duration of a status quo. With a population of under 50 million, Britain could not maintain dominance over nations the size of Russia or the United States (with populations over 200 million), and these nations, in turn, ultimately cannot expect to lead China or India, which have populations exceeding a billion. The reason for dominance at different periods in history is based on variations in the rate at which nations develop. Earlier development by some nations provided them with a temporary predominance. As economic convergence diminishes the differences in productivity across nations, challengers to the status quo leadership will emerge. The primary question is not whether the conditions for such challenges will occur but whether they can be resolved and what the outcome of a conflict might be.

From the perspective of Power Transition, a dominant nation that successfully co-opts potential challengers ensures that the international status quo will be preserved. Economic growth, however, is not determined primarily by foreign policy interaction. Domestic decisions, such as adopting market reforms, allow nations to travel faster through the endogenous growth path and ultimately converge in the rates of output.[30] Similar patterns drive political convergence. The literature on transitions to democracy shows that domestic factors are instrumental in the evolution of democratic regimes. However, there is a concurrent trend towards democracy based on the efficiency of these regimes in preserving continuity and ensuring the survival of leaders in relatively affluent societies.[31]

Faced with a challenge from a fast-growing dissatisfied nation, and failing co-option, the dominant nation can still preserve preponderance via alliances. It must persuade nations to "bandwagon" and thus expand support for the status quo. Such expansions may prove costly or untenable in the long-term because the dominant nation is declining in power. When a dominant nation fails to incorporate an overtaking challenger into its coalition, the dissatisfaction generated by such a transition may lead to military challenges. The defender may have to wage war to preserve the status quo or face the prospects that it will be replaced.

Growth is directly related to the development of cooperative relations in the international system. These in turn are linked to domestic regimes. At the domestic level, research shows that economic development is tied to the transition to democracy, yet the mere presence of democracy does not secure sustained growth.[32] In most economies that sustain growth, reversion from democracy to authoritarian rule is infrequent. In England, Germany, the United States, and Japan the process of economic growth is tied to the development of democracy. In Latin America and Asia, the most successful economies are becoming democracies.[33] Given the increase in the number of democracies, the international system should be far more stable in the future as more and more nations coordinate their domestic regime types. Research on the democratic peace supports this argument.[34]

There is, however, an exception. Some democracies fail to reach sustained growth. India, a democracy for half a century and a budding great power, has not fully implemented a market economy and has thus far failed to achieve sustained growth. Forecasts based on population structure suggest it will not do so in the first half of this century.[35] Furthermore, India is not a satisfied nation. Democracy by itself, therefore, does not guarantee stability. Likewise, China is modernizing its economy, moving very fast into a market economy but failing to develop national democratic structures. While some democratic activity is present at the local level, the central government remains a well-entrenched autocracy.[36] If economic institutions continue to converge, but the political institutions remain at odds, the consequences for cooperation are unclear. China, like India, may remain noncooperative, move toward neutrality, or become competitive. From a Power Transition perspective, an evolving status quo resulting from the coordination of political and economic structures is the key to ensuring peace.

Power Transition recognizes that nations favoring the status quo are far less likely to engage in conflict. For this reason it is not surprising that liberal democracies seldom engage in war. Evidence now has emerged that nations with similar political systems — authoritarian and democratic — do not wage war or wage it far less frequently against one another. Democracies, however, wage war at the same rate as other governments, but they concentrate this activity against nations with different regime types.

Power Transition accounts for the democratic peace thesis, noting that a successful dominant nation imposes common preferences on its allies. When the defender is successful in adjusting domestic political regimes within its alliance to one type, as the United States has been, members do not fight one another. As such an aggregation becomes preponderant, the probability of war is reduced dramatically. Supporters of the status quo reinforce their economic growth through trade benefits, fiscal stability, investments, technology transfer, labor mobility, and security. The democratic peace is consistent with Power Transition, but the existing link may be fragile and dependent on the presence of liberal democracies and market economies. If democracies fail to adopt open economies (India) or if open economies fail to become democracies (China), the tie between regime types, economic growth, and peace could unravel. Today, the democratic and market economic principles of the preponderant U.S.-led coalition ensure the perpetuation of the *Pax Americana*. In the future, there could be challenges.

Integration

Power Transition advocates economic and political integration among status quo nations because such arrangements support stability, but the theory warns against integration among challengers. Political and economic integration produces joint benefits in the long-term among status quo nations willing to pursue a cooperative relationship. Integration is in the interest of the dominant nation because the economic gains accrued by major powers strengthen their support for the status quo.

As economic and security arrangements are formalized, as with the EU or NAFTA, relationships consistent with the goals of the dominant nation are institutionalized, increasing the probability of the preservation of established rules even beyond the period of dominance by the defender. The democratic peace is related to this argument. In the case of integration, nations formalize their cooperative postures. In the case of the democratic peace, they adopt conciliatory security policies toward one another. In each case cooperation is driven by positive evaluations of the status quo.

Integration tends to either follow peaceful power transitions or emerge after dramatic reductions in the degree of conflict among contending parties. Integration of status quo nations assures further reductions of instability because it creates institutional channels for the resolution of policy differences. Advancing integration is beneficial to the dominant power because it creates satisfaction, enhances the pool of resources in the alliance, and maintains systemic stability. U.S. support for the EU, and U.S. participation in NAFTA, are completely consistent with the interests of the dominant nation. By advancing integration among status quo nations, the United States ensures consistent support for market economies, patent restrictions, financial structures, and other forms of economic behavior that advance the integrity of the international status quo. By expanding its market, the United States guarantees stability within its own region.

Consider the long-term implications of a unified EU. A strong Europe would provide support for the very structures that have made the United States successful in the postwar era. The United States consolidated its international political and economic position with the recovery of Western Europe. These nations became its primary trading partners. A strong Europe meant that NATO was an effective fighting force. Security did not depend exclusively on troops and equipment supplied by the United States. As their economies recovered, the financial and logistical responsibilities have increasingly shifted to the Western European nations.[37]

The United States should continue to support European integration. This includes the monetary union in Europe. Adjustments to the dollar may follow, but both sides are likely to operate well within the rules established by the current international status quo. A stable European currency should reinforce satisfaction within the international system.

U.S. support provides the international monetary system with credibility. With a single European monetary unit, the United States can take advantage of substantial rewards from seigniorage that would be more equally distributed among European partners with two internationally accepted currencies. Europeans may use the euro, as the Japanese have used the yen, to advance their trade advantage. To preserve the status quo, therefore, Europe and the United States must find equitable agreements that ensure the stability of both currencies.[38] A stable European monetary union would help cultivate satisfaction for the status quo along the economic dimension.

Given Western interest in favor of integration, what are the consequences of further expansion of the EU? Expansion by the EU reinforces the commitment of Western European nations to stability, *provided* that satisfaction with the status quo is maintained. Challenges could come if Europe were to renege on its commitments to NATO or if it were to adopt a different set of rules for economic interactions. This is a very unlikely scenario because of the long-standing security arrangements as well as the economic ties between the United States and the EU that are so profitable for both. Figure 5.2 (p. 111) anticipates that conflict along the economic dimension will grow as the EU becomes a global economic contender, but that overall relations will remain cooperative, anchored by security collaboration. The development of institutions like the Organization for Economic Cooperation and Development (OECD) and GATT/WTO help ensure that economic disputes, even difficult ones, can be resolved through negotiations. Integration and the institutionalization of cooperative solutions to dispute therefore are useful tools in the maintenance of stability.

There are additional gains from integration. Economic theory suggests that when the factors of production are approximately equal across countries, increasing capital flows and trade will generate larger economic rewards for partners. After a devastating war, the Marshall Plan and economic integration rekindled the economies of Europe.[39] The early coal and steel community was enlarged at the Treaty of Rome because the continental European nations understood that a larger market gave them a competitive edge.

Economic integration among nations with dramatically different factors of production will also favor faster growth rates in nations with lower production costs. In recent years, Ireland, for example, has led all EU nations in growth. Successful integration accelerates economic convergence among nations with different production capabilities. Under NAFTA the fastest growth rates should be enjoyed first by Mexico, then Canada, and finally the United States. Power Transition suggests that enhancing economic convergence, while fostering behavior congruent with the international status quo, is a strategy that will ensure continued stability.

Integration, nevertheless, is not a panacea. Conflict can be generated when challengers to the status quo pursue integration. Economic cooperation among dissatisfied countries enhances their power, and the product can be used to challenge the dominant nation and its coalition.[40] This was the strategy adopted by the USSR during the Cold War. Although the Soviet Union could not challenge the United States at the global level by itself, it created a competing coalition. Even though the Soviet-controlled Council for Mutual Economic Aid (COMECON) fell short of its sponsor's expectations and never challenged the U.S.-led Western coalition, COMECON economic institutions helped consolidate the hold of the USSR over Eastern Europe.

We now know, and should have known earlier, that centrally planned economies are not economically viable in the long term. They are not competitive with open economies. Yet, had COMECON survived, had the USSR managed to liberalize its economy without abandoning political centralization (as China has), and had the Sino-Soviet split been amicably resolved, then the economic and political power of these challengers might well have been far more difficult to overcome. Successful integration among dissatisfied nations can be a recipe for war.

Given its current preponderance in the power hierarchy, the United States should seek to increase integration among satisfied nations. A more risky and higher reward strategy is to seek integration with nations currently in transition from competition to cooperation — such as Russia, China, and India. The challenge for U.S. policy is to be bold and forward-looking. Positive responses to changing international dynamics include U.S. support for the expansion of the EU to Eastern Europe, the incorporation of Russia into NATO and the EU, the enlargement of NAFTA to include Mercosur, and future expansion of the Asia-Pacific Economic Cooperation forum (APEC). Incorporation of China into the WTO is a first step toward eventual acceptance as a full partner, provided it accepts the fundamental principles embedded in the international status quo. Economic and political integration among satisfied nations generates not only a stable policy environment but also reinforces the power structure of the international system.

From the Power Transition perspective, the most effective means to preserve the integrity of the international system is to reinforce commitments to the status quo. The original designer of the status quo cannot forever remain the dominant nation. The EU has shown that integration can bring old enemies together by generating favorable economies of scale and positive spillovers. Encouraging an old competitor, like Russia, to join the EU enhances hierarchical stability. The same strategy of economic engagement and integration that succeeded in Western Europe could reinforce Russia's drift toward democracy and strengthen its commitment to the status quo. Through integration, the *Pax Americana* could continue unchallenged well into the twenty-first century. Through integration of China and perhaps India, the U.S.-designed international status quo could last beyond the period of American dominance.

Economic Consequences of War

Integration and coalition building are critical elements in maintaining peace. The first steps toward cooperation should be taken as soon as war with a former enemy is concluded. After a war has reduced the power of one of the nations, the factors that increase the probability of renewed conflict already are at work. This section reports the effect of war on a nation's economy. It argues that support for the status quo should be generated as soon as is possible among former enemies. Our remarks are directed largely to the consequences of conventional conflicts, but they should apply as well to limited nuclear encounters. Fortunately, there is no experience to guide us in evaluating the consequences of a major nuclear war.

A nation's power is dependent on its population, economic productivity, and political capacity. Figure 5.5 illustrates empirical findings that for an advanced nation losing a war, the time necessary to catch up to its prewar growth pattern is less than twenty years.[41] The implication of the Phoenix Factor is that wars do not have a long-term effect of eliminating potential challengers among the economically developed powers. A nation defeated on the battlefield can rise to its previous level within one generation. Because of this recovery, great powers, such as Germany, challenge for supremacy repeatedly. This happens because the wartime costs, though terrible, are transitory, and power is regained quickly.[42] Empirical research has shown that losers recover from war as fast or faster than winners, whether or not they were occupied during the war.

The process of recovery has structural characteristics that relate changes in the status quo to economic growth. When the challenger is successful or when, as a consequence of the war, the challenger becomes a satisfied member of the international status quo, conflict acts as a boost for economic growth in the long term. After recovery to prewar growth rates, economic expansion is driven to an even higher rate by the incorporation of the previously rejected challenger into the international economic structure, defined by the international status quo.[43] The economic relationships that benefited the defender at the expense of the challenger are now altered by the settlement following the war. For example, the creation of the EU generated the conditions for enormous growth in Europe, including Germany and Italy. On the other hand, constraints imposed on Germany following World War I allowed that country to recover but did not diminish its dissatisfaction thus generating the conditions that led to World War II.

In developing societies, the Phoenix Factor is enormously attenuated. These societies, hovering at the edge of the poverty trap, may very easily fall back into the self-destructive syndrome of high fertility and low growth

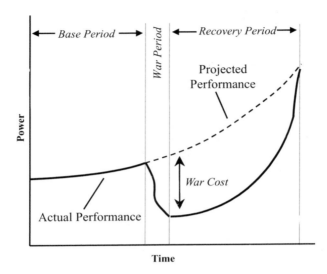

Figure 5.5   The Consequences of War: The Phoenix Factor

produced by the intellectual and capital losses imposed by war. Pakistan, North Korea, and North Vietnam are good examples of nations whose recovery from war was partial. Losers of great power wars can overcome these losses, since their productive base is sturdy.

The important policy implication of the Phoenix Factor is that wartime power losses are short term. This is the only time when a dominant country, through intervention, can affect the challengers' future behavior, by transforming the regime of the defeated nation to coordinate with the norms of the international status quo. The newly established status quo, created by the dominant nation, can distribute security and economic gains to those nations that now choose to support it, including losers. In the case of former enemies, this must be done during the period immediately after the war when the enemy's power position has been temporarily reduced, and well before the former enemy has an opportunity to regenerate its strength and reassert its dissatisfaction.

The fundamental difference between World War I and World War II was the effective management of the peace. In the former, the Europeans imposed sanctions on Germany that maintained its dissatisfaction but were insufficient to prevent its recovery and the recurrence of war. In the latter, the United States, through the Marshall Plan and the provision of a security umbrella through NATO and the Mutual Security Treaty, integrated the primary losers, Germany, Italy, and Japan, into the international status quo. The result has been fifty years of stability. In the Middle East on the other hand, Israel missed a very important opportunity by not imposing a settlement in the West Bank concurrently with the settlement with Egypt following the Seven Days' War. The longer a settlement is delayed, the less advantageous will be the conditions of peace for the Israelis, as dissatisfied Palestinians and their Arab allies move toward a power transition with Israel. As nations approach parity, negotiations favorable to the dominant nation become increasingly difficult.

Conclusions and Policy Implications

Power Transition demonstrates that the domestic dynamics of economic expansion reshape the structures of the international arena. Specific changes in structures associated with power overtakings increase the probability that wars are waged. Political elites can take advantage of periods of preponderance to establish strong common bonds with allies and eliminate tensions with opponents. The use of economic instruments that facilitate trade, stabilize currencies, manage labor mobility, and increase technological transfers are the tools with which dominant nations can enhance support for the status quo. When such tools are used successfully, as demonstrated by the United States following World War II, transitions are peaceful and the periods that follow are increasingly stable. If, on the other hand, the dominant nations and their key allies fail to take advantage of their preponderance to establish workable relations with potential opponents, as Great Britain failed to do in its interactions with Germany during the *Pax Britannica*, then stability is challenged and war is likely.

To preserve peace it is important to reconcile the preferences of competing nations. Economic interactions can be used to generate support for the status quo when the elites of dominant nations pursue a cooperative strategy. While such strategies do not maximize the immediate economic interests of the dominant power, they build the trust that is essential for an "internationalist" perspective. The process of economic and political integration that is frequently vaunted for its economic spillovers has more important security implications. Nations undergoing the process of economic integration establish a cooperative relationship, eliminating the need to use conflict to resolve disputes. As the record of Europe before and after World War II attests, the integration process eliminates the need to rely on military power to ensure one's safety against neighboring countries. The additional payoff of integration is the creation of supranational units. This concentrated power ensures that participants are preponderant over a larger set of opponents.

Power Transition suggests that the convergence of preferences is conducive to peace. Stability is achieved when the dominant nation and its preponderant coalition support the status quo. The dominant nation is torn because it has a greater interest in preserving stability than in advancing its particular preferences. Testimony to the primacy of stability over common values abounds. During the Cold War, U.S. support for regional pro-American dictatorships was based on the fear that the Soviets would step into the vacuum. When the Soviet Union was collapsing, the United States *did not* actively support independence for the Baltic nations and did not favor the dissolution of the USSR into Russia and the former Soviet Republics. In the long term, the successful international status quo can only be preserved by constructing a status quo that allows flexibility in relations and incorporates the changing preferences of nations as different countries become the dominant nations in the international system.

Finally, empirical work resulting from Power Transition theory indicates that even the most determined attempts to change the international hierarchy by force are short-lived. The implication of a Phoenix Factor is startling: Major wars do not eliminate potential challengers among the economically developed powers. A nation defeated on the battlefield will rise again within one generation and if it remains dissatisfied, it *can and most likely will* challenge again for supremacy. It is not through war that political leaders restructure relations in world politics. Rather peace is shaped by the changes in economic and diplomatic policies implemented *after* war.

Nations can win the war and lose the peace.

Part III

Policy Challenges

CHAPTER 6

The Realignment Challenge: The Expansion of NATO

I am not an advocate for frequent changes in laws and constitutions, but laws and institutions must go hand in hand with the progress of the human mind. As that becomes more developed, more enlightened, as new discoveries are made, new truths discovered and manners and opinions change, with the change of circumstances, institutions must advance also to keep pace with the times. — THOMAS JEFFERSON

Power Transitions and the Expansion of NATO

In the U.S. executive branch and in Congress, the process of NATO expansion continues. For a combination of reasons — domestic politics, organizational inertia, sloppy strategic analysis — NATO expansion up to but not beyond the boundaries of the former Soviet Union is a reality.[1] Plans include the possibility of incorporating a second stage of possible entrants, including Romania, Bulgaria, Slovakia, and perhaps the Baltic states. By limiting NATO expansion to small Eastern European states, however, NATO leaders preclude the alliance from developing the power it will need to confront the coming security challenges of the twenty-first century — a potential transition with China.

From a Power Transition theory perspective, current plans for limited NATO expansion ignore the biggest future security problem for the West, which is not Russia itself, but the long-run possibility of a U.S.-China power transition sometime in this century. In this geostrategic scenario, Russia matters because of the potential power of a Russian-Chinese alliance. The need to prevent any such alignment should be central to all thinking about the future of NATO. In the short run, the problem of securing Russian respect for the boundaries of its neighbors in Eastern Europe is best managed within the context of NATO's proven capacity for reducing and resolving conflicts among its members, of whom Russia should be one.

We do not review the standard objections to limited NATO expansion without Russia. They were, for example laid out well by forty-eight senior analysts in their 26 June 1997 statement[2] and, in any event, are now largely moot. For small gain, limited expansion poses great risks. Whatever Western analysts may say, the only justification for that kind of expansion is an at least hypothetical danger from Russia. It has no compelling purpose otherwise. It is too late to stop the first round of NATO expansion, but it is not too late to consider including Russia in the next. Many Russians see an extended NATO as a direct threat against them as the rising anti-American rhetoric during the Kosovo war illustrated. This perceived threat risks reviving old Russian fears of the West, strengthening Russian militarists and nationalists and inducing greater instability in Russian domestic politics and foreign policy.

For the near future, the risks may appear tolerable. Right now, Russia can do little more than complain.[3] Over time, likely results include intransigence on arms control issues, an increase in the resources Russia devotes to rebuilding its military capabilities, and a turn of its diplomatic orientation in a hostile direction.[4] Expanding NATO as currently planned may ultimately *create* a threat from Russia that is now absent.[5] The best-case future includes a hostile and isolated Russia. Power Transition theory suggests that these unpleasant circumstances are manageable, because a dissatisfied Russia would still lack the power to overtake or credibly threaten the United States.

More plausible is a much worse outcome: an emergent alliance of Russia and China, where they are drawn together by their common dissatisfaction with the status quo.[6] Such an alliance would look very attractive to two big powers that may see themselves as excluded from a hegemonic Western community. Taking a long-term view, only a form of NATO expansion that ties Russia securely to the West ensures peace.

From a cost-benefit perspective, it is not only about what the Russians might bring to NATO, but what NATO brings to the Russians, and what the Russians then *do not* bring to the Chinese. A future round of NATO expansion that fully incorporated Russia into NATO — not just in a second-class NATO-Russia Joint Council — would eliminate Russian concern about Western encirclement and address the long-term problem of growing Chinese power and a possible U.S.-China power transition. It would allow Russia to become a normal democratic state within the Euro-Atlantic community.[7] That would firmly bind Russia's future to Western Europe's and ensure substantial global peace for the next century.

Russia's Options

From a geostrategic perspective, expanding NATO without Russia runs the risk of creating a severe security dilemma for *both* the East and the West.[8] What are the choices available to a state faced with an alliance far stronger than it is or can hope to be?

Alliance Expansion

One possible reaction is *bandwagoning*.[9] A state may try to join in cooperation with those who might otherwise threaten it. This is, in essence, the policy that Mikhail Gorbachev began and is the policy that led to the end of the Cold War. To date, Boris Yeltsin and other Russian democrats have largely followed Gorbachev's precedent, albeit in fits and starts. Russian integration into NATO would be a giant step in that direction.

Russia's second option is to *hide* or to withdraw into heavily armed isolation greatly dependent on its nuclear weapons and rooted in a perception of being surrounded by potential enemies (Western, Islamic, Asian). Some evidence of this can be found in the Russian Duma's unwillingness to ratify the latest strategic arms limitation treaty (START). A Russian xenophobia based in some degree on reality (many paranoids do have enemies), an economy once again autarkic and burdened by militarization, and the revival of an autocratic government is surely not in Western interests. Nor are Russians likely to see it as a viable option for the long run.

If NATO does not take Russia in, their third choice will become more attractive: to look eastward for a partner with whom parity can be achieved against the perceived threat from the West. NATO expansion without Russia will likely lead to a Russo-Sino rapprochement and even a formal military alliance between the two. True, there is a long history of trouble in Russian-Chinese relations,[10] and such an alliance would experience real friction, but it would not be a type of alliance without precedent.

To protect their interests, states will find allies where they can and must. Russian leaders have never liked to face adversaries on two fronts.[11] It is naive to think they would not eventually turn to China. Imagine Russia allied with a hugely populous partner, for whom Russian military technology represents the high end of what is available to the new partnership. A Russo-Sino alliance would vitiate the single most effective foreign policy initiative of the Cold War: Nixon's opening to China, a move that then deprived the Soviet Union of any hope of recovering its most powerful potential ally. Limited NATO expansion risks re-creating the world of parity that Nixon deftly managed to shatter.

Such an alliance is not so implausible that the West can safely ignore the possibility. It would have big benefits for each side. For Russia, China's expanding economy and 1.2 billion people would provide a counterweight to NATO. For China, a Russian partner with 150 million people, great natural resources, and a GNP with significant growth potential, would be a big catch.

Russia's military technology, while now largely inferior to that of the West, remains the most modern part of the Russian economy and has the potential to serve as a catalyst for future military development. In virtually every category, Russia's capabilities are far superior to China's. From submarines, to communications, to missiles and aircraft, to nuclear weapons, the Russians have much to offer a large and increasingly wealthy state. Easy access to Russian technology would hasten Chinese military modernization, at reduced cost. It would also reduce incentives for the continued contraction of Russia's military industrial complex.

Evidence for improved Chinese-Russian relations can already be found in arms sales and diplomatic efforts alike.[12] China agreed to buy seventy-two advanced SU-27 fighter planes from Russia[13] and build a production line in Shenyang to make more.[14] A similar agreement on the SU-30 may be next, and Moscow recently announced a new sale of two advanced cruise missile warships.[15] In the context of recent Chinese espionage, even more unsettling is evidence pointing to renewed missile sales between the two countries.[16] With China now assumed to possess advanced nuclear weapons designs, missile launch and guidance technology is all that stands in the way of China becoming a nuclear power of the same rank as the United States and Russia. A desperately cash-strapped Russia has much to offer China.

On the diplomatic front, Russia has been flirting with Beijing. In December 1996, President Yeltsin and Chinese Foreign Minister Li Peng announced a package of large troop cuts on their borders, trade agreements, and further arms deals. The April 1997 meeting in Moscow between Yeltsin and Chinese President Jiang Zemin called for a "multipolar" world in contrast to a unipolar one where, in Yeltsin's terms, "someone else is going to dictate conditions."[17] While disavowing any causal linkage from NATO expansion, Russian Defense Minister Igor Rodionov affirmed the development of neighborly relations with China, which "even bind Russia to strengthen relations of partnership also in the military sphere." A Russia-China partnership would place the destiny of much of the Eurasian landmass and the western Pacific in the hands of an antidemocratic alliance.[18] This alliance would operate outside the structure of international law and the norms of universal human rights associated with *Pax Americana* for the past two centuries.

Avoiding the Dangers of a Russia-China Alliance

Power Transition theory suggests that China, not Russia, presents the most severe long-term credible potential threat to Western (and global) peace and security. As noted earlier, a state's intentions or its satisfaction with the status quo is as important as power parity concerns. This is *not* said to impute particular intentions or malice to the Chinese people or to its current leaders. Nor does it imply that the Chinese government's intentions are fundamentally more than defensive, to secure a territorial integrity that includes but does not exceed historic Chinese regional claims. Rather, it is stated simply to recognize what diplomats and scholars have long understood.

The period of transition from dominance by one great power system leader to another is marked by tremendous potential for instability and cataclysmic conflict as a challenger catches up and ultimately surpasses the power base of the previously dominant state. If the rising power is dissatisfied with its place in the international system, war between the system leader and the challenger may well result.[19] Germany's ambitions earlier in this century illustrate, but by no means exhaust, the list of challenges. Moreover, the dangers exist even when the challenger is not particularly aggressive or expansionist. The fears, uncertainties, and potential miscalculations of each other's intentions and power provide danger enough. Experience suggests two essential and complementary strategies for managing the approaching dangers of Western-Sino military and economic parity.

One strategy is to prevent the rising state from being able to approach the dominant state's power. A preponderance of power concentrated in the hands of the system leader will deter the initiation of overt conflict. Deterrence can work as long as the power of the dominant alliance exceeds that of the rising state's by a considerable margin. However, a pure deterrence strategy — associated with mutual assured destruction — emphasizing counterthreat and military containment can intensify conflicts and increase the challenger's commitment eventually to achieve its own dominance.[20] Pure deterrence cannot be relied on indefinitely, and so long as it is practiced, can become a self-defeating strategy. Nevertheless, preponderant deterrence can buy valuable time, during which other means of ensuring the peace can be brought to bear.

Enhancing the Status Quo

The one factor that most constrains a state's potential power is its population.[21] With but 150 million people, Russia is a fragment of its former self. Even a reconstituted Soviet Union, developing economically once again, could pose no fundamental danger to NATO's roughly 700 million people. Russia is not today, nor could it be in the future, a threat to the demographic and economic preponderance of the West. China is another matter. An economically growing China, with 1.2 billion citizens, is the single state that could pose a threat to the future security and prosperity of the NATO countries.

Expanding NATO to include the Visegrad countries and Russia would produce a population base of more than 900 million people. More important, the combined wealth and technological superiority of the alliance would postpone the day of reckoning with China's overtaking of the West. China can only achieve geostrategic parity by growing its economy to the point at which its national income approaches that of the West, a development that is possible in the near term, though its translation to national power will take much longer.

Over the long run, if the Chinese economy were to grow at 8 percent a year while the expanded NATO's grew at 2 percent per year, it would take nearly until the year 2030 to reach parity with the West.[22] As noted in chapter 7, we judge these rates as unlikely. There is no historical precedent — Japan included — for a long-sustained growth rate as high as 8 percent.[23] Nor is there much chance that China could maintain that rate with growing environmental problems[24] and, as its technological gap with the West narrowed, with less room for catching up simply by copying Western goods and services. Given an expanded NATO's power preponderance, a growing mercantilist China[25] would find it very hard to develop the military or economic capabilities needed to challenge America and NATO for system leadership, by force *or* beggar-thy-neighbor policies.

The second strategy is to ensure that the rising power and the dominant power have few quarrels over the nature of the international order and the distribution of goods therein. This kind of transition occurred when the United States passed Great Britain as a world power. America did not fundamentally oppose the system that Britain had put in place. In turn, Britain was not willing to fight to oppose the marginal changes to the international system that resulted from subsequent U.S. leadership. Both states shared many common interests and values, and both British and American leaders made a deliberate decision to strengthen Anglo-American ties.[26] Integrating Russia into NATO provides time and means to guard against the rising power of China in the short run. In the longer run, it creates a mechanism and a model by which China can, over time, become fully integrated into the international system, allowing the future rising power to be accommodated without cataclysmic conflict.

As for potential Chinese fears, the Chinese have their safeguards against Russian or Western aggression. An invasion and occupation of China's vast territory and population is unimaginable, particularly by a NATO limited to a defense or limited-offense orientation. China also possesses the world's third-largest nuclear force. In this scenario, both sides would have ample time to develop a long-term solution to the parity problem, which will require a convergence of both preferences and interests.

Managing Russian Entry into NATO

There are some standard objections to admitting Russia to NATO, which we list and then rebut. Carefully considered, the logic behind the argument to admit Russia is compelling and far outweighs the concerns. Consider the main objections.

1. The Russian military establishment is too degraded to meet NATO countries' high standards. Thus, the costs of bringing Russia's military up to NATO's level are too high and the potential benefits too low. Russia, with a population more closely resembling Brazil's and a GDP currently the size of the Netherlands, does not appear to be a nation that could threaten or substantially contribute to one of the most powerful, stable, and enduring alliances in history.[27]

2. Even if the Russians were allowed into the alliance, the West could not trust them to behave as loyal members. NATO members must be able to depend on one another to meet their commitments during potential crises. NATO cannot rely on the Russians because their only real interest lies in blocking NATO's expansion, not in actually joining an alliance that would compromise their sovereignty and military secrecy.[28]

3. Russia's economy is insufficiently market oriented and too corrupt to provide a match with the West. Nor is Russia's political system sufficiently democratic, stable, or even governable to provide any meaningful contribution to NATO's overall security.

The logic of Power Transition refutes such arguments. Cost and benefits analysis shows that today the Russian military is in bad shape. The Red Army's poor performance in Chechnya does not presage a serious Russian threat to NATO now or in the reasonable future. Nor does it provide a basis for confidence that Russia will be able to meet the high military standards necessary for incorporation into NATO. Nevertheless, in the history of admissions to NATO — which includes Greece, Turkey, and Spain — the yardstick correctly applied was not the standard of a state's existing military capability. Rather, it was the potential of that state once integrated into the alliance, for a range of political as well as military contributions. On the ground of potential, Russia rates highly.

Russia — the West's greatest former threat — over time can contribute greatly to the overall security of NATO. The equation of Russia with Brazil misses one big point. Russia possesses something quite significant that Brazil does not: its own high-technology military industrial complex with associated research and development potential, waiting for the opportunity to be exploited again as it was during the Cold War.

Estimates of the costs of integrating the new Eastern European members vary wildly, for political as well as technical reasons. The RAND Corporation study put the price at approximately $42 billion over ten years. This is the cost for upgrading their forces and readying NATO for rapid deployment to their territory in a crisis, but without stationing NATO troops there otherwise.[29] The Defense Department's estimate for the most comparable upgrading is a little lower: $35 billion over twelve years, whereas the Congressional Budget Office's closest option comes in much higher, at $61 billion. For the sake of an illustration, let us take the DOD figure.

Let us speculate that for Russia, with two-and-a-half times as many people, the cost of upgrading its military systems to bring them into line with NATO standards were as high as $100 billion. (This is probably too high, since increased costs for NATO rapid deployment would not be proportional.) While that is a significant sum, in the context of President Reagan's historic $4 trillion arms buildup it would represent a tremendous bargain, far more than the return from bringing in just the East Europeans. Those states have no indigenous aircraft industry, no submarine manufacturing industry, no nuclear weapons, and no ability to make a self-sustainable contribution to their defense and security obligations.

Although the costs cannot be ignored, neither can the potential gains from Russian integration. A major benefit would be the reduced burden of acquiring information through covert means. How much has the West paid in the past and is it planning to pay in the future to get information on Russian intentions and power covertly? To be able to integrate Russian nuclear weapons into NATO's nuclear command and control system would alone be worth the price. One of the greatest fears about Russia concerns the loss of control of its nuclear weapons. Admitting it to NATO provides the means to control its fissile materials more directly than by buying up excess warheads or trusting the Russians to convert surplus plutonium to reactor fuel. By contrast, leaving Russia out encourages its continued reliance on nuclear deterrence, maintaining thousands of warheads on alert and immensely complicating all high-priority arms control efforts to reduce nuclear weaponry.[30]

Lack of trust and murky motives are not sufficient justification to refuse a dissatisfied power willing to join the status quo. France was brought into the Quintuple Alliance in 1818 to reduce its dislike of the status quo imposed after Napoleon.[31] Germans were not trusted forty years ago following World War II. One of the principal reasons for bringing West Germany into NATO in 1955 was fear of revived and unconstrained German nationalism. In Lord Ismay's phrase, Germany belonged in NATO to "keep the Germans down" as well as to "keep the Russians out." The allies recognized that the best way to contain German expansionism was to include the Germans in security structures, not to exclude them.[32] Similar concerns brought West Germany into the whole range of European institutions, led to Gorbachev's acceptance of a United Germany in NATO,[33] and continue to motivate French and German policy today.

These same motivations should hold toward Russia. NATO should bring the Russians in precisely *because* the West does not fully trust their intentions. Integrating Russian and NATO military forces will require a convergence of doctrine, command, training, and equipment. For example, NATO aircraft have IFF (identify friend or foe) devices to prevent them from firing on one another. This integration of standards and equipment will require and create a level of openness impossible to obtain otherwise.

Openness exposes secrets, creating conditions in which no hidden preparations, as those for Barbarossa in 1941, are possible. A large-scale German surprise attack on any current NATO member is simply inconceivable today. Much of the explanation lies in changed German intentions. Nevertheless, in no small part, our dismissal of such a scenario stems from the openness that NATO provides and in the institutional binding of Germany to Europe and the United States, including the unified NATO command. Military integration into NATO will become a guarantee of effective civilian control of the Russian military.[34]

Will Russia simply obstruct NATO's now relatively smooth operations and sow seeds of dissent among the alliance members? There are real conflicts of interest within the alliance, but NATO has a decent record of handling them. Consider the seemingly intractable dispute between Greece and Turkey. Although NATO has not been able to resolve all their problems, NATO's conflict-resolution techniques — a combination of mediation (as by Cyrus Vance and NATO Secretary-General Manlio Brosio in 1967) and deterrence — have kept them from going to war.[35] Without NATO, they probably would have done so by now. Fears of conflict within NATO should not preclude the expansion of one of the few organizations that truly can make a difference in solving the thorniest security dilemma the major powers will face in the coming century.

Do the Russians really want to come in? Although in 1991 Boris Yeltsin repeatedly requested NATO admission for Russia,[36] maybe today, after Kosovo, they are not serious. Joining NATO imposes significant constraints on a state's ability to exercise privacy rights and sovereignty. While the loss of autonomy for NATO members does not match that embodied in the EU, Russian entry into NATO would bring a substantial loss of control. Indeed, that would be part of NATO's motivation in inviting the Russians.

Russia could decline the invitation just as it declined Marshall Plan aid following World War II. However, if it does refuse a sincere offer, it will be by its own choice, not by way of NATO exclusion.[37] This should defuse many Russian objections, and hence reduce the political backlash in Russia to limited expansion of NATO. A refusal to accept an offer of NATO membership would be a useful early indicator of the future direction of Russian foreign policy, making NATO expansion to the borders of Russia more justifiable.

Alternatively, Russia could accept the offer but not in good faith. What happens if NATO lets the Russians in and the expanded partnership does not work as planned? Alternatively, what if the differences in the two cultures are so great that they cannot be bridged by intrusive NATO institutions? Certainly, the Russians would have learned a lot about Western military doctrine and weapons. Nevertheless, the West will have learned a great deal about the Russians' command postures and intentions as well.

Or Russia might join, even intending to stay, but then throw sand in NATO's gears, with the alliance losing much of its capacity for joint action in situations such as those in Bosnia and Kosovo. Because of the consensus clause in the NATO charter, unanimity is required for all significant decisions. In this scenario, the Russians could effectively veto NATO actions, or otherwise obstruct NATO's already limited capacity for out-of-area operations. The United States and other NATO leaders chose not to pose the possibility of NATO action in Kosovo before the United Nations, knowing that Russia would veto the action. If Russia were a member of NATO, it would be able to exercise similar veto power over NATO actions.

Even in this admittedly dismal situation, Russia would not and could not pose a credible threat to NATO's security. It would chiefly limit NATO's proactive offensive capacity, a risk worth taking by an alliance whose principal purpose is providing for the common defense of its members. Nor would a continuation of a security frontier in Europe — like the Cold War's, only farther east — exist to feed irrational fears and resentments within Russia's borders. By including Russia into NATO, the current debate about the future of NATO, whether it should be a defensive alliance or a proactive collective security police force for Europe would largely be ended.

Ultimately none of these objections carries much weight. If the Russians do prove obstructive, NATO would simply become a defense-only alliance, albeit one still serving to protect its members from attacks both from the outside and from each other. Ironically, this scenario produces a new NATO, which is, in the end, what it has claimed to be from the outset. NATO, in this situation, will evolve into a transparent defensive alliance with little offensive capacity, a collection of states that pose no aggressive threat to anyone.

It will, however, have evolved into a structure that can both inwardly and outwardly guarantee the borders of its members. Indeed, it should include a general guarantee of borders in Eastern Europe, avoiding the mistake of the Locarno treaties of 1925.[38] In 1999, had Serbia been a member of NATO it is likely that the breakdown in talks that led to the war in Kosovo would not have occurred in the same manner. By creating a division of labor, pushing states to pursue technical specialization and military comparative advantage, NATO hampers its members (other than the United States) from acting alone. NATO provides powerful restraints on adventurism by its members.

Furthermore, cooperation of the sort NATO demands of its members has already begun to grow in many nonmilitary areas between Russia and current NATO members.[39] The United States is risking the lives of its astronauts in cooperative aerospace projects. Russian rockets will launch critical components of the planned space station and components of private firms' global communications systems. NATO expansion would merely extend the type of cooperation already underway between the Russian space agency and NASA. Civilian firms also are cooperating in joint ventures that require exchange of technology and human resources.[40] Boeing technology and equipment will be used on Russian and Ukrainian rockets to launch communications satellites.[41] Allied Signal has established two joint ventures, to design and manufacture avionics and landing systems for Russian-built aircraft and a software development center in Zhukovsky.[42] Additional partnerships are in progress for cooperative development of environmental controls, auxiliary power, fluid systems, and engines.

Political and economic institutions can endure Russian incorporation into NATO. Fears of political instability in Russia are not unfounded — but limited NATO expansion will exacerbate the conditions that generate those fears. Rather than increase the risks of political instability, rising ultranationalism, and the general decline of democratic institutions, including Russia in NATO as a full partner would defuse the aura of external threat that strengthens the hands of the radical conservatives in Russia. It would also eliminate the greatest external threat the Russian military can point to in the internal battles for budgetary and political influence.

Concerns about Russia's political compatibility with democratic regimes in the West should not preclude consideration of its suitability as an alliance partner. Although most NATO members have been free-market democracies, Portugal joined under the Salazar dictatorship and neither Greece nor Turkey was expelled during its periods of military rule.[43] NATO does not maintain the very high admission standards for democracy and free markets that we associate with the European Union. Russian democracy and free-market economics are surely as well developed as those of Romania, where hopes for inclusion in the next round of NATO expansion are being fanned.

If the United States expects to strengthen commitment to the status quo, it needs to aid the Russians in the continued development of open political and economic institutions by addressing their security fears. In the end, the best way to promote sustainable democracy is to integrate Russia into Western political, economic, and security institutions, NATO in particular, with the prospect of further integration when its democracy becomes firmly established. Including Russia follows directly from Secretary of State Madeleine Albright's characterization of more limited expansion, when she declared, "The purpose of NATO enlargement is to do for Europe's east what NATO did fifty years ago for Europe's west: to integrate new democracies, defeat old hatreds, provide confidence in economic recovery, and deter conflict."[44]

Russian entry into NATO will not and cannot happen immediately. It will take years of preparation, as did European integration.[45] The point is to start that process now, with a firm commitment and a credible timetable. If the United States wishes to remain the leader of NATO, this is the issue on which to exercise leadership and persuade reluctant Europeans. Bringing Russia into NATO would finally complete what Tsar Peter the Great and other westernizers aimed to do from the eighteenth century onward: integrate Russia with the West, to their mutual benefit. It would bring security and enhanced stability at a lower cost than would bringing Russia into the EU, and it more directly addresses concern over the rising power of the military within Russia.

Managing the Chinese Reaction

Both the United States and the Soviet Union exacerbated the Cold War conflict by being insensitive to the fears of the other. Would our proposed grand expansion of NATO simply create a replay of the old Cold War, with a potentially more powerful adversary?[46] It should not, and need not. Any coming confrontation with China will be fundamentally different from the old ideological conflict between NATO and the Warsaw Pact. During the Cold War, U.S.-Soviet ideological differences made conflict virtually inevitable, as the two systems not only differed in their domestic and worldviews, but also were fundamentally opposed to the continued existence of the opposition.

Leninist doctrine, which provided the theoretical underpinnings of the Soviet system, was based on a revolutionary world ideology — despite its rejection of Leon Trotsky's overt call for world revolution.[47] The endgame in the Leninist framework was to be world revolution driven by inevitable class struggle among a growing urban proletariat. The communist system would win out in the end in part because Lenin and his followers argued that the Soviet state had the superior economic system.

The ideological foundations of the Chinese system do not carry those ambitions. Mao Zedong's ideological goals were fundamentally local; driven not by an ever-expanding worldwide urban revolution that could spread from one city to another like wildfire before a strong wind, but by his vision of a rural revolution. Today's Chinese leaders have largely abandoned Marxist economics and, in an attempt to modernize rapidly, vigorously embrace capitalism and more open markets. In China, we are left not with an expansionist regime driven by an ideology fundamentally opposed to the continued existence of the West, but rather confront a growing power governed by what is essentially a variant of Asian authoritarianism. The Asian authoritarian model does pose an ideological challenge to Western liberalism, and to some provides an attractive organizing principle for the relationship between economics and politics.[48] It does not, however, carry a fundamentally subversive and mutually exclusive ideological appeal, as did the old Marxism/Leninism.[49]

Consider how states gauge or measure success in the international arena. For the Soviet Union, success was in being a new communist country with a centralized economy. Not so for contemporary China, where Mao's communist ideology is no longer at its core. Today, the Chinese gauge success by making money and increasing their influence abroad. Of course, no one should discount the antagonism of an expanding democratic ideology and a growing authoritarian ideology.[50] Democracies prefer to be surrounded by other democracies in an inherently peaceful relationship.[51] The Western democracies should continue to engage China on human rights and democracy by indirect means through the creation of domestic interest groups. Those advocates will, in time, gain influence. Nevertheless, democracies also are accustomed to surviving in relationships with non-aggressive autocracies. Economic insularity today is much more difficult for both democracies and autocracies to sustain.

Confronted with a growing NATO, China will have the same three basic options as does Russia. China could try to achieve parity with the West and challenge for dominance, increasing the risk of war in the future. Fear of Russian movement toward parity drives Western willingness to have Russia join NATO. For those in China who wish to match the Western alliance, if NATO follows our prescriptions it will have taken China's obvious partner, Russia.[52] China might conceivably attempt to move toward parity by striking an accord with India or Japan, but it is difficult to see Japan, ever more integrated economically and institutionally with the West, as throwing its weight to the Chinese side. In fact, Chinese economic and military growth should eventually bring the Japanese into a closer arrangement with NATO.[53] A Sino-Indian alliance is unlikely for a number of historical and regional hierarchy reasons, as discussed in the next chapter. Shut off from Russia, India, and Japan, China would have little hope of gaining parity against an expanding NATO for at least the next half century.

In the Asian Pacific Rim hierarchy, Chinese efforts to expand regionally against weaker neighbors are likely regardless of whether Russia joins NATO. Threats to nearby Pacific islands, including Taiwan, are to be expected.[54] For small nations on China's border, security will lie with a strong U.S. regional presence, a clear U.S. power preponderance, and artful diplomacy — strategies already recognized and practiced by many of China's neighbors. The original NATO members would not be much involved, nor do they posses the capacity or physical proximity needed to have much influence over these Pacific Rim affairs.

Russia, however, could be an invaluable NATO member in this regard given its geographic proximity, naval and military bases in the Far East, and potentially respectable military capabilities.[55] Denying these potentially valuable strategic assets to China will help restrain it.[56] The inclusion of Russia would make NATO the first truly global alliance. Both northern oceans would have a NATO state on each side, with a stable Europe as the keystone. Articles 5 and 6 of the NATO Treaty exclude Asia from those regions in which an armed attack against any member "shall be considered an attack against them all." While this could be amended, an amendment could be seen as a provocation to China. It is already understood that common action may occur elsewhere, outside the narrow boundaries of the North Atlantic Ocean, if unanimously approved as a Combined Joint Task Force operation.

Beijing's next possible response could be *hiding,* or pursuing an isolationist policy. A Chinese foreign policy stance of armed political, if not economic, isolationism would pose some difficulties for the United States and NATO. Indeed, in the short run this may well be the policy reaction to a broad expansion of NATO. Yet, this short-term increase in Chinese dissatisfaction pales in comparison to the absence of a long-term solution. To the contrary, it solves the thorniest dilemmas of the coming global power transition. An isolationist China would confront an intractable political predicament.

The new leaders in China would face a series of political challenges and tradeoffs that they will be forced to confront in the near future. These choices will be impelled by the high and competing costs associated with military modernization, the economic and technical difficulties associated with rapid economic modernization, and the problems of maintaining an autarchic regime in the face of a growing middle class. In the emerging global economy, with its constant competitive pressures, the challenge of attempting to grow the Chinese economy while simultaneously expanding its immediate military base may prove intractable. Unlike the current Russian leaders, who have so far survived a near-stagnant economy, the legitimacy of the Chinese rulers depends almost entirely on their continued ability to deliver rapid growth.

If China aspired to match the Western alliance in military power and economic capacity, armed isolation would be very costly, espionage of the past ten years notwithstanding. Chinese leaders would have to reverse current priorities and devote proportionally more resources to the military. Even then, it will be many years before China can match U.S. military spending and capability levels, not to mention those of a U.S.-NATO-Russia coalition. Although the Chinese army is numerically large, the Gulf War in 1991 demonstrated that sheer numbers no longer carry the same weight in conventional war that they did during the Korean War, which was the last large-scale direct conflict between China and the West.[57] China's military is now in far worse shape even than the Soviet Union's was before its collapse. To try to match the West's overwhelming capability, China would be forced into either of two courses of action.

If the Chinese decided to be isolationist and to rely principally on domestic investment, they would likely have to choose between the military and domestic consumption and investment.[58] Given the growing strains on China's internal stability, diverting significant resources to the military is not a viable alternative if the Chinese truly hope to achieve strategic parity with the West. The history of the Soviet Union's collapse suggests what would happen to a China that tried simultaneously to catch up militarily, satisfy growing civilian consumer expectations, *and* sustain the economic growth-rate needed to bring itself up to par with a far richer Western alliance.

Alternatively, China might turn to outside sources of direct investment by continuing and expanding on its current policy. Doing so could free up domestic capital to be invested in the military, but this policy also serves Western interests. An economy sufficiently robust to be able to support high levels of military investment would need Western investment on the civilian side. From the perspective of NATO — an alliance seeking both global stability and the maintenance of the global territorial status quo — opening up the Chinese economy would be beneficial. All else being equal, economically interdependent states are more likely than others to live in peace with one another.[59]

Would Western investment keep flowing to a hostile China?[60] Marx long ago claimed that the capitalists would end up making the rope with which to hang themselves. Of late, European firms have demonstrated great willingness to invest in potentially unstable areas of the world. However, they do so at a price to the investment recipient. Bellicose states and political adversaries pay a high cost for the foreign capital they import. Investors put a higher discount on politically risky investments, with demands for higher interest rates and expected profits. Such penalties will raise the costs to China to develop its military *or* grow its economy at a pace sufficient to allow it to catch up with the West. Therefore the Chinese become bound by strong incentives to maintain stability and to keep sending reassuring signals to Western investors.

The Chinese dilemma is this: If they do not want to be dependent on Western investment, then they cannot afford the rapid military buildup needed to confront the West in the near term. If they rely on Western investment and thus divert domestic capital to support the military, then they become, over time, interdependent with the West. The second choice inevitably draws them closer to the status quo. Already China's dependence on foreign trade and its eagerness to participate in multilateral international organizations like the WTO put it on a path of cooperative relationships that will be strongly resistant to reversal. Such growing interdependence reduces the likelihood that China will choose a confrontational military and foreign policy, absent some cataclysmic event.

China's final alternative would be to *bandwagon*. Indeed, China may itself seek to join NATO, binding its security interests with those of former adversaries. The Chinese have bandwagoned in the past. They turned West with the Nixon initiatives, although the United States at the time anchored the dominant pole in the international system. In doing so, the Chinese did not simply seek parity to ward off an immediate military threat.[61] They could have interpreted Western outposts around China — South Korea, South Vietnam, Taiwan, Southeast Asia Treaty Organization (SEATO) — as being fully as threatening as their Soviet neighbor was. Instead, they saw improved relations with the United States as the key to building their economic and long-term military security. China bandwagoned west in a way that presaged the Soviet bandwagoning that ended the Cold War because the Chinese realized that joining the preponderant power ensures stability and maintains opportunities for growth.

If Russia is to be kept out of NATO for fear of antagonizing China, much the same logic should have stopped NATO expansion into Eastern Europe for fear of antagonizing Russia. Rather, the first round of NATO expansion should be the first step toward one last big cycle of bandwagoning. NATO would then expand to include a democratizing Russia. Until China is also ready to join, it is important that NATO not gratuitously threaten Chinese security. The Chinese leaders should be encouraged to see their security vested in a policy of increasing political and economic openness.[62]

China should be engaged in an ever-deepening network of international organizations and economic interdependence.[63] Given the proper combination of political and economic reforms, eventually China should join NATO. Ultimately, this great alliance might come to include all but the rogue states. In a sense, that *would* be the end of international political history. Perhaps Francis Fukuyama[64] called it one move too soon, with not quite enough attention to geostrategic matters. Such an alliance would constitute a triumph both of Western ideology and of Western power and organization.

Conclusions: The Future of NATO

In order to confront the changing environment of the twenty-first century, NATO may be forced to choose between two sometimes compatible, but sometimes conflicting missions. NATO exists first and foremost to provide for the security of its members against attack by an external or internal foe. Second in purpose and importance, NATO holds the possibility of providing for the internal stability of its nonmember neighbors. For the former purpose, considerable benefits would accrue from extending an offer of membership to Russia even at the possible cost of losing the ability to pursue the second mission.

Such an offer would integrate a potentially threatening state into NATO and increase the overall power base of the alliance. For Russia, the new NATO would provide security assurances on its western front and deterrent power vis-à-vis its eastern front. Membership criteria should be, on both political and economic grounds, similar to those required for membership in the EU. But rather than raising the bar to such heights as to preclude marginal states from joining the new NATO, the membership hurdle should be set just a notch lower than the stringent conditions for the EU.

It is far easier for states to reform their economies and polities in the absence of security concerns than when faced with powerful and potentially bellicose neighbors. Integration into the NATO alliance provides stability to a state's domestic political regime and external security that allows it to focus on the tough job of political and economic development. Any defensive alliance serves two purposes. The first is to prevent an external power from trying to alter the global status quo. The second is to prevent any of the member states from wishing to do the same. NATO supplies greater physical security for all its members by integrating them into the full NATO system. Key is the integration of command, doctrine, training, and equipment. The NATO system is much more than just a traditional alliance — it creates common expectations and notions of defense versus offense and common beliefs in the stability of the interstate system. That means integration and interdependence in the broadest possible sense — ideological, institutional, and economic.

The bigger the alliance becomes, the lighter the burden on any single state and the greater the security provided.[65] If smaller states "cheat" on defense expenditures — as some did and do in NATO past and present[66] — those states will then become even less able to mount any serious threat on their own. This potential demilitarization would provide a downward spiral of the security fears of neighboring states. Why should not other states, such as Japan, Russia, and ultimately China or India, be attracted to this and be welcome?

Wider NATO expansion will and must proceed slowly. Japan is clearly a potential member, an outcome to be encouraged later. Japanese domestic politics are not ready, and for now, Japan's ties to the other industrial countries are strong enough to allow NATO membership to remain a low priority.[67] Rapid global NATO expansion would only feed historically well-founded Chinese fears of encirclement and Western imperialism. The challenge of managing the peaceful power transition that China may present is a long-term one that does not require a policy of "containing" China and Russia. Engagement with Russia and China by America and Japan is much to be preferred.

Expansion of NATO to include Russia risks some losses as well as offering considerable gains. The downside risk is that Russia would hamstring NATO in many respects. For example, the war in Kosovo would likely not have been possible in the guise it followed had Russia been a member of NATO. Even so, Russia would still be in a security system for moderating conflicts within the NATO alliance. With Russia no longer a potential ally of China, large net gains accrue to the West. Western ideological and institutional principles will lie at the core of world organization, even more so than now. In effect, a continually expanding NATO provides an essential supplement to the United Nations, one with military teeth and an organizational structure to support them. It is a multilateral structure, in which American leadership is strong but tempered by common perceptions and the experience of negotiated cooperation.

If NATO chooses to include Russia, the very enemy it was created to guard against, what is the potential limit to NATO's expansion? NATO should, in time, welcome all states that meet certain criteria of economic and political stability. Potential members should be well into the democratization process, avoiding instability and any consequent tendency toward external disputation.[68] Democratic states have less internal violence and civil war than do other states,[69] and once established, democratic regimes become permanent if the democracies are also reasonably wealthy.[70] New NATO recruits would have to do what Germany, Japan and now Eastern Europe did to enter the Western alliance: grow their economies and reform their politics. This is the kind of post–Cold War security system worth striving for. NATO should expand to include *anyone* who meets the criteria, most certainly including Asians, and especially the Chinese.[71]

CHAPTER 7
The Asian Challenge

The question is not whether China will become the most powerful nation on earth, but rather how long it will take her to achieve this status.... The United States will retain world leadership for at least the remainder of the twentieth century, perhaps even for a longer time, but the position will eventually pass to China.
                                                    — A.F.K. ORGANSKI

There has been a geological shift in the locus of international conflict. No longer is great power conflict Eurocentric. It has migrated to the Asian landmass where it will remain centered. This chapter investigates in detail the first and most important challenge that will arise in the Asian theater, China as a superpower. Specific strategies are offered for the United States to manage the seismic events associated with this shift in world politics. Following China, we briefly focus our attention on India as it asserts its eventual right to superpower status.[1]

Managing Power: The Primacy of China

Since the dissolution of the Soviet Union in 1991, the United States has been uncontested in its position as world leader. This respite may well be relatively short. Upon finishing with one comparatively weak challenger, China has surfaced as the new threat to U.S. dominance of world affairs. As the Chinese challenge develops during this century, the tectonic plates on which international relations rest will move irreversibly.

The phenomenon of China's modernization — its reduced fertility rates, the increase in its political capacity, and its economic growth — signaled the future of international relations for the past three decades.[2] For the most part, the consequences of these signals were overlooked as attention was focused on the Cold War. No longer is that the case.

The U.S.-China rivalry has become the dominant foreign policy problem, not only for each nation, but also for the world in this century.[3] It is no accident that this conclusion is shared in Washington, D.C., and Beijing. Former U.S. ambassador to China Winston Lord summarized the U.S. view as follows: "The question is not whether China will be a major player in global as well as regional security affairs but rather when and how. China's

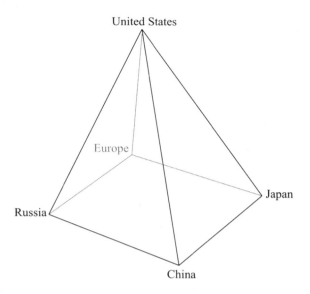

Figure 7.1 The Global Hierarchy: A Chinese Perspective

rapid economic development, its growing military capabilities and its historical international role will make it a major power in the coming century. The challenge we face is to assure that as China develops as a global actor, it does so constructively, as a country integrated into international institutions and committed to practices enshrined in international law."[4]

Wang Jisi, the director of the Institute of American Studies at the Chinese Academy of Social Sciences, offered the Chinese counterpart perspective by observing that the United States will remain the single superpower in the world for the next decade or two and "the only nation capable of wielding military power and political influence in every corner of the globe."[5] The vice-president of the Society of Asia-African Studies, Xue Mouhang, visually represents the centrality of the United States in world affairs by placing the United States at the heart of a global hierarchy composed of four triangular relationships (see figure 7.1).[6]

Centering on the primary link within this hierarchical perspective, the U.S.-China relationship can be formulated as follows. China has the demographic, economic, and political potential to catch and overtake the United States, first in the size of its economy and then in power. "If" this is to happen, China's overtaking of the U.S. economy, in terms of GDP, will occur considerably earlier than its overtaking in power. The former is expected in the first quarter of the twenty-first century.[7] The latter would take substantially longer (see figure 7.2).[8] The fact that economic power only

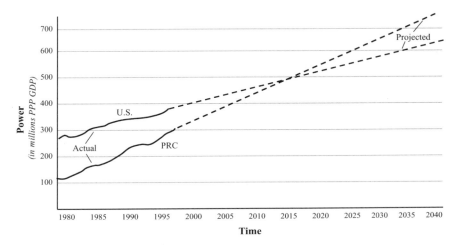

Figure 7.2 U.S. and PRC Power Shifts, 1980-2040

subsequently translates into national power will provide a breathing space for both nations to adjust to the new realities.

Since China is in the very initial stages of economic parity, which is a precondition for the eventual but still distant power overtaking, a number of major questions arise. First and foremost, what conditions would allow this passage to occur peacefully? Equally important, what policies should the United States follow prior to and during a transition? And what policies should China follow? Below we address all three questions from the Power Transition perspective.

First, however, let us deal with the "if" we noted above. There are two conditions under which China will not catch or overtake the United States. The size of China's future economy will vary with the rate and duration of its economic growth. Therefore the first condition stipulates that if either variable is seriously reduced before the society is transformed from a peasant to an urban system with a highly productive economy, China may not catch, let alone overtake, the United States. Since we cannot deny the possibility of a dramatic slowdown or even a collapse, for the purposes of our analysis we assume a Chinese GDP growth rate of 5.5 percent over the next decade or two,[9] and slightly lower growth rates in the very long run.[10] It should be recognized that this growth rate is substantially lower than official Chinese figures,[11] which we believe have been artificially inflated not only for national political purposes but also as a consequence of inadequate internal controls.[12]

The second reason for our "if" is the possibility that China will fragment and/or the central government will lose economic power to its provinces. The Chinese political system has been subjected to powerful centrifugal social, economic, and political forces for almost two decades. There is some question whether China's political system will be able to withstand the internal and external pressures rapid growth will bring.[13] For example, there is evidence that tax revenues, as a percentage of GDP, are dropping rapidly — a danger sign for a central government intent on developing national power.[14] Yet fast-growth countries traditionally do not fragment; they consolidate power at the national level. Therefore, we assume a normal rapid growth rate based on a strong united China.[15]

To repeat the assumptions underlying the following analysis: first, China will continue to grow economically at relatively rapid rates; and second, China will not fragment politically or devolve to regional economic units fiscally independent of the central government.

The Dynamics of China's Power Transition

China's power rose spectacularly at the end of the 1940s. The source of China's increase in national power was the radical change in its political system.[16] The communist system provided China with political institutions able to mobilize a much larger fraction of the Chinese population and resources than had ever been possible in the modern era. The presence of these institutions accounts for the Chinese army's success in fighting American forces to a standstill in Korea despite huge losses.

A process of elimination makes us confident that political change was the source of newfound Chinese strength. Economic and demographic variables did not change significantly in the late 1940s. The Chinese population remained roughly the same, and Chinese economic productivity did not rise appreciably. China was still a poor, peasant, economically nonproductive country. Yet China was able to take on the United States in Korea by 1950.[17] The one variable that did change was the political system. The ruthless discipline and efficiency of the Communist Party permitted the fielding of a large, motivated ground army.

In evaluating the Chinese style of communism, the West focused on its dictatorial and repressive nature. It was clearly all of that. However, the form of government was less significant than the emergence of new institutions, particularly a mass political party that enabled the central leadership to mobilize vast levels of human resources.

Since the Korean War, China has progressed substantially in the three critical areas of power: population, productivity, and political capacity. It has the political institutions necessary to mobilize large portions of the Chinese masses. The huge increments of political capacity that have taken place since World War II represent only about one-half of the political modernization process, but completing that push up the endogenous growth trajectory will be far more costly and difficult to implement.

What accounts for this rapid growth phase? First, the drop in fertility rates. This is an unusual achievement, one with a direct impact on the development of power. Controlling population growth eventually translates into higher per-capita productivity. This shift has occurred in advance of the socioeconomic changes usually responsible for bringing about such decreases. It is an important measure of the capacity of the political system, a predictor of future Chinese economic growth and international power, and, although obviously controversial, a new model for the developing world.[18]

With success managing population growth, the second most important developmental change is the creation of an embryonic but fast developing free market system.[19] The portion of the economy liberated of government control, although generating only about 10 percent of GDP in 1999, is the engine of growth that is responsible for China's extraordinary economic performance and it will be the major factor propelling it to the next rung on the ladder of international power. This can be seen in the phenomenal growth rate in private businesses. While the number of state-owned enterprises has remained relatively constant and collective-owned enterprises have grown modestly, individually owned enterprises have more than doubled and the trend is accelerating.[20] An additional benefit of privatization flows from the fact that key segments of the U.S. business community have gained a stake in Chinese economic production and in the huge Chinese market.

To date, China's rapid growth has not permitted it to project power much beyond its geographical borders. That occurs only after the resources produced by political controls are combined with demographic resources and rising economic productivity. Then a nation goes through its power transition and realizes its full potential to project power at great distances. For China, that time is coming.

Managing the Transition

With China's rising power and changed conditions in the United States, the most important question for U.S. policymakers is what policies should be followed to manage the emergence of China? If China does overtake the United States in the size of its economy and then in power, is it possible to neutralize the conditions for conflict brought about by the overtaking process? The Power Transition theory informs us there are three strategies to be followed.

One is to foster conditions where the leaders of the two sides do not wish to fight. In the terminology of Power Transition theory, this requires the managing of the transition so that both countries remain satisfied during the process.[21] We explore what can be done in this regard.

The second strategy focuses on the management of flashpoints related to territorial claims. We distinguish this strategy from a general readjustment of the status quo because even satisfied nations may confront each other when territorial disputes are severe.[22]

The third strategy seeks to change the total power available to the two sides so that, over time, China's increase in power will be shadowed by increased U.S. power. The core task is to ensure that the U.S. alliance offsets Chinese advances to the greatest extent possible. Such engineering could deflect the Chinese challenge altogether or simply blunt or postpone the overtaking.

These three strategies should be considered concurrently since there are synergies that increase the effectiveness of each.

Strategy 1: Engineering Satisfaction with "Realignment"

The creation of a satisfied China rests on the successful accomplishment of a specific foreign policy goal, albeit one with domestic characteristics. The United States should assist in the expansion of the Chinese private sector and encourage the development of a powerful Chinese business class. While this may sound like a by-product of the Clinton administration's policy of "constructive engagement" or even George W. Bush's "strategic competition," we suggest a more accurate description of our concept is "realignment." It is a policy designed to accomplish a fundamental and far-reaching objective — the realignment and harmonization of the ruling coalitions in both countries. The first stage of this adjustment already has occurred in the United States. The goal now is to cause a reciprocal event in China. This will not be easy to do. Despite its strategic importance, support for increasing the economic power of China is a controversial policy that faces powerful American domestic opposition.[23]

We should be clear about what can and what cannot be done. The United States, and the rest of the world for that matter, can only affect the economic growth of a society the size of China at the margins. Nicholas R. Lardy points out that despite dramatic increases in foreign investment, the net capital inflow into China may be less than 1 percent of the its cumulative output over a recent twelve-year period.[24] Thus only a tiny fraction of the human and material resources China needs to grow will come from external sources. The vast bulk of the resources have to be found internally. Progress toward privatization and expansion can be made only if China's leaders understand this phenomenon. The United States can help or hinder this process only modestly, but the commitment to do so is critically important since it will be a central ingredient in China's ultimate sense of satisfaction or dissatisfaction.

The task of the U.S. government is to prod the Chinese leadership to make and implement the necessary decisions to open the marketplace, boost efficiency, and increase public participation and consumer benefits. The transfer of economic resources into the Chinese economy is the task of the U.S. private sector and the multinational business community.

On the U.S. side of the equation, a relatively new coalition of political and economic leaders leads the effort to engage China. They have put in place a family of trade and investment policies that will have the effect of demonstrating positive involvement by the United States while easing China's historical and cultural fears of the West.

This new foreign policy coalition has come to power at a fruitful time in China's development. China's market is operating in ever-wider portions of their productive system. At the September 1997 Communist Party Congress, President Jiang Zemin announced the sale, over five years, of some ten thousand of the thirteen thousand large state enterprises that had been previously excluded from transfer into the market economy. Vice Premier Zhu Rongji, elevated to premier in 1998, was placed in charge of this transformation, and he promptly stated the task could be accomplished in three years using mergers, acquisitions, and bankruptcies, although at a cost of higher unemployment.[25]

Two points need to be emphasized. First, the task of privatization is just beginning, and if successful, will revolutionize the Chinese economy and society. Agriculture will need to follow industry. Second, this drive to privatize is not in response to any pressures from abroad. It is a tacit recognition by the Chinese government that a centralized command economy cannot produce the wealth and resources necessary for the next phase of world power.

The Chinese opened the foreign investment door with a series of economic reforms announced in 1978. Specifically, the government established six special economic zones, fourteen cities, and three deltas under favorable import-export rules. As a consequence, direct foreign investment soared from nearly nothing to $45.3 billion in 1998[26] before nose-diving to an estimated $35 billion in 1999. But there are geographical dislocations. Since 1989, about 90 percent of this investment has been funneled to the coastal region. Exports generated from this foreign investment jumped from 1 percent of total exports in 1985 to 47 percent in 1996. Trade volume increased from $28 billion in 1979 to $323 billion in 1998, causing the percentage of the GNP attributed to trade to jump from 10 percent to 30 percent in the same period.[27]

These initial reforms paid immediate dividends, and they promise future rewards. From 1978 to 1995, the economy charged forward at an average annual growth rate of 7.5 percent using adjusted estimates or 9.8 percent using Chinese official data. China's GDP doubled in the eight years from 1978 to 1986, tripled by 1991, quadrupled by 1993, and quintupled by 1995, based on official data.[28] Using the adjusted lower historical figure and our assumed future grown rate of 5.5 percent,[29] China will account for

17 percent of the world's GDP by 2015.[30] By whichever standard, official or adjusted, this is an impressive growth record.

As soon as the initial trend became apparent, the U.S. business community responded. U.S. exports to China grew 144 percent from 1990 to 1995. With a total of $11.7 billion in 1995, the United States became the largest non-Chinese investor in China, ranking third behind Hong Kong and Taiwan.[31] Thanks to a growing population expected to exceed 1.4 billion in 2015 and estimated future per-capita income growth of 4.5 percent (down from the 6 percent annual rate from 1978 to 1995), China will continue to be an economic magnet. This will position the Asian region to strongly influence world economic activity by 2025 with 55 to 60 percent of the world's income.[32]

Growth of the Chinese private sector has important political implications for long-term U.S.-Chinese relations. The expansion of the private sector will spur the growth and strength of business leaders with broader interests than those of the political-military authorities who have run China since the communist take over. The expectation is that this new business elite will have a heavy stake in orderly and predictable relations with their counterparts in other nations and that consequently they will apply their influence in national debates and decisions. Of course, Chinese business leaders may defy this prediction and operate under other rules of the road, but we would assume that both as individuals and a class they would act in their own self-interest.

Why would the privileged and powerful in the Chinese ruling establishment, the Communist Party, government, military leaders, and heads of state enterprises, concede to demands of a much weaker emerging business community? Why would they consent to relinquish some of their privileges and power to accommodate demands that might conflict with more nationalistic attitudes? We suggest that they can be expected to do so for two reasons.

The first is the same internal justification for changing course in 1978 and initiating economic reform. Political elites convert economic growth into political resources. The market economy and its private sector provide the ruling establishment with substantial benefits, domestically and internationally, at a relatively "cheap" cost. It simultaneously satisfies emerging popular demand for higher living standards while rapidly accelerating international power — a hard-to-resist combination.

The second reason flows from the fact that the ruling elite already is involved in the marketplace. Senior political leaders have their own private business ventures. And their siblings, the so-called princelings, have extensive business ties developed typically as a result of preferential treatment.[33] The same pattern occurs within the military and police establishments. The People's Liberation Army (PLA) offers a good case study.

The Chinese military, fortunately for the West, has been drawn deeply into the civilian market. Prior to 1979, PLA private market exposure did not exceed more than about 8 percent of total military production. By the early 1990s the military establishment was using some 70 to 80 percent of its productive assets for civilian goods. In 1996, it operated more than 10,000 enterprises, the lowest estimate, with about 700,000 employees and generated earnings estimated at $6 billion to $10 billion. The extent of the penetration of the military enterprises is astonishing. By one estimate they produce 30 percent of the color televisions, 50 percent of the refrigerators, 65 percent of the motorcycles, and 75 percent of the taxicabs in China. Some PLA-produced goods are exported to the United States.[34]

This involvement by the PLA in the emerging private sector created resentment, or at least concern, among the business and political elites of China. In July 1998, President Jiang Zemin ordered the PLA to give up its nonmilitary private enterprise ventures and additionally to engage in a crackdown against smuggling, which may cost the government at least $12 billion a year. Coming on the heels of a charge by the official party organ, the *People's Daily,* that both the PLA and the People's Armed Police were engaged in illegal activities, this order struck at the heart of the PLA's financial operations. Profits from private and state-run enterprises owned by the PLA not only subsidize the military budget but provide illegal income to high-ranking officers and their units. Subsequent statements by senior Chinese officials indicated that major PLA firms are to be transferred to the State Economic and Trade Commission. Provincial governments will run smaller firms.

If these policies hold, and that is not clear since so much is at stake for the PLA and its political/business allies, it will have two ramifications. First, the PLA may become more isolated from free market reforms and thus more hostile to the allure of reciprocal business ties to the United States. Second, it will free considerable manpower resources in the PLA for more traditional military activity, thus increasing the power of the PLA as a military force.[35]

The PLA and leading government officials have reasons to be both respectful and fearful of the emerging market system. The power and legitimacy of the Chinese ruling establishment stems from the recognition that its policies have brought the country dramatic economic growth and the promise of substantial benefits to an ever-larger segment of the population. Moreover, the political stability of the system and the security of the same leaders could be threatened by major social upheavals if rates of growth were substantially diminished.

By opening up the rural and urban economy to market forces, the political leadership has precipitated a tsunami wave of migration from countryside to city and from the "traditional" to the "modern" portion of the economy. This migration provides new labor for the modern economic sector, a growing market for the economy's products, and the replacement of rural belief systems with values more congruent with modern life. It has also substantially reduced Communist Party controls in rural areas.[36] Rural-to-city migration is a phenomenon at the heart of the development process. The modern portion of the economy must continue to grow in order to absorb the "floating" migrants from the countryside who now may number 150 million.[37] The increasing differential between urban and rural per-capita income fuels this internal migration. Rural unemployment rates were near 35 percent in mid-1997 compared to 8 percent in the urban areas. The latest round of reforms may force 8 to 10 million layoffs at state-owned enterprises over three years. Should this mass of relatively uneducated mobile workers find no place in the new economy, they could seriously destabilize the political order.[38] Top government officials have indicated that an 8 percent growth rate is necessary to avoid domestic unrest, a rate that may not be sustainable.[39]

Assessing these trends en bloc, our conclusion is that the long-term U.S.-China relationship is extremely sensitive to current policies. Therefore, we consider a sustained, multifaceted, American economic investment in China as a vital element of current U.S. national security.[40] Ultimately, it could determine whether the world is at peace or war.[41]

The U.S. Side

Power Transition theory suggests that during periods of parity the opportunity exists to manage and potentially defuse a conflictual overtaking. At this point in time, this is the task of the United States. In order to minimize the chances of a military conflict with China as that nation moves through its power transition, the most productive policy for the U.S. government will be to make the growth of the Chinese private sector a matter of the highest priority. This policy will be difficult to agree on and implement. A consensus must develop among all three of the key foreign policy players — the political, economic and military elites.[42] One is reminded of the kind of coalition that structured American purpose during the Cold War.[43]

The rise of China comes about simultaneously with an internal shift in power in the United States. There has been a structural shake-up in the coalition running U.S. foreign policy. During the Cold War, the U.S. leadership coalition was composed of political, military, and economic elites, in that order of power and authority. The economic elites were by far the junior partners. That now has changed. The political leadership is still dominant in the domestic power hierarchy, but the business sector has taken the place of the military establishment as the second most powerful player. In the new pecking order, the military rank third at best. As a result, business interests generally now take priority over national security interests.[44]

Through the Cold War years the business community saw its interests largely neglected.[45] It watched the extension of subsidies to competitors' economies, the opening of the American marketplace, U.S. tacit support for protectionist policies abroad, and government interference in the marketplace, all in the name of meeting the challenge of communism. With the collapse of the Soviet Union, the political mechanism that gave the political-military tandem priority over the business community disappeared. Now, in the struggle over resources, the military leadership is disadvantaged. Business interests come first because the success of the political leadership is directly linked to the success of the business community in keeping the economy vibrant. As noted earlier:

> The new international strategy of the United States has profoundly reorganized international priorities. Top priority has been withdrawn from security and extended to economic issues. The business of the government is again business: removing barriers to American goods and services. Opening new markets to American exports has replaced stopping Communism as the first priority of foreign affairs. Similarly, the fear of loss of jobs, or the hope of creating new ones through expanding exports, has replaced the fear of Soviet expansion. Jobs, the new political all-purpose justification for much that is done in the field of foreign affairs, is the political motive for American activities abroad.[46]

In this new political environment, containment policies, arms buildups, and the subordination of social and economic needs to security considerations are no longer sustainable politically.[47] For all of these reasons, the future of U.S.-China relations will follow a different path.

Both in the U.S. executive branch and in the growing portion of the business community with international ties, there is strong support for the policy of investment in China. The intent appears to be to protect such policies from attack and even expand them. The continuing success of this policy is contingent upon the political and economic sectors maintaining their preeminence in the coalition. But that is not guaranteed. How long the military elite remains the junior partner in the coalition depends on perceptions of the international threat.

American political leaders are well aware of the role of the business community as the new agent of U.S. foreign policy and power projection. They also recognize the risks involved in providing economic support to a possible challenger. For its part, the business community understands its dependence on the government for market penetration and the risks that would flow from making China a Cold War-type enemy.[48]

If U.S.-China relations can be turned into a security issue, military leaders would regain center stage in the foreign policy coalition. It would be a familiar and comfortable role. In this new environment, resource constraints would be lifted and new appropriations would be made available for military needs. Military views and contingency plans would be powerful factors in structuring relations with China.

This revamped foreign policy coalition, no less than its predecessor, would seek to minimize the chance of a military confrontation because the military leaders understand the high risk and potential costs to military institutions involved in the use of force. In fact, they have insisted that political leaders protect them from criticism.[49] While remaining cautious about a military confrontation with China, however, the military establishment will insist on substantial real growth in military expenditures for advanced technology and force multipliers to counter Chinese manpower advantages and growing technological competence.

The U.S. business community will find its interests threatened under these conditions. Investments in China might be severely limited by U.S. action or subject to expropriation as a response to perceived U.S. hostility. The many industries with exposure in China could suffer substantial losses. If the business community finds itself being displaced by the military sector in the coalition, the resulting internal debate over national strategy would be extraordinarily contentious because the stakes would be so high. For the first time, the business community may challenge the military establishment directly.

The Chinese emergence will be more difficult to meet politically than that of the USSR. One should not forget that the policy to deter the USSR only appeared to bring results because the Soviet Union never came close to the United States in power. Since we assume that China may not just challenge but gain parity with and then pass the United States, the threat will be of a much larger magnitude. The immediate reaction of some U.S. opinion leaders will be to fall back on familiar Cold War rhetoric and policies such as containment.[50] That would push China further into a state of dissatisfaction and dramatically raise the prospects for war.

The Chinese Side

Decentralization. China faces a number of critical domestic issues. The United States is substantially superior in power over China at the present time. This power imbalance governs how each country deals with the other. The United States recognizes that since its superiority is not absolute, there are limits on its range of options. The ability of China to resist U.S. demands and eventually challenge for global leadership correlates with the capacity of its central government to mobilize resources.

Given sufficient internal resources and growing international power, increasingly Chinese leaders will be able to ignore U.S. demands. Certainly that now is the case with regard to China's vital Mainland national security interests. But the United States still maintains some leverage on certain important issues such as Taiwan, missile and nuclear technology exports, trade, and even in the human rights arena.

On the other hand, if the Chinese central government finds that it is unable to aggregate national financial assets because they are being withheld from Beijing at the regional level, then this will have an impact on China's ability to challenge the United States. There are some early indications that national allocation decisions are being negotiated between the central government and regional authorities.[51] If this trend continues, and even assuming that national security issues would remain the prerogative of the central government, the resource demands of the regions could compete with the military for priority.[52]

A weakened central government in Beijing would find itself unable to directly challenge other major powers, let alone the United States. Nor would it necessarily want to do so since its economic concerns would be paramount. Should China grow rapidly under decentralization and pass the United States, it would resemble the peaceful overtaking of the United Kingdom by the United States. Thus decentralization, with or without rapid power gains, would enhance the prospects for peace.

International Norms. The development of a strong private sector in China must be accompanied by a commitment to abide by international commercial rules. The Chinese government is only now beginning to understand the benefits of that linkage and to make corresponding changes.[53] It is a difficult conversion since it involves closing certain illegal copyright, royalty, and gray-market operations that may be owned in whole or part by important national figures or organizations. In addition, corruption must be curtailed and a uniform body of legal and tax rules promulgated. China's entry into the World Trade Organization (WTO) may help institutionalize these reforms.

It is essential that the Chinese central government supervise and apply these international rules. It will need to guarantee that its own leaders are not allowed to make the playing field too arbitrary and uneven. Without the application of accepted standards, investment will dry up as foreign economic players find property rights dismissed, laws and regulations misapplied, bribes demanded, and profits limited. Imposing a stable environment for economic activity requires an active and effective government. If decentralization proceeds, at best it will make this process quite uneven throughout the country.

The issue of human rights and individual liberties is closely associated with economic development. A fully open and free system provides optimal conditions for the social and geographic mobility that helps generate economic growth. China will not be able to become a fully developed society until the rule of law protects individual liberties.

That said, this process is long, difficult and almost entirely internal in nature. External forces can have influence only on the margins of this issue. For this reason, the linkage of human rights and economic issues is destined to fail. Human rights reforms will flow naturally from an expansion of the modern economy and the appearance of countless new organizations with the power and determination to protect their self-interests. In the absence of such stakeholders within the political system, outside influence will be at best marginal and at worst negative. Therefore the strategy human rights organizations should follow to modify Chinese behavior is: (a) support the growth of the free market economy; (b) stimulate the creation of Western-style interest groups in China; and (c) rethink their public relations campaigns. Put another way, human rights groups should substitute action and institution building for rhetoric.

Free Enterprise and Democratization. A central dilemma for the Chinese elites turns on the question of democracy and free enterprise. At what point will the free market economic reforms force change in the underlying political system? Can a nation enjoy a free market system under a single party system? These are questions not only of ideology but personal preference and benefit.

China has engaged in low-level experiments with democracy. About half of China's 928,000 villages, averaging one thousand people each, have conducted "free" local elections. While the Communist Party is the only party allowed to participate, there is open competition for office, grass-roots campaigning, promises and slogans, and an emphasis on local politics. To date this is an experiment that has been limited to isolated, nonurban regions. Nonetheless, it involves the fundamentals of expression of opinion without retaliation, some degree of free choice, and an emerging sense of electoral responsibility.[54]

This experiment, when coupled with the opening of the Chinese marketplace to private ownership and competition, raises fundamental questions about the scope of control of the central government. The government, at least temporarily, has ceded autonomy to certain segments of its society. It is a modest beginning, but a beginning nonetheless. At some point, this experiment with rudimentary democracy may gain an irreversible momentum. This does not mean that China will become a democratic nation by Western standards. But it does hold out the possibility that Chinese society will move incrementally toward a more pluralistic society.

For the governing Chinese elites, the issue fashions itself as a tradeoff between relaxing controls and unleashing productive capacity.[55] As with any fundamental economic shift, there will be winners and losers in this equation. It will be a battle between the old and the new, the traditional and the modern, orthodoxy and pragmatism. Government leaders undoubtedly will seek to find transitions that service their need to become a world-class power while maintaining their firm grip on leadership. It will be a difficult and often unmanageable process once China moves up the endogenous growth trajectory. At some point, the creation of wealth by a few and the expectation of wealth by the many will drive national decisions as much as party loyalty or ideological purity.

This opening of China is the key to satisfaction. The United States cannot play a direct role in this transformation, indeed an overt attempt to manipulate could create a strong backlash. But the United States can help indirectly to create the conditions wherein a strong domestic faction develops that is tied to the international marketplace, accepts international business norms, exerts some degree of influence over its friends and allies in the central government, and perhaps, over time, becomes part of the governing coalition or buys into that coalition with relationships of its own.

Strategy 2: Controlling Territorial Flashpoints

Sound economic policies will not be sufficient to guarantee that China rises to power under peaceful conditions. If relations between China and the United States are plagued by political and security quarrels and particularly by disputes over territory,[56] U.S. business will not risk investment in China. This will mute conditions for an expansion of the Chinese private sector and, more importantly, deny the benefits of interlocking business communities exercising restraint within each political system.

China and the United States, of course, share no borders and have no direct dispute over territory. On three occasions, however, the United States and China have engaged each other, either directly or indirectly, in arenas with sensitive border implications: Korea, Vietnam, and Taiwan.[57] Despite China's recent initiatives to reconcile border issues, its record of border skirmishes is substantial, suggesting that territorial issues have broad leadership support and a high national security priority.[58] There also is preliminary evidence that China may be more dispute-prone and violence-prone in disputes than all other major powers except for the United States in terms of disputes and India in terms of violence.[59] Prior disputes notwithstanding, the most dangerous flashpoint for U.S.-China relations is the issue of Taiwan's future.[60]

The Taiwan Problem

Three questions dominate this explosive issue: (1) Will Taiwan declare its independence of China? And if it does, will it act in the near future or in later stages of the overtaking process? (2) If independence is asserted, will China use military force against Taiwan? (3) Will the United States intervene on behalf of Taiwan if China moves militarily against Taiwan? Power Transition provides a perspective on each of these questions.

These three questions are examined in the context of two scenarios. In the first scenario, Taiwan declares its independence, China undertakes military action to make Taiwan back down, and the United States interposes its forces between China and Taiwan. The second scenario has three contingencies but one common outcome: (a) Taiwan does not assert its independence; (b) Taiwan declares independence and China does not retaliate militarily, and (c) Taiwan voluntarily associates itself with China.

In the first scenario, if Taiwan declares its independence of China in the early part of the overtaking process, or roughly during the next two decades before China passes the United States in GDP, Power Transition provides important information about what outcomes can be expected. First, China will be defeated in its attempt to force Taiwan to back down. The power advantage of the United States over China at this point will be substantial enough to ensure that America will prevail. Second, China's capabilities will be limited, and, therefore, if there is a military struggle, that will be limited as well. The contest will center on Taiwan's future rather than the broader issue of leadership of the international order. Third, the costs of a military confrontation will be substantial for both combatants, but China, the weaker player, will pay the higher costs in actual losses and missed opportunities. Power Transition theory holds a chilling message for leaders in Taiwan, China, and the United States: the longer a declaration of independence is postponed in this early phase, the larger and the more deadly the potential struggle.[61] The logic of this first scenario also applies to the situation where China decides to take unilateral military action against Taiwan in the early overtaking period.

Despite success by the United States in the early period of this scenario, Power Transition theory argues that the victory would be temporary. It would only postpone the time when China will reacquire control over Taiwan. That outcome is inevitable once China has passed the United States. But the early U.S. victory would have other consequences. China's dissatisfaction with the status quo would be deepened, and even mutually advantageous economic ties most likely would not be strong enough to outweigh more nationalistic considerations.

If Taiwan declares its independence at a later period in the overtaking, the United States would be confronting an opponent as strong as or stronger than itself. Recognizing the costs and being a satisfied great power, the United States may choose not to engage in war. If, for domestic or regional reasons war did erupt, that conflict would no longer be limited to the issue of Taiwan. This time the underlying issue would be the leadership of the world order and the war likely would be both massive and worldwide.

The second scenario offers a series of contingencies, all of which share the common result that U.S.-Chinese relations and the opening up of the Chinese private sector could develop unimpeded. If Taiwanese leaders, having tested the waters, conclude that U.S. support for independence is too uncertain, they may decide to forego that option. In that case, U.S.-Chinese-

Taiwanese relations could remain static for some time, at least until China's relative power position improved greatly.

If Taiwan declared independence and China declined to intervene in order to avoid conflict with the United States, to preserve its emerging economy, to defer to its Asian neighbors, or to adhere to a longer-term strategy, then again there should be no fundamental change in the U.S.-China relationships for a time.[62]

Finally, it is possible, maybe even likely, that Taiwan will negotiate a private deal with China specifying the conditions under which Taiwan would rejoin the Mainland while retaining certain unique qualities.[63] The complex set of personal and business relationships linking Taiwan, China including Hong Kong, and Singapore could facilitate such a "merger." Under these circumstances, the United States and China would avoid any territorial dispute. This outcome also would relieve some of the domestic pressures on leaders in both countries.

Options for Taiwan

Taiwan's leaders differ in their preferences with regard to China. Economic elites have made substantial investments on the Mainland since the ban on such investments was lifted in 1991.[64] They benefit directly from preserving economic ties. From 1978 to 1995, Taiwan businesses invested $30.1 billion in contracted value and $11.4 billion in actual investment in China involving 32,000 projects. This makes Taiwan the second largest investor in China, Hong Kong being the first in the preunification period.[65] This investment occurred despite the overt political obstructions erected by the Taiwanese government. The Taiwanese political elite, on the other hand, has an interest in safeguarding its own political power, which would be greatly diminished if Taiwan and China were to unify. Over time, there may be a convergence between the economic and political elites. James Soong, a Nationalist Party figure, may be the agent for that transformation.

Taiwan's leaders have three broad policy options: The first option is to postpone *sine die* any declaration of independence and/or talk independence but take no action. This strategy would be congruent with accepting eventual unification with the Mainland or at least passing the problem off to successors while gaining the support of pro-independence groups. The strategy could also be designed to obtain concessions from both China and a United States anxious to head off the crisis that would inevitably follow an independence declaration.

This first policy has risks because it leaves Taiwan's leaders vulnerable to committed supporters of secession. The risk, however, is limited to the point in time when China has achieved power parity with the United States, after which it would be clear to all concerned that independence was no longer an option.

Taiwan's leaders can follow a second option and declare independence from the Mainland while the United States maintains an overwhelming lead over China in power. If they make this calculation, their protective fuse resides in the U.S. political system where, they would assume, their allies would mount a political campaign to come to their rescue.[66] They are fully aware that a U.S. military intervention is their only hope for survival. Their judgment on this issue will be informed.

The Taiwanese leaders are quite skilled at interpreting the U.S. political system and at mobilizing U.S. support. In this they have a decided, though declining, advantage over their Mainland cousins. The Taiwanese leaders have proved exceptionally adroit in manipulating the U.S. political system. Despite operating without an embassy or official presence, they have established a sophisticated infrastructure in the United States that supports their interests.[67]

This infrastructure consists of those who supported Taiwan as part of an anticommunist ideology; those who wish to support the new democratic traditions being established there; and those who by association find themselves predisposed to support Taiwan. This latter category consists of thousands of U.S. opinion makers and political leaders at the federal, state, and local levels who have accepted paid trips to Taiwan over the past thirty years. Without question, the Taiwanese have operated one of the most effective public relations operations in the United States.[68]

In effect, Taiwanese leaders have gone through a dress rehearsal for the independence option. The 1995–96 Taiwan Straits crisis, the worst flare-up in twenty years, was precipitated by the "private" visit of Taiwanese President Lee Teng-hui to speak at his alma mater, Cornell University.[69] In the subsequent confrontation, the PLA tested missiles close to Taiwan, and the United States parried by sending two naval task forces to the Taiwan Straits, although, contrary to many press reports, both did not arrive at the same time. It was clear in retrospect that all parties were only signaling each other. Nonetheless, this event fairly represents the initial conditions of a future conflict.

Based on this crisis, subsequent public statements and private messages between Taipei and Washington, Taiwanese leaders undoubtedly have assessed the likelihood of U.S. support should they decide to declare independence. We speculate that assessment as negative. That is, we believe the Taiwanese probably calculate there is insufficient political will in the United States to support Taiwan in the aftermath of an independence decree, should that mean all-out war with the People's Republic of China (PRC).[70] The danger is that they may erroneously conclude they can finesse the declaration so that the United States would be drawn incrementally into a supporting role in the resulting conflict.[71]

The third option for Taiwanese leaders is to enter into a negotiation with China on the conditions for a peaceful association or unification.

Such negotiations occur on two levels, public and private. At the public level, leaders on both sides will interpret statements from the other, assessing what is meant for domestic public consumption and what is meant for direct diplomatic impact. They will engage in formalized meetings designed for posturing and signaling. From that standpoint, it would appear that both sides have established a hard-line negotiating position.[72] Real progress, however, will occur out of sight. It is impossible to analyze the nature of any private negotiation but it may be presumed to be highly skilled, nuanced, and laced with personal and business interrelations among Taiwan, China, Hong Kong, and Singapore. If James Soong wins the presidential elections in the spring of 2000, that could be the catalyst for a new relationship, although one that would pose challenges for the PRC as well as Taiwan.

Options for China

Power Transition theory clarifies the options available to China's leaders. It tells them that over the long run, with reasonable growth rates and maintenance of central authority, they will overtake the United States and reunite Taiwan to the Mainland with or without the use of force. Doing so will conclude the last territorial issue of their civil war and erase a bitter memory of defeat at the hands of the Japanese. But what if Taiwan declares independence within the next two decades or so? Will China seek to subdue Taiwan now or wait until its own power is overwhelming? That is the fundamental choice that China must make. The preferences, power, and the resulting tug-of-war among the Chinese ruling coalition will shape this decision.

Will China risk using force if Taiwan declares its independence while the United States dominates China in military strength and power? Obviously it is foolhardy to count on China backing down and opting not to use force to bring Taiwan to heel. Remember that a far weaker and more isolated China decided to repulse the United States from the Yalu. But there are also good reasons to conjecture that Chinese restraint is not to be excluded altogether.[73]

Chinese officials often discuss the value of strategic planning. More so than other nations, China seems to respect the sanctity of time. It may recognize that time works on its behalf with regard to Taiwan and that it is not now in a position to oppose the United States militarily.[74]

The Chinese place a priority on economic development even over military needs. This strategy is reflected in the statement *"Fu guo qiang bing,"* or "Rich country, strong army," a philosophy adopted by the PLA.[75] This strategy, which was successfully pioneered by the United States, has allowed China to become a great power and may eventually permit it to challenge for dominant power status. The policy of emphasizing the military at the expense of the economy brought the Soviet Union to ruin, a lesson that could not have gone unnoticed in Beijing. On the other side of the equation, this strategy will postpone China's becoming a world-class military power until the middle of this century. It will make China unprepared to confront the United States for several decades to come. Thus it is a strategy with a long-term vision and short-term liabilities.[76] These liabilities, most notably the disparity in military technology, were noted by Chinese military officials in the aftermath of the Persian Gulf War, and their fears were reinforced by the U.S. air war in Kosovo and Serbia. The Balkans air war stimulated the PLA to lobby for more funding and more political standing.[77] The accidental bombing of the Chinese embassy in Belgrade on 7 May 1999 provided an additional pretext for anti-American rhetoric and posturing.

Another drawback to confronting the United States early is the decentralization problem. If China's central government does not maintain leverage over regional authorities, it may not acquire the necessary resources for a confrontation with the United States. The decentralization of power in China could create a situation where the society in total would have the necessary resources to take on the United States, but the regional political and economic elites would deny their use to the central government. This would force the central government to find solutions other than a military confrontation with the United States. In this situation, Taiwan's move to independence might, and the conditional tense is used advisedly, not eventuate in war. Were that to happen, Taiwan could count on a few more decades of independence before returning or being returned to China's control.

But China's decision also could go the other way. China could decide to confront the United States early on. We noted earlier that if it did so in the near term, China would lose the fight and pay a high cost in military capability, market shares, foreign investment, and the opportunity costs related to the redirection of resources from investment to security.

The most serious long-range consequences for U.S.-China relations flowing from an early fight would be the restructuring of the coalition running China. Leaders concerned with national security would have the opportunity to move farther up the power ladder and those running the economy and commercial affairs would be downgraded. This would ensure that resources would be deflected from the economy and economic growth to the purchase of defense goods and services.

The clash with the United States could affect the leadership of China in another way. The central elites could succeed in using the opportunity presented by the external threat to reverse the power ceded to regional authorities in any ongoing decentralization.

Should China choose to wait until after the overtaking, it might not need to fight, for the change in the power of the two superpowers should make it obvious that Taiwan's independence is not an option. China's patience and restraint will be critical variables. The worse case will occur if Taiwan declares independence after the overtaking. Should the United States and China fight at that time, the war would likely be extremely violent and widespread. The victor would lead the international system.

Options for the United States

How should the United States view the Taiwan situation from a Power Transition perspective? First the overview. The United States remains the dominant nation in the international system, commanding a very strong alliance system. China is a growing great power but will not be in a position to challenge the United States for international leadership for several decades. Recognizing China's potential, the United States is attempting to manage its emergence on a basis favorable to itself and its allies. The most important foreign policy objective of the United States is to create a satisfied China.

With that as prelude, Power Transition argues that the most promising Taiwan strategy for the United States to follow is an adaptation of the medical term "watchful waiting." A military engagement with China over Taiwan, even if successful during this early transition period, would not guarantee long-term security for that island. Furthermore, it could create an environment between the United States and China so poisoned that normal relations would not be possible. It would cede authority to the military and political leaders most dissatisfied with the international system. It would fuel nationalism and cultural xenophobia. Business leaders would be put on the defensive, dissipating any moderating influence that they may be exercising on the government. Counterintuitively, a U.S. military victory would damage long-term U.S. security interests.

Maintaining the status quo via watchful waiting means using the strongest diplomatic and, if necessary, economic pressures and incentives to dissuade Taiwan from declaring independence over the next two decades or so.[78] After that time, Power Transition suggests that all parties to the dispute, the United States, China, and Taiwan would recognize the futility of an independence effort and act accordingly. In the meantime, the United States must take every available precaution not to allow immediate crises to degenerate into war — the winner notwithstanding. What the United States must understand is that China is not a normal nation. It is a potential challenger. Therefore our vital national interests are at stake every time we take an action that directly or indirectly establishes the predicate for that challenge.

As distasteful as this message might be for some, it should be remembered that the strategic imperative of the United States is to add China to its alliance structure or, if that is not possible, to socialize China into the existing international system by gradually having it accept prevailing rules and norms. Today's policies have to be directed toward tomorrow's goals.

Domestic political considerations will play a central role in the success of this postponement strategy. Powerful political factions have an interest in the China-Taiwan equation. The Chinese question has attracted a loose coalition of interest groups sharing strongly critical views about China's role in the world. This coalition has many components. At one time or another, its unofficial membership consists of human rights organizations, the Christian Coalition and other conservative groups, right-to-life organizations, the Free Tibet movement, some labor unions, exiled Chinese students, Cold War anticommunists cut adrift by the fall of the Soviet Union, and some GOP political leaders.

Public campaigns initiated by these disparate groups, some coordinated, some not, have the consequence of measuring China as the new enemy.[79] China's size and power potential makes it a more believable threat to U.S. dominance than the Soviet Union.[80] Maneuvering China into the role of enemy, however, is rendered difficult because the source of threat to U.S. dominance currently is from China's domestic economic growth. The economic challenge of China does not generate the same set of national security fears that a military challenge would provoke. All that would change dramatically following a declaration of independence by Taiwan. A U.S.-Chinese clash immediately would realign politics in the United States. National security factors would take precedence over business interests. Cold War-type anticommunism would reappear.

Even without a U.S.-Chinese confrontation, the new anti-Chinese forces in American society will make it increasingly difficult to carry out a long-term strategy managing the emergence of China as a satisfied international power. The rhetoric accompanying the alleged Chinese campaign contributions, defense lab spying incidents, and the WTO debate indicates that anti-Chinese feelings run close to the surface in some political circles. These political leaders and interest groups may find it useful to elevate China to the status of an enemy. There would be many benefits for them. It would represent the galvanizing issue lost by the dissolution of the Soviet empire.[81] It would be a beneficial tool for membership and financial purposes. And it could be viewed as a coalition builder.

If anti-Chinese forces in the United States dominate the political landscape, it will have dangerous consequences for U.S. security. China will read that development as confirming its worst fears about containment and Western domination.[82] Its sense of dissatisfaction will grow proportionately and, should Chinese power continue to accelerate, the stage will be set for a violent overtaking. As former Defense Secretary William Perry has argued, "If we treat China as an enemy, it will surely become one."[83]

With domestic political dynamics expected to be a disruptive influence, it is imperative that responsible political, business, and military leaders openly discuss China's potential and the resulting implications for U.S. strategy. This must be done now, before positions harden irreversibly along political, ideological, and religious lines.[84]

Strategy 3: Reengineering Power Distributions

One option for reengineering power is through the structuring of alliances. If a dominant nation cannot maintain its economic leadership over a fast-growing challenger and that challenger steadfastly remains dissatisfied, then the only option for preserving its dominance is to increase its power with an expanded alliance system. In terms of the U.S.-China relationship, how should the United States respond to the worst-case scenario where: (a) China does not respond to efforts encouraging its full and open participation in the current international system; (b) China's growth rate threatens to overtake the United States in power; and (c) China, for whatever reasons, remains a dissatisfied challenger?

If the policy options explored earlier in this chapter are ignored or fail, then the United States has only one course of action in the Power Transition view. The United States must find a way to maintain clear power superiority or preponderance over the fast-growing China. The endogenous growth trajectory dictates that this cannot be accomplished by a spurt of renewed economic vitality in the United States. On the contrary, the growth rates of mature economies such as the United States tend to fall off. The United States, however, is the leader of a great international coalition. Augmentation of this alliance offers the United States a potent device to head off the Chinese challenge.

There are three long-term national security options that address this situation. In the first, the United States encourages European unification and some form of affiliation or formal political cooperation with the United States. The United States, in effect, would add a unified Europe to its coalition as the first step toward the creation of a "superbloc." Combining the resources of Europe with those of the United States would approximately double the power available against any external source.

The second national security choice also would increase the power of the U.S. alliance system by adding the potentially large resource unit of Russia. Integrating Russia into NATO and gradually binding it to Europe would have several positive outcomes. It would add to the power of the superbloc, help ensure that Russia does not revert to its former status as a dissatisfied country, and deny China the opportunity to reestablish an anti-American alliance with Russia.

The third national security choice, well off in the future, is the integration of India and its enormous potential into the Western alliance. This would be important not only from the perspective of diluting the potential for direct U.S.-Chinese conflict but also in order to limit the conditions for conflict between India and China as they vie for leadership in Asia.

In addition to these three options, the United States should continue the negotiation of bilateral and multilateral economic agreements as a device to encourage political convergence. NAFTA, GATT, APEC, and similar agreements not only tie countries closer to the United States economically, but they have powerful political implications.[85] They encourage countries to adopt business rules established by the United States. They create institutions in the host countries with U.S. interests. They dry up the reservoir of nations available to align themselves with a rising challenger.

We do not wish to overstate the case. The obstacles to these strategies are daunting. If China continues to grow rapidly and appears to be on a path to challenge the United States, the U.S. alliance system will witness defectors, first in Asia and then possibly elsewhere.[86] China will begin constructing its own alliance system. Meanwhile, the building of a superbloc may turn out to be extraordinarily difficult given the complexities of national interests, prestige, and different operating systems.

The United States enters this period of Chinese challenge with significant advantages. It has a clear superiority in power. It is a technological leader moving quickly into the information age. It has a large, economically viable alliance system. It has the resources to penetrate economies and create new coalitions. Its most important asset, however, is time.

Managing Power: The Emergence of India

With China entering the steep growth phase of development, perhaps to be followed by India, both countries could be superpowers in the latter half of the twenty-first century, challenging not only for regional but also global dominance. As with China, the case of India requires a number of assumptions. It is very early in the development cycle to project India into the front rank of nations. That India must be considered at this time is the consequence of important Power Transition factors. First, India has a population of about 1 billion,[87] which will exceed that of China, given current projections, in about 2040. Second, India is showing signs of developing the kind of economic vitality that generates the conditions for an economic takeoff.[88] Its huge middle class, which is estimated at between 150 to 300 million and thus larger than the entire working class of the United States, is relatively well-trained and productive.[89] It has more scientists and engineers than any country but the United States, and it has demonstrated technological competence both in military and commercial applications. India is making a successful transition to a market economy, yet it faces staggering problems.

In order to generate vast amounts of power, India must control its population growth, raise per-capita income, increase political capacity, and manage the urban-rural migration problem association with development. If it can accomplish this formidable agenda, then it has the potential to achieve superpower status. Is it far-fetched to even think about such a possibility? A snapshot of the growing pains of the United States in the mid to late 1800s would argue that the possibility should not be overlooked.

The timing of India's potential ascendancy to global power is a critical factor.[90] The overtaking of China by India would lag far behind the overtaking of the United States by China. Therefore, depending on the outcome of the previous competition, the Indian challenge may be either a regional or global one. If China were to become a member of NATO or somehow aligned with the United States, the transition of India and China would be restricted to a regional domain. Even if India were to be dissatisfied, this would not necessarily produce conflict because of the overwhelming alliance that would then be arrayed in China's favor.

If, on the other hand, there is a NATO alliance that includes the United States, Europe, and Russia but excludes China and India, the competition at the regional level between these two now-dissatisfied nations would generate the most dangerous preconditions for regional war. Indeed, India has long been China's greatest regional rival. It is unlikely that a Sino-Indian alliance can be constructed to avoid a regional war given a transition and their traditional geopolitical rivalry. Such an alliance would not bring China the advanced industrial and technological support it needs nor satisfy India's growing need for regional and world recognition. Thus the likelihood of a conflict under parity and overtaking appears to be high.

The future of Sino-Indian relations has been foreshadowed by their history. While relations between India and China were cordial from 1949 to 1959, it was clear, even then, that both were contenders for the role of the major power in the region. Relations deteriorated because of disputes of the borders demarcated by the United Kingdom.[91] India had confidence that the existing boundary between the two countries was correct but the dispute quickly erupted in the Sino-Indian War of 1962, during a time when the two nations were close to parity.

China emerged victorious from this dispute, reinforcing its role as the dominant power in the Asian region. The border conflict with China was a turning point in India's relations with the rest of the world for two reasons. First, China widened the gap with India in terms of power, becoming a great power in the global hierarchy. This position was confirmed by China's nuclear tests, the Sino-Soviet fallout, and the growing strategic alliance between the United States and China following Nixon's visit.

Second, these historical factors are important since in combination they helped push India into the status of a dissatisfied nation. Other challenges to Indian security emerged. Despite the Indian democratic tradition, the United States tilted toward Pakistan, partially in response to India's economic and military ties to the USSR. India, in effect, alienated itself from the dominant power, reinforcing its dissatisfied status. When the political and economic inadequacies of nonalignment later became apparent, India found itself both without an effective supporter in Moscow and without an international coalition of similar nonaligned nations to lead. Now it was cut off from all significant international support and leadership opportunities. Having attempted to carve out for itself a unique role in the world independent of the global power hierarchy, through a succession of ill-fated strategic choices, India found itself in virtual isolation and dissatisfied with its role and status in the world.

At home, India faced a serious economic crisis. The central-planning economic system ran out of steam.[92] Recognizing world trends, both economic and political, India turned to a market system to ignite its economy.[93] The last decade witnessed India's change in economic policy from an import substitution industrialization strategy to an export-oriented industrialization path. This sets the stage for India's economic modernization in this century.

India's defense program demonstrates its status as a dissatisfied nation. In 1974, India conducted its first "peaceful" nuclear tests, but it did not then press its advantage beyond a refusal to sign the Non-Proliferation Treaty and the Comprehensive Test Ban Treaty. That changed in 1998 when a series of nuclear tests signaled the willingness of the new Hindi leadership to demonstrate national power, warn Pakistan, and challenge China's preeminence in the region. Indian public response to the tests reinforced the impression that India was seeking global great power status and would do so despite international approbation, sanctions, and the inevitable Pakistani reaction. Testing of the medium-range Agni II missile in April 1999 further reinforced this perception. All these events are classic signs of dissatisfaction.

As the world's largest democracy, India is poised to enter the high-growth phase of the endogenous growth trajectory. Its power potential is enormous. The long-forgotten giant, India will be a significant factor in the international system of this century if its internal growth dynamic continues. Coming late to free enterprise and still lagging China's accelerated growth rates, yet with the fifth largest economy in the world, India is a superpower in waiting.

India's potential emergence raises serious implications for a future competition with China. Despite its democratic regime, India has not been incorporated into the global hierarchy, nor has it fully reconciled its territorial and political differences with China.[94] If current trends continue, a confrontation is possible, even likely. As with the case of China, U.S. actions can either defuse or delay the possibility of conflict. Defusing the potential conflict would involve moving India from dissatisfied to satisfied status. For example, the United States can help accelerate the democratic and free market factors within India. Or the United States could coax India, over time, into considering a membership in an expanded NATO. Both strategies have the potential for creating a satisfied India such that should a power transition occur between India and China, or in the very long-run between India and the United States, the transition would be peaceful.

If the attempt to bring India into the global hierarchy run by the United States is unsuccessful, and if India remains a dissatisfied nation, then the U.S. (or Chinese) response should be to create an expanded international coalition so large that even a superpower India could not successfully challenge. That might be a U.S.-NATO-Russian coalition or a U.S.-China coalition.

For grand strategists, the central regional issue for the next fifty years will be the contest between China and the United States with India looming in the backdrop. Driven by internal growth rates, framed by long-standing territorial disputes, conditioned by dissatisfaction and nationalism, vying for leadership of the most dynamic economic region in the world, this contest for dominance has all the aspects of classic great power conflict. As the dominant power, the United States has a large stake in the outcome of this competition. Though the challenge of China may come first, it is impossible to ignore the next and perhaps last great power transition — India. By midcentury, the U.S.-China-India relationship may be the most important in the world.

Conclusions: China, India, and the United States

The Asian challenge is twofold. China is the most immediate danger to the United States and the international system. India is a secondary danger, first to the region and later to the global hierarchy. Solving the former danger is an important step toward resolving the latter.

If China continues its dramatic increase in power, and we have indicated there are legitimate questions about this, it will overtake the United States, first in the size of its economy, and, after a time, in power. This will be a period of great instability and will greatly increase the probability of war.

Challengers do not frequently overtake dominant countries. These are rare events. We know that the overtaking may be peaceful as was the case with the United Kingdom and United States. The critical lesson learned from that transition is the need to ensure that China moves into the world as a satisfied rather than a dissatisfied nation.

China must be socialized into the existing international community.[95] This includes accepting the rules and norms established by the U.S.-led coalition. Expanding foreign investment in China and revitalizing its private sector are two tools to accomplish this objective. This will create a progressively more powerful business elite. The interests of this new business class, in parallel with its counterpart in the United States, will moderate the more extreme views of the political, military, and internal security elites.

Every effort must be made to avoid making Taiwan a flashpoint that could disrupt the long-term U.S. strategy toward China. A declaration of independence by Taiwan could trigger actions by China and the United States that would destroy the chances of China becoming a responsible, satisfied member of the international community. The United States can defend Taiwan at the present stage in the power relationship, but once China's power approaches that of the United States, it will be impossible to do so without going to war. If a war occurs at that time, it will not just be over Taiwan, but will also include control of the international system.

If the effort to bring China into the current international system fails, the only other option available to head off a Chinese challenge is to strengthen the U.S. alliance system. That can be done by creating a superbloc of U.S.-led nations to include a unified Europe, Russia, and eventually India. Concurrently, the United States can add to its pool of power by expanding multilateral economic associations such as NAFTA. These agreements tie countries to the United States politically as well as economically.

All of these strategies — creating a satisfied China, reducing flashpoints, and adding to U.S. power — face significant political obstacles.[96] Powerful political factions and interest groups in the United States would profit from an anti-Chinese agenda. They already are at work to make China the next enemy. In China, the business sector is not yet powerful enough to force restraint on the political and military coalition when it comes to volatile national security issues such as Taiwan. Rising nationalism and anti-U.S. feelings may be generated or used by political leaders to offset the rising power of the business sector.[97] Increasing U.S. power by adding a unified Europe and Russia to the U.S.-led coalition poses political risks of its own. The NATO expansion debate offers an insight into the modern form of the old isolation-internationalist divide.

Behind China, India waits in the wings. Largely overlooked by Western strategists, India has the key components for rapid power growth: a large population coupled with the dynamics of an emerging free marketplace. India can ride the rapid phase of the endogenous growth trajectory if it broadens its economic base, curbs population growth, successfully manages the rural-urban migration, and increases governmental political capacity. A formidable list of challenges, but similar in many ways to those faced by the United States in the late 1800s and by China today.

If India meets these challenges, its power potential is enormous, competing with that of China and the United States. It is not mere speculation to project India and China as superpowers in the mid to late part of this century. Should that come to be, the implications for regional and world peace are ominous. Both China and India currently are dissatisfied nations. Continuation of that disposition, coupled with an overtaking, would greatly increase the probability of war.

The United States has leverage on this situation, particularly during the early period of rapid growth. It can take action to help India obtain positive economic benefits in the international system and to wean it away from its peculiar form of political isolation. It can address the Indian need for international recognition. It can slowly bring India into new forms of political and military cooperation so that over time India sheds its status as a dissatisfied nation and moves comfortably into the U.S.-led international system. Specifically, the United States must give recognition to the important power disparities in South Asia by treating India collegially with dignity and respect, and by designing a strategy that anticipates long-term benefits from an Indo-U.S. alliance. In the case of India, perceptions, language, and status may be of equal importance to specific actions.

Power Transition does not predict that an overtaking or war with China or India is inevitable, but both are sufficiently realistic possibilities to warrant systematic attention. The United States, China, and India must examine these realities in a farsighted strategic context. It takes extraordinary discipline to think strategically in a political environment where immediate costs must be weighed against very long-term benefits. Yet that is precisely what the leaders of China, India, and the United States must do. Time is an ally, but it is not inexhaustible. The stakes could not be higher.

CHAPTER 8
The World to Come

We shall see strange things before we die. Dare we guess at what they will be?
— A.F.K. ORGANSKI

The State of the World

Power Transition theory is one the most powerful intellectual tools for policymakers to understand the dynamics of world politics in this century. Unlike other theories, it captures both the structure and the dynamics of the international system. This characteristic permits policymakers to anticipate events that must be managed in world politics.

This theory has three unique characteristics. It has a strong empirical base that has been subjected to rigorous testing against two centuries' worth of data. Its theoretical description of the world is consistent with real political events and policies. And it provides insights into the future that can guide policymakers in their international management roles.

With breadth and versatility, Power Transition accounts equally well for both World Wars, the Cold War, and the post–Cold War era. It is applicable to the prenuclear and nuclear ages. It merges economic and security factors into one argument. It is a general theory of world politics that forms the basis of a grand strategy.

Power Transition theory describes the international system as a hierarchy based on power. Atop this hierarchy sits the dominant power, which organizes the global status quo. This status quo is the combined pattern of economic, military, and other interactions by which the members of the international system come into contact with one another. Within the global hierarchy some states associate with and are benefited by their relationship to the dominant power. Others, dissatisfied with their role and share of benefits in the system, seek to alter the status quo.

The power hierarchy of the international system is dynamic. States grow at different rates, thereby altering their relative positions in the hierarchy. The relationship between the dominant power and other countries, satisfied and dissatisfied, is in flux. From time to time a challenger manages to overtake the dominant power. If this challenger emerges from the ranks of the dissatisfied, the probability of war rises sharply. Such wars are likely to be both severe and long, but they are rare events. If the challenger emerges victorious, the international system is altered to its benefit.

In the alternative, if the challenger emerges from the ranks of the satisfied, cooperation prevails and the status quo is maintained without conflict.

The arguments we have made in this book demonstrate the versatility of Power Transition theory to address not only global but also regional concerns. At the global level, it offered an effective guide, in retrospect, for the management of relations between the United States and USSR in the Cold War era. Today it is a useful tool for understanding the complexity of future U.S.-Chinese interactions, as well as those involving NATO, Europe, and India.

After the collapse of the Soviet Union, policymakers refocused attention on and elevated the importance of regional politics. In this environment of heightened sensitivity to regional concerns, Power Transition theory outlines when and where regional conflicts are likely to occur, offers implications about the interaction between great and regional powers, and addresses questions of intervention, resolution of conflict, and the diffusion of war.

International economics has assumed a more important role in relation to security concerns. Some analysts even argue that economics have become the coin of national security.[1] Power Transition theory provides tools to understand interaction between states competing over economic concerns or security concerns or both. The theory outlines the conditions conducive to economic and security integration while establishing the predicate for continuity of the prevailing international regime.

While the reduction in tensions between the United States and Russia has diminished concerns about deterrence, the problems raised by nuclear proliferation have been elevated. Power Transition argues that deterrence is unstable. It also tells us that proliferation is extraordinarily dangerous because during an overtaking by a dissatisfied state, nuclear weapons may be used. That is why the theory recommends that so much emphasis be placed on blocking the proliferation of nuclear weapons.

Turning from what the theory says to how we can use it, we see that the United States, as the dominant power, continues to manage the international system. Therefore, we must understand what strategies will ensure peace and stability in this century. The United States has followed a successful strategy in Europe by encouraging democracy and integration. Power Transition theory views further NATO and EU integration into Eastern Europe as a beneficial achievement, *provided* it does not preclude Russia from also joining this system. A long-term extension of this strategy includes the incorporation of China, and then India, into the U.S.-led alliance system. The consequence of that would be the creation of an ultrastable superbloc of satisfied states holding a vast preponderance of power.

An all-encompassing superbloc may be impossible to achieve. China or India could very well decide on a more independent course of action. In this circumstance, the United States can follow two counterstrategies. First, it can attempt to manage satisfaction by encouraging China to identify with existing international norms. The management of satisfaction requires the reduction of territorial flashpoints, the adoption of market economies, and the expansion of democracy. If this strategy fails, America should attempt to realign the international power distribution into the U.S.-European-Russian superbloc variant described in chapter 6. This would increase its pool of resources and ensure sufficient preponderance to postpone a future Asian challenger.

World Institutional Structures

Though imperfect in many respects, the United Nations is the best approximation available of an institution that can help manage the global status quo. It was created to reflect the power hierarchy in place at the end of World War II. The permanent members of the Security Council were, as they should have been, the nations with the most power in the global hierarchy. The dissatisfied, defeated nations were excluded. The postwar period was dominated by supporters of the status quo, with the exception of the USSR, which despite its dissatisfaction had a voice and a veto in the Security Council. The institution has evolved modestly over time, reflecting some of the changes in the global hierarchy driven by endogenous growth. China's replacement of Taiwan as a permanent member of the Security Council was a long overdue recognition of the power hierarchy.

To be effective, however, the Security Council permanent membership should represent the changing power hierarchy rather than a mirror on the past. The composition of the Security Council should reflect actual power distributions. This would help create widespread acceptance of Security Council actions. American preponderance over decision making in the Security Council accurately reflects the current hierarchy of power, with the U.S. coalition represented by the United States, United Kingdom, and France. But this arrangement cannot last. The continued exclusion of Germany and Japan weakens the institution. Given the current global hierarchy, either Germany or the EU should be represented. So should Japan. As India and, in the distant future, other nations such as Brazil gain power, these too should be represented in the Security Council. Expansion, however, has its limits. Britain and France are likely candidates for exclusion as the EU gains direct representation.[2]

An even bolder and more speculative conclusion would follow if democracy spreads to all the major regions of the world at the same time that national economies converge. Then the types of policies selected by the dominant nation will be universally accepted by the international system. Endogenous growth implies convergence in the per-capita economic growth rate of countries. As this convergence becomes global, somewhere far into the future, it is possible to speculate that the voting power of the permanent members of the Security Council will be changed to more closely approximate the size of their populations, making for a sort of "one person, one vote" system with protected rights and a satisfied international community. This would resemble a democratic system predicated upon great power peace where all nations would share common goals and values.

Until that utopian period, international politics will continue to unfold as in the past. Although dramatic change in the international system is possible, it is premature to assume an "end of history" or a fundamental redefinition of the nature of power. Nations will continue to grow and contract, continually changing their power relationships to one another. International institutions should reflect these changing realities of power.

Global and Regional Hierarchies

Interactions within and between the global and regional hierarchies will determine the level of international conflict in the future. Once Asian states such as China or India establish their preponderance, the probability of further power transitions at the global level will diminish dramatically. The reason is that these Asian states have such enormous populations that no contenders will be able to overtake them. The only chance for power transitions after Chinese or Indian dominance is established will be if integration creates new "super" countries or if the Chinese or Indian states suffer disintegration along the lines of the collapse of the Soviet Union.

In the meantime, transitions within regional hierarchies are inevitable. Conflict will shift, we believe, from the global to the regional arena. If this assumption proves correct, then great power war participation will be characterized mainly by intervention in regional conflicts. An important issue for consideration is how the current dominant power can stabilize regions in order to avoid great power intervention.

What can a dominant nation do to increase regional stability? Power Transition suggests that the dominant nation's central concern is the promotion of stability and satisfaction at the global level. This will be complemented by stability within regions. A globally dominant nation interested in regional stability should seek the support of the local dominant nation and continue that relationship for as long as the local power's preponderance is assured. By such action, the dominant nation reinforces regional peace and stability. Assuming the new local dominant nation is not an opponent of the global status quo, when a regional power transition takes place, the global dominant nation should consider a shift in strategy and support the rising challenger after the overtaking has been completed. Such action will limit the probability that war would again be waged within the regional hierarchy.

A concurrent goal of the globally dominant nation is to attain support from the regional dominant nation for the global status quo. The findings regarding the democratic peace suggest that nations with similar regimes sharply reduce their willingness to wage war.[3] Authoritarian regimes are also less likely to fight each other than are mixed dyads.[4] Power Transition suggests that domestic regime coordination leads to the emergence of similar attitudes towards the global status quo.[5] The fundamental point is that to preserve stability, the global dominant nation should seek out potential allies among the dominant states of each region, and work to create common concerns with each.

Future Hierarchies

The global hierarchy of the future may look startlingly different. New dominant powers will emerge, and they may refashion the international system in unfamiliar ways. The locus of power is moving to Asia, the land of new challengers. We cannot say for sure if the transfer of power will be peaceful or violent, but we can see the outlines, the shadows, of the primary events through the lens of Power Transition theory.

Figure 8.1 traces the international system from the year 1900 and projects it through the end of this century. The figure illustrates how hierarchies change over time. The consequences of these changes account for the most significant events in international politics.

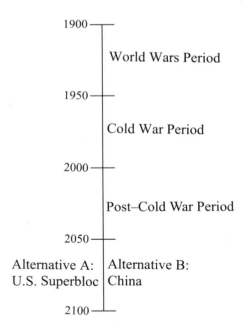

Figure 8.1 Evolution of the Global Hierarchy

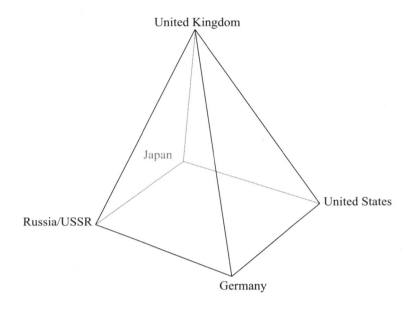

Figure 8.2   The Global Hierarchy in the World Wars Period

The century began with a period of intense competition where global wars dominated international interactions. In the second period, the Cold War threatened humanity, but American preponderance precluded the catastrophes associated with the two previous World Wars. We currently stand at the beginning of the post–Cold War era, a period of time striking in that it has not yet been given its own name. Some have suggested the Information Age, others the Second American Century. Whatever name is attached to this time, American preponderance continues to ensure the absence of global war. But this period will not last forever. If a dissatisfied China threatens to overtake the United States, we can expect to see precursor conditions similar to the Cold War. With a successful challenge, a dissatisfied China would undoubtedly establish a new world order.

Looking at the evolution of the global hierarchy in more detail, the World Wars period depicted in figure 8.2 was dominated by the United Kingdom. But the British-led global hierarchy was not managed effectively. The failure to create a satisfied Germany or to construct a cohesive prewar alliance to deter Germany led to World Wars I and II. Perhaps the most serious mistake was the failure to integrate the United States into active defense of the status quo prior to the outbreak of hostilities. British exhaustion coupled with the tremendous growth in American relative power

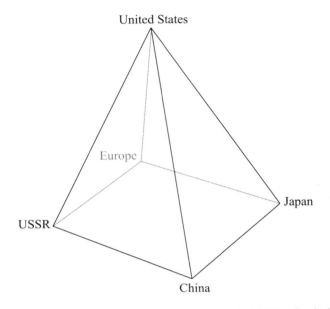

Figure 8.3 The Global Hierarchy in the Cold War Period

led to the emergence of the United States as the dominant power of the international system in the next period.

In contrast with Great Britain's failure following World War I, the United States transformed Germany and Japan into democracies after World War II, removing potential challengers from the system described in figure 8.3. China and the USSR remained outside of the satisfied international coalition, resulting in a protracted Cold War. The United States responded to the Sino-Soviet rift by taking the first steps to engage China and thereby attempt to reduce its dissatisfaction. Similar initiatives were directed toward the Soviet Union during détente. The preponderance of NATO, combined with these U.S. initiatives to engage potential opponents, stabilized the international system. The Cold War period ended abruptly as the pressures of competition with the U.S.-NATO alliance exposed the weaknesses of the Soviet system and revealed the hidden reality of American preponderance.

The collapse of the Soviet Union restructured the U.S.-led international system (figure 8.4) but, unlike the case of the British-led system at century's dawn, did not reduce its stability.

Given its enormous relative increase in power leading to the establishment of preponderance, the United States now should move to integrate Russia into the international economic community and into NATO. This is not based on Russia's current GDP, the size of a small European nation,

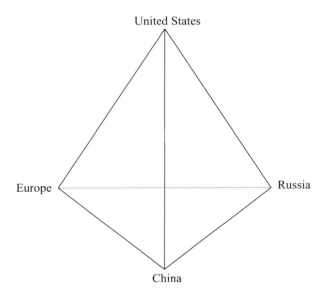

Figure 8.4   The Global Hierarchy in the Post–Cold War Period

but on the expectation that Russia, despite a diminished population, will resume its place on the growth curve within a decade or two. The United States also should expand its program of external constructive engagement and "internal realignment" with China. If these initiatives succeed, the stability of the current system will be ensured within this hierarchy for the first half of this century and perhaps beyond.

The Next International Period

The future structure of the global hierarchy will be determined largely by the continued economic expansion of the great powers. As endogenous growth fosters convergence in the growth of per-capita economic output, the size of a nation's population will ultimately set the limit on the size of its economy. Each of the next three figures adjust the size of each continent based on the share of the particular resource focused on. Figure 8.5 (p. 190) displays each continent's share of world demographic resources.[6] Asia is clearly preponderant in terms of population. The dramatic difference in the demographic bases of each continent sets the foundation for the next global hierarchy. As per-capita growth rates converge, Asia will have no rivals for its preeminence in world politics.

Despite the wide disparity in populations, the global distribution of wealth favors the West. Figure 8.6 (p. 190) illustrates the current world shares of GDP for each continent.[7] Today, the Western alliance of Europe

Figure 8.5   Current World Population Shares

Figure 8.6   Current World GDP Shares

and North America is economically preponderant over the Asian region. Because of this preponderance, the United States is the unrivaled global leader. It is not surprising to find that it has assembled the most powerful coalition in support of the status quo.

   According to the model of endogenous growth, the distribution of the world's economic resources will shift over time. The majority of the world's wealth will shift to Asia as per-capita GDP converges. Figure 8.7 forecasts the world shares of GDP in the middle of this century.[8] Given its dramatic advantage in population resources, Asia should hold a *larger* share of GDP than both Europe and North America *combined*.

   The global hierarchy needs to accommodate these changes in the distribution of power. The issue is not whether a transition will occur, but

Figure 8.7   Mid-Century World GDP Shares

whether it will be peaceful or conflictual. The goal of U.S. policymakers should be to foster a peaceful power transition that incorporates the Asian power center into the existing status quo. If such efforts fail, the probability of a global war increases dramatically.

A number of structural arrangements are possible in the twenty-first century. Specifically, two ideal types represent opposite ends of the spectrum of possible hierarchies, the U.S.-led superbloc in figure 8.8 (p. 192) and Greater China in figure 8.9. There are many possible types in between, but these two define the range. The first scenario, wherein the United States can greatly increase its power by expanding NATO into a superbloc via incorporation of Russia, China, and India, is illustrated in figure 8.8.

In a U.S.-led superbloc, all members of the hierarchy have been persuaded to be part of a common international coalition, where democracy and the marketplace are the distinguishing features. These are central because they are the goals of the current dominant power. Constructing a superbloc in which bloc members are encouraged or peacefully persuaded to adopt these goals will produce a system in which all are satisfied. This distinguishes this scenario from the strategy of hostility and appeasement followed by the previous dominant power in the 1930s. In that case, the British failed to bring the German challengers into agreement with their goals. The greatest tragedy may be that the British simultaneously failed to construct a superbloc with the United States, a country available because it generally shared British goals and preferences.

The preponderant superbloc system in figure 8.8 is ultrastable. American leadership of this superbloc would be expected for decades to come. However, given demographic trends, the most powerful member of the superbloc late in this century is likely to be either China or India. This

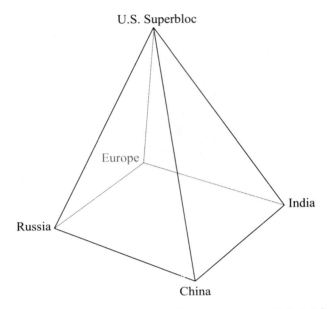

Figure 8.8 Alternative A: The Global Hierarchy under a U.S.-led Superbloc

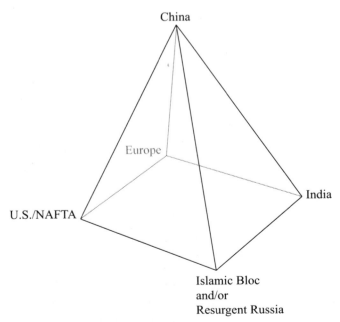

Figure 8.9   Alternative B: The Global Hierarchy under China

will make the superbloc an Asian-led alliance, but one that has been conditioned to be consistent with American interests.

At the opposite end of the spectrum, illustrated in figure 8.9, we find a dissatisfied China imposing a very different international order. In this scenario, China overtakes the United States as its coalition proves stronger than that of the satisfied states. This raises the prospects for global war.

China can establish this new hierarchical order, but in so doing it has to supplant the U.S.-established global status quo. Power Transition theory implies that the means by which a dissatisfied China would impose a new status quo is through war against the United States and its allies. Successfully besting the United States would establish China as the dominant power. The threat to China then would be an eventual challenge by India, perhaps in alignment with another emerging power, for argument's sake, a resurgent Russia.

The fundamental result of this hierarchical analysis is that *in war or peace* Asia eventually emerges as the center of the international system with an Asian state as the dominant power. While the ultimate outcome of Asia's emergence is inevitable, the alternate paths to that future are very distinct. Which course is followed is, to a substantial degree, in the hands of U.S. decision makers today. Every dominant power eventually passes the mantle of leadership to another. The prudential dominant power makes sure that this transition occurs on its own terms.

Notes

Chapter 1: Power Transition Theory for the Twenty-first Century

1. For a list of articles that specifically take traditional and neorealist theories to task for this failure, see Jervis 1991; Singer and Wildavsky 1993; Lebow 1994; and Ray and Russett 1996. For realist and neorealist counter-claims, see Huntington 1989; Mearsheimer 1990; or Waltz 1993.

2. An extraordinary amount of new research has validated and extended the theory in the past two decades. The original basic statement of the Power Transition perspective is found in A.F.K. Organski's *World Politics* (1958), with extensions to the nuclear era in the second edition (1968). The fundamental test is found in Organski and Kugler's *The War Ledger* (1980). For an overview of recent work and extensions see Kugler and Lemke's *Parity and War* (1996).

3. See Dougherty and Pfaltzgraff 1996 for a systematic categorization of international relations theories.

4. Described in more detail in chapter 3, but originally presented in Lemke 1993, 1995a, 1996; and Lemke and Werner 1996.

5. Organski and Kugler 1980, 19; see also Organski 1968; and Kugler and Arbetman 1989a.

6. The preceding should not be interpreted to mean that being powerful but not the dominant power automatically means that a state will be dissatisfied. Furthermore, the act of growing more powerful, even more powerful than the dominant country itself, does not automatically mean that the growing state will be satisfied. Were that the case, Power Transition would be internally inconsistent, because it would then be impossible for an overtaking by a dissatisfied state to occur. Power Transition would then logically preclude the hypothesized condition conducive to war from possibly occurring. A recent article by de Soysa, Oneal, and Park 1997 misrepresents Power Transition theory by claiming that power or growth causes states to be satisfied with the status quo. Lemke and Reed 1998 point out the logical inconsistency associated with such claims and demonstrate by a Granger causality analysis that there is no statistical relationship between power level, or growth in power, and evaluations of the status quo for all states over the 1816–1985 time period. The logic and intuition of Lemke and Reed's argument is simple to comprehend. Although it is clearly plausible to expect growth or power would be associated with being satisfied with how the international system operates, it is not necessarily the case. It could well be that the powerful or growing state became powerful or has experienced growth *in spite of* an unfavorable international status quo or even in the fact of overt hostility from the dominant state. Nazi Germany in the 1930s or the Soviet Union of the 1950s experienced dramatic growth in power but did so within very hostile international atmospheres. Becoming more powerful made neither state satisfied with the status quo. Although power and wealth may be generally satisfying in some broad sense, they do not guarantee that a state will be satisfied with the status quo. In fact, it is possible to conceive of an international system in which most of the great powers will be dissatisfied (in contrast to the shading in figure 1.3). Imagine a "Robin Hood" dominant power that reallocated from the great powers to struggling developing world states. In such a system the proportion of satisfied states would *increase* as we moved lower in the international power pyramid.

7. See Lemke and Reed 1996; and Russett 1993.

8. Power can be expressed as follows: Domestic Power = Population* Productivity *Political Capacity. This specification can be extend to include external aid: Power = (Population * Productivity * Political Capacity) + (Foreign Aid * Political Capacity of Recipient). See Organski and Kugler 1980.

9. Given the importance of power, both conceptually and in practice, a vast literature addressing questions of the statistical measurement of national power has been produced over the years. The Composite Capabilities Index of the Correlates of War Project (first described in Singer, Bremer, and Stuckey 1972) is the most common measure employed in statistical analyses. It aggregates national shares of world population, urban population, military expenditures, military personnel, iron/steel production, and coal/oil consumption. It does so in attempt to capture the importance of demographic, military, and industrial components of national power. Power Transition theory focuses on domestically available resources and the government's ability to mobilize those resources. Thus, most Power Transition research has employed GDP, usually weighted by the political capacity of the government. Not surprisingly, the Correlates of War and GDP measures of national power are highly correlated (Kugler and Arbetman 1989a, Merritt and Zinnes 1989), and both measures have been used to validate Power Transition expectations. Lemke and Werner 1996) specifically report that both measures of power support Power Transition expectations, but de Soysa, Oneal and Park 1997, employing a different spatial domain, report somewhat more qualified support.

A related literature addresses efforts to measure the political capacity of governments (see, inter alia, Bahl 1971; Chelliah 1971, Organski and Kugler 1980, chap. 2; Jackman 1993; and the recent comprehensive summary and survey edited by Arbetman and Kugler 1997). The general thrust of these efforts is that the ability of a government to mobilize national resources, its "political capacity," can be effectively gauged by comparing how well it does penetrating national society and extracting resources (in the form of taxes) therefrom, to what it might have been expected to achieve based on statistical models of penetration and extraction. Governments that play a large role in the everyday life of their citizens and are able to extract taxes from them are more politically capable than governments isolated from and unable to tax their populations.

10. For similar arguments about national growth from economics, see Organski 1965; Solow 1987; Romer 1986; and Lucas 1988. For contrasting arguments, see Barro and Sala-i-Martin 1992.

11. This figure is derived in Feng, Kugler, and Zak 2000. Their paper proposes a formal dynamic model of politics and economic growth based on fertility, physical, and human capital accumulation. In their model, human capital provides the foundation for sustained increases in living standards as individuals with new ideas enter into the production processes. They show that politics critically affect fertility choices, which in turn determine the transmission of human capital from parents to children.

12. Feng, Kugler, and Zak 2000 show that politics may be a primary cause of countries falling into a low-income poverty trap. Indeed, an expectation of political instability increases the likelihood of a poverty trap because it adversely affects income and thus raises fertility. Similarly, governments with low political capacity will allocate low levels of taxes to increasingly generate output from the public sector and preserve high levels of fertility, thus allowing human capital to decrease over generations and causing reductions in future output.

13. Intriguing analyses of the extent to which governments can control their populations' demographic rates have been offered by Organski and Organski 1961; Organski, Kugler, Johnson, and Cohen 1984; Rouyer 1987; Arbetman, Kugler and Organski 1997; and Feng, Kugler, and Zak 2000.

14. Chapter 3 extends this argument. For more detailed arguments about extraction of resources by governments and the relationship between this and war, see Organski and Kugler 1980, chap. 2; Kugler and Domke 1986; and Ray and Vural 1986.

15. Organski and Kugler 1980.

16. Numerous studies find that satisfied dyads do not fight wars (Kim 1991; Werner and Kugler 1996). More generally, studies have begun to find that satisfied states may be less conflictual in general (Rousseau, Gelpi, Reiter, and Huth 1996) and in specific dyadic interactions (Ray 1995, chap. 5). In fact, Lemke and Reed 1996 argue that the much-researched democratic peace proposition (summarized in Maoz and Russett 1993, and Ray 1995) may be anticipated by Power Transition theory. Specifically, Lemke and Reed argue since the dominant powers of the past two hundred years (United Kingdom until 1945 and United States since) were democracies, it is probably the case that democracies

are disproportionately satisfied with the international status quo since they are likely to benefit from whatever benefits their politically similar dominant power. Lemke and Reed report that democracies have been disproportionately likely to be satisfied states and that the resultant "satisfied peace" may subsume the democratic peace.

17. This overtaking in power is what many think of as *the* power transition. That such overtakings are important correlates of war was established by Organski and Kugler (1980, chap. 1). More recently, Wayman (1996) has argued that the general category of "power shifts" (including both overtakings and rapid approaches) is a very dangerous one.

18. See chapter 3, and Kugler and Arbetman 1989a.

19. This surface is formally derived, with robust empirical support, in Efird and Kugler 1999. For details and extensions see Efird 2000. For details on the role of integration, see Efird and Genna 2000.

20. This claim is based on research reported in Bueno de Mesquita 1981, chap. 5; Wang and Ray 1994; and Bennett and Stam 1998. See also Organski and Kugler 1980, chap. 1.

21. See Walt 1987; and Hwang 1993.

22. See Alsharabati 1997 for a formal proof supporting this logic. In a recent study, Reiter (1995) reports that preemptive wars (where one side attacks because it fears it will be attacked subsequently if it does not act now) virtually never occur. Dominant powers are not the only myopic actors. For a more general and conceptual rather than empirical treatment of preventive and preemptive wars, see Levy 1987. Schweller (1992) argues that democratic states have a very difficult time waging preventive wars (especially against rising democracies) because being an international bully proves impossible to justify domestically. Since Power Transition's dominant powers of the past two centuries have been democracies, Schweller's arguments might also help to explain their myopia.

23. Organski 1958.

24. See Organski and Kugler 1980; and Bueno de Mesquita and Lalman 1992.

25. This more recent research is rigorously developed in Alsharabati 1997, which builds upon and extends Abdollahian 1996.

26. Organski and Kugler 1980.

27. See Alsharabati 1997 for a detailed discussion and evaluation of the relationship between the speed of overtaking and the likelihood of war.

28. In his 1920 book *The Economic Consequences of the Peace,* John Maynard Keynes argues that war creates an incrementally increasing economic gap between the winners and losers — spreading to the winners in the very long term. The short-term effects of war are discussed in more detail by the U.S. Strategic Bombing Survey 1945 and 1946. See Organski and Kugler 1980, 253–54.

29. See Organski and Kugler 1980, chap. 3; and Kugler and Arbetman 1989b.

30. Werner 1996, 1998; and Siverson and Starr 1994 discuss how defeated states have their leadership and international commitments revised by their conquerors. Although not Power Transition studies per se, both suggest how dominant powers might recast defeated challengers to affect their status quo evaluations.

31. Churchill 1955.

32. See Brodie 1946, 1959; Kissinger 1957; and Waltz 1990.

33. Some proponents of the value of MAD have recognized this chilling implication of their theory, see Rosen 1977; Waltz 1981; Intriligator and Brito 1981; Bueno de Mesquita and Riker 1982; and Mearsheimer 1990.

34. For prior Power Transition analyses on the role of nuclear deterrence and proliferation, see Organski 1968; Organski and Kugler 1980, chap. 4; Kugler 1984, 1996; Zagare 1987; and Kugler and Zagare 1990.

35. See Russett and Stam 1998.

36. A growing body of research (which includes Vasquez 1993; Hensel 1996; and Huth 1996) argues that territorial disagreements are the most war-prone of all international issues.

37. This has been a central argument of Kim's 1989, 1991, 1992, 1996 research on Power Transition theory.

38. Here we have in mind forecasting models applicable to specific situations. See Bueno de

Mesquita, Newman, and Rabushka 1985, 1996; Bueno de Mesquita and Stokman 1994; and Kugler and Feng 1997a and b.

Chapter 2: Power Transition Theory Tested in the Nineteenth and Twentieth Centuries

This chapter is an extension of Organski, Kugler, and Abdollahian 1995. The data are described and defined in Bairoch 1976.

1. Werner and Kugler (1996) utilize the measure of arms buildups to reflect hostile competition between rival dyads preceding transitions and wars. For new alternatives, see Signorino and Ritter 1997; and Benson 1998.

2. We utilize Bairoch's (1976) period scheme of European economic growth as a guideline. He identifies 1800–1913, 1913–1950, and post-1950 as three distinct periods of economic performance. Bairoch suggests that nineteenth century Europe witnessed slow growth, followed by uneven economic development in the interwar period and sustained growth after World War II.

3. Comparable time series data for Austria-Hungary are highly unreliable so they are excluded from figure 2.2. Data for Austria-Hungary used in figure 2.1 are very sketchy and do not show yearly variations in growth rates.

4. Note that what primarily enabled the United Kingdom to overtake France, the largest and most powerful of its competitors, was its two-to-one advantage in economic productivity. In 1851, the U.K. GDP per capita was 1,673 international dollars while French GDP per capita was 847 international dollars (1980 prices). This advantage was a function of the United Kingdom's increasing economic returns from the modernization process by going through the industrial revolution first. This advantage more than made up for a population between a fifth and more than a third smaller than any of its principal competitors. Higher economic productivity also reflected a more capable government in terms of efficiency than continental powers. It is accepted that among the major powers of the eighteenth century the Prussian government was the most powerful followed by that of France with the British government weakest. We propose that the proportions setting off that order should be reversed. The British political system may have been "weakest" in some sense, but it was the most effective. Data are not available to measure directly the capability of governments at such early dates. However, a number of indications suggest that the order we propose is correct. See Organski, Kugler, Johnson, and Cohen 1984; and Arbetman and Kugler 1997.

5. Our data provide no direct evidence of this U.K. overtaking of France since the series do not extend back far enough. We do know, however, that the two preceding decades were times of almost constant war between Revolutionary and Imperial France and the coalition of nations led by the United Kingdom. We expect the data would show an overtaking to have taken place if the GDP series used in our research were extrapolated back several decades.

6. The United States overtook every major European nation in economic and international power. The United States passed Prussia in 1834, Austria in 1836, France in 1858, and the United Kingdom in 1879. The United States also overtook Russia in 1880 and China in 1890. Comparisons between the GDP of the United States and those of China and Russia need to be interpreted carefully however, as Chinese and Russian economic data in the nineteenth century are of questionable accuracy.

7. Werner and Kugler (1996) list the arms buildups that precipitate major wars in their table 11.8.

8. See also Organski 1958.

9. The analyses of the coalition politics that shaped the behavior of the two nations is presented in Organski (n.d.).

10. According to Huntington (1997): "Historically the United States has been a strong country with a weak government. Apart from the military, most of the resources cited as evidence of American power are not easily subject to the control of the American government."

11. We should raise another possibly relevant point about the avoidance of a U.S.-U.K. confrontation over leadership of the international order. The U.S. refusal to claim leadership could legitimately be thought as having signaled to a truculent and rapidly growing Germany that the leader was still the United Kingdom, a competitor Germany could overtake, as in fact it did. We contend that the U.S. decision to spurn leadership was the result of bitter disputes among U.S. elites over foreign policy direction. Had the outcome of that struggle been different and had the United States made its own claim to leadership plain, Germany would have known it had no hope to catch and overtake America as leader. One could also argue that U.S. isolationism after World War I again misled Germany. It is clearly fatuous to rerun history, but the implications of this hypothesis for the evolution of the order of great powers in the first half of the twentieth century should be obvious.

12. Richardson 1994, 106–34.

13. Werner and Kugler 1996, table 11.8.

14. The population of Germany was 62 million compared to the 44 million of the United Kingdom, and the per-capita product of Germany was $1,833 compared to the British $2,720 in 1907.

15. Werner and Kugler 1996, table 11.8.

16. See Abdollahian 1996 and Efird 2000 on the structural constraints of war initiation and the stability of peace, regardless of foreign policy crises or incidents.

17. Organski and Kugler 1977.

18. See Organski and Kugler 1980; Kugler and Arbetman 1989b; and Arbetman 1996.

19. For an alternative explanation of why the Cold War was peaceful, see Gaddis 1987.

20. Soviet academician Oleg Bogamolov put the question as follows: "How could a country (the USSR) whose GNP was one-third of another country (the United States) believe itself as strong as the other country? One is duty bound to ask the inverse question. How could a country (the United States) with an economy (and, therefore, national capabilities) two or three or more times larger than another country (the Soviet Union) possibly believe that its opponent was its equal in national capabilities and therefore in power?" quoted in Organski and Arbetman 1993.

21. Werner and Kugler 1996, table 11.8.

22. Estimates are from Kugler and Arbetman 1989a.

Chapter 3: Regional Applications

1. See the studies reviewed in Kugler and Lemke 1999.

2. The multiple hierarchy model was introduced in Lemke 1993, 1996; and evaluated in Lemke 1997b, forthcoming.

3. For an extensive review of such efforts, see Lemke 1993, Appendix A.

4. See Siverson and Starr 1991 for a good summary.

5. Bremer 1992 is generally considered to offer the strongest evidence that contiguity increases the probability of a militarized dispute between states.

6. See Vasquez 1993 for a definitive treatment of these ideas. For an early, non-political science presentation of these ideas, see Lorenz 1966.

7. The actual formula is an exponent to which a state's share of power is raised, resulting in "adjusted power":

   Adjusted Power = Power $^{\log[(\text{miles})/(\text{miles per day})+(10\text{-}e)]}$

8. A much more detailed presentation of the loss-of-strength formula and its use in defining regional hierarchies is offered in Lemke 1993, 1995b. The formula employed is a variation on Bueno de Mesquita's (1981) exponent, which in turn is based on the conceptualization of the loss-of-strength gradient originally advanced by Boulding (1962).

9. Bueno de Mesquita 1981, 104 offered these transit ranges based on consultation with military officers and historians.

10. It may be excessively overoptimistic for great powers as well. Consider the following: the distance between Washington, D.C., and Riyadh, Saudi Arabia (arguably the average beginning and endpoints of the American deployment for the Gulf War) is roughly 8,500

miles. In August 1990 President Bush ordered General Schwarzkopf to determine how long it would take before the American military could be in position to defend Saudi Arabia against Iraqi aggression. The general's answer was seventeen weeks (Woodward 1991, 303). This distance and time-frame suggests an American transit range of just over 70 miles per day in 1990. Obviously there are logistic hurdles specific only to this mobilization, but it seems quite clear that 500 miles per day is an over-statement.

11. See Lemke 1995a.

12. Available through the Correlates of War Project at the University of Michigan and described in detail in Jones, Bremer, and Singer 1996.

13. Small and Singer 1982 define "great powers" via a standardized list of states so designated by consensus of historians.

14. Corroborating evidence is also available. In an analysis of Latin American interstate relations, Hensel (1994, footnote 2) notes that of militarized interstate disputes initiated by two Latin American states there is not a single instance of subsequent great power militarized participation. Popular perception suggests that there has been a great deal of interference in Latin American affairs by one of the Great Powers — the United States. Contrary to the popular view, such interference has *never* occurred in militarized fashion in Latin American *interstate* disputes.

15. The results described and summarized in this section of the chapter are drawn from Lemke (forthcoming), which offers a much more empirically rigorous presentation and elaboration.

16. In the analyses that are summarized below, power has generally been measured as GDP weighted by Relative Political Capacity (RPC), described in Arbetman and Kugler 1997. When GDP data are unavailable, measures derived from the Correlates of War Project's Composite Capabilities Index are used. In general the results are consistent regardless of the measure of power parity employed. Dissatisfaction with the status quo has been gauged by employing the extraordinary military buildup measure discussed in the footnotes to chapter 1. The time spans for each regional analysis vary somewhat, based either on political reality (e.g., most African states did not achieve independence until after 1960) or by the availability of data. The analyses summarized below include South American regional hierarchies 1865–1990, those of the Middle East, and Africa and the Far East for 1960–90. Additionally, analysis of the great powers (occupants of the overall international hierarchy) covers the years 1816–1990.

17. As is traditional in most empirical scholarly treatments of international war, the studies described here employ the Correlates of War Project's definition of interstate war (Small and Singer 1982, chap. 2): sustained, officially sanctioned conflict between two recognized members of the international system in which at least one thousand battle fatalities occurred.

18. The Correlates of War Project lists the 1962 Sino-Indian War and two wars between China and Vietnam (1979, and 1985–87) as occurring during the study period for the Far East. None of these wars is included in the analyses described here because Vietnam and India were both calculated to be unable to move military resources to Beijing. These wars are either indications of need for refinement in the operational definition of regional hierarchies or else serve to indicate how China's position in East Asia is fundamentally different from that of other Asian states in that it can make war on Asian states regardless of their regional hierarchy, but other Asian states could not carry a war to China's core territory.

19. Table 3.1 summarizes work that employs a statistical technique known as logistic regression analysis; for a discussion of this technique, see Aldrich and Nelson 1984; and Liao 1994.

20. These probabilities are calculated based on an estimation that employs Correlates of War rather than GDP power data. Much more detail about these analyses is presented in Lemke 1997b; and Lemke (forthcoming).

21. In a reply to a criticism of his expected utility theory as trivial because so few dyads with positive expected utility for war actually go to war, Bruce Bueno de Mesquita (1984, 354–55) pointed out that the rates of war given positive expected utility are similar to the rates of lung cancer given that a person smokes. For cigarette smokers the proportion who develop lung cancer is 156 per 100,000. For nonsmokers the proportion

who develop lung cancer is 7.8 per 100,000. This suggests that smoking increases the average person's risk of developing lung cancer from 0.0078 percent to 0.156 percent. Smoking increases a person's risk of lung cancer something on the order of twenty times, yet the risk of lung cancer is still extremely low in absolute terms (just over one-tenth of 1 percent). The fact that the absolute increase in the risk of cancer is small has not prevented the federal government from aggressively acting to suppress the tobacco industry. Similarly, the seemingly small absolute increase in the probability of war in some minor power regions should not make us disregard the importance of power parity and dissatisfaction with the status quo.

22. By power share is meant the proportion of both countries' combined power held by either country (North Vietnam's "power share," for example, would be [North Vietnam's Power]/[North Vietnam's + South Vietnam's Power]). Any time these two shares are between 0.6 and 0.4 the two states are defined as at parity. If both sides' shares were 0.5 they would be exactly equal.
23. Organski and Kugler (1980) estimate that the financial costs exceeded $180 billion.
24. See Organski and Kugler 1980, chap. 1.
25. In fact, in a pair of studies, Kinsella (1994, 1995) has offered evidence that the United States and the USSR transferred resources to Israel and Egypt, respectively, in a roughly offsetting and reactive fashion.
26. Some 14,000 lives were lost in the Pacific and 130,000 in the Chaco.

Chapter 4: Security Applications

1. HNL See Organski 1958, 1968; Organski and Kugler 1980; Kugler 1984, 1996; Kugler and Zagare 1990; Powell 1990, 1996; and Zagare and Kilgour 1993, 2000.
2. See Kugler 1996.
3. To some degree, the limitations of systematic research are at fault. It is both dangerous and improper to allow incomplete results to affect policy, only to discover that the oversimplification required to achieve scientific deductions has obscured important elements in the real world. The shadow of scientific misapplications during the Vietnam War inhibits such usage. However, inaction is merely an alternative form of action. When conditions that reduce the likelihood of war are identified, but practical options to avoid them are not explored; when opportunities to strengthen collaborative efforts that reduce regional conflict are discovered, but no action is taken to exercise them; when conditions that reduce the danger of nuclear proliferation and war are isolated, but no action is taken to advance them; then silence is as dangerous as advocacy.
4. Rathjens and Kistiakowsky 1970.
5. Speed 1979.
6. Sagan 1989.
7. These estimates are from Urlanis 1971, 295. We are aware that these losses were much higher for the Jewish and Gypsy populations in these countries.
8. This position is supported by Brodie 1946, 1959. For extensions see Intriligator and Brito 1984; Fearon 1994; and Waltz and Sagan 1995. For the purposes of this analysis, we will use the original classic definition of deterrence rather than subsequent variations. We recognize that some of the inconsistencies we address have been "adjusted" in subsequent variations.
9. This graph is adapted from Intriligator and Brito 1984. We are aware that with increased proliferation nuclear weapons will generate complex multilateral interactions that need to be more fully explored.
10. The most stable region in the figure (p. 202) is along the line of parity, extending from MAD, passing through the balance of terror, and ending in the cone of war. Under MAD, as in classical deterrence, the costs of war are so prohibitive that neither opponent will initiate or retaliate. For this reason classical deterrence and balance of power both argue that MAD is ultrastable and peaceful. The Cold War did not heat up under MAD because the terror of nuclear retaliation averted wars that otherwise would be waged. For this reason, advocates of balance of power generally opposed the Strategic Defense Initiative since this would reintroduce the dangerous connotations of massive retaliation,

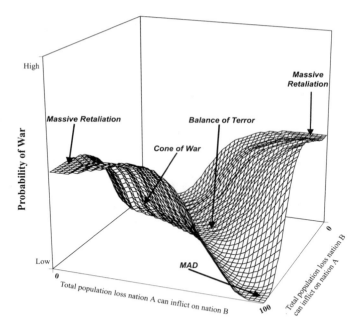

High

Massive
Retaliation

Massive Retaliation

Balance of Terror

Cone of War

Probability of War

Low

0

MAD

Total population loss nation A can inflict on nation B

100

0

Total population loss nation B
can inflict on nation A

Balance of Power and the Probability of Nuclear War

where one nation could unilaterally destroy its major opponent. Simply stated, this perspective argues that increasing equivalent costs enhances stability. Massive retaliation is unstable.

The balance of power perspective proposes that massive retaliation is unstable. The preponderant power can and will take advantage of its superiority to impose its political preferences in an environment of anarchy. Nuclear preemption is likely under massive retaliation because leaders are driven by uncertainty about an opponent's intentions; see Wohlstetter 1959 and Powell 1990. Only under massive retaliation can a preemptive strike be undertaken without fear of reciprocation. As nuclear proliferation proceeds, this advantage is lost. Preemptive strikes are anticipated in situations like the Middle East today or between the United States and USSR early in the Cold War since there is nothing to stop the advantaged nuclear state from stopping its rival from changing the nuclear imbalance to balance.

11. Casualties may be enormous, as during World Wars I and II, but still relatively low compared to nuclear exchanges.

12. Anarchy is the absence of government rules, whereby each state decides by itself whether or not to use force (Waltz 1979, chap. 6).

13. See Brodie 1946.

14. See Gibelterra 1998.

15. Alsharabati (1997) provides a formal explanation for this potential anomaly. She shows that if an overtaking takes place very swiftly, because of the collapse of one of the contenders, the challenger then becomes the dominant nation so quickly that it may be able to redress the local status quo without conflict.

16. See Gibelterra 1998.

17. See Rosen 1977 for the most explicit advocacy of stability through nuclear balance in the Middle East

18. Abdollahian 1996; and Alsharabati 1997.

19. The logic of this argument follows this pattern: In a political context would you prefer

to wage nuclear war in 1950 when the USSR just acquired nuclear weapons or in the future when it becomes certain that the United States would be in peril. Would you rather fight today or would you rather wait for 2050 when the challenge from China may reach maturity? Decision makers seem to engage in conflict when they expect to obtain the highest payoffs.

20. Fearon (1994) introduces this powerful representation of the deterrence sequence and solves this structure from the static perspective of balance of power. He is careful to point out that he only considers conventional conflict, but there appears to be no logical reason to preclude a nuclear extension.

21. Threats can consist of troop movements, diplomatic moves, or any act that may signal the possibility of a hostile action in the future.

22. Extensive work in crisis decision making shows that leaders do make a difference and outcomes can be changed by their intervention. See Bueno de Mesquita 1981; Bueno de Mesquita and Lalman 1992; and Kugler and Feng 1997b.

23. The necessary nuclear technology has been re-created in any number of countries. Replication becomes a much easier task for any aspiring nation to become a nuclear power. The collapse of the Soviet Union has made available the plutonium and scientists necessary to fill whatever gaps remain in the nuclear programs of nations seeking to acquire nuclear weapons. In the long term nuclear proliferation is not likely to be stopped on the supply side. As figure 4.6 demonstrates, there are (and have been) a number of countries on the verge of nuclear proliferation, and yet the number of nuclear powers remain small. Why has the set of nuclear countries remained so limited? The Power Transition perspective argues that proliferation is most likely when a nation has the opportunity (near parity) and the willingness (when they are dissatisfied with the status quo) to fight the defender. When these two conditions are met, proliferation is most likely to occur, but it is not an inevitable fact.

24. Modifications are extrapolations based on Meyer 1984.

25. Intriligator and Brito 1987. Note that this argument is consistent only with the balance of power notion of deterrence (see note 10). It does not fit well with the classical version that assumes no first strike, because there should be no increase in the probability of war when one nation has exclusive possession of nuclear weapons. Moreover, the inclusion of risk also destroys the stability of classical deterrence. Kugler and Zagare 1990.

26. Bueno de Mesquita and Riker 1982.

27. Some consistent proponents/analysts of classical nuclear deterrence make this logical connection, for example, Rosen 1977; Waltz 1981; Bueno de Mesquita and Riker 1982; Intriligator and Brito 1987; and Waltz and Sagan 1995.

28. See Kugler 1996. See also Organski 1968; Kugler 1984; Huth and Russett 1984, 1990; Kugler and Zagare 1987, 1990; Zagare and Kilgour 1993, 2000; Alsharabati and Kugler 1995, 1996; Zagare 1996; and Alsharabati 1997.

29. See Kugler 1984; and Huth and Russett 1984, 1990.

30. Bueno de Mesquita 1985; Bueno de Mesquita and Lalman 1992; and Kugler and Feng 1997b.

31. Kugler and Zagare 1990.

32. The history of the SDI concept and the informal way it was presented to the president convinces us that it was intuition rather than profound strategic calculus that led to its adoption.

33. We do not argue that the United States needs to deploy a ballistic missile defense at this time. The U.S. nuclear and conventional advantage is overwhelming. Should that change or a substantial challenger arise, that would change the equation.

34. The removal of nuclear weapons from South Africa was due to domestic changes. Argentina and Brazil seem to have acted to reduce regional tensions. International pressures, therefore, are not the only means to solve the proliferation dilemma.

Chapter 5: Economic Applications

1. Unlike advocates of realism who argue that security considerations are paramount (reflecting "high" politics) while economic considerations are secondary (or "low"

politics), Power Transition considers these as equivalent components. The Power Transition approach argues that dissatisfied nations will compete on security and economic fronts, attempting to foster competitive relationships despite the risk of war, while satisfied nations will approach similar issues utilizing cooperative relationships, minimizing the risk of conflict. For example, economic and security exchanges between Iran and the United States are now shrouded in conflict as both use a competitive strategy with each other, while in relations between Canada and the United States such exchanges are cooperative.

2. The literature on absolute and relative gains deals with similar issues. We loosely equate the notion of absolute gains with cooperative relations because participants are willing to engage in mutually beneficial interactions even when one side gains more than the other. On the other hand, we relate relative gains with noncooperative relations because the participants enter into interactions only when they see a direct unilateral advantage from doing so. For a discussion of this point see Grieco 1988; Powell 1991; Snidal 1991; Grieco, Powell, and Snidal 1993; and Huntington 1993. Morrow, Siverson, and Tabares (1998) argue that relative gains do not imply purely exclusionary behavior by showing that concern with relative gains does not prevent trade between rivals. Our continuum suggests the opposite of cooperative behavior is noncooperative behavior — not exclusion or pure animosity.

3. Bueno de Mesquita, Newman, and Rabushka (1985) elaborate this point to its extreme conclusion when they argue that all economic interactions are cooperative while political interactions are conflictual. They point out correctly that during a sale, the consumer can choose to pay the asking price and take the desired product or walk away with the money. In either case the outcome is cooperative. On the other hand, political interactions are typically conflictual. When a police officer is giving a ticket to a speeder who passed you on the road, a sense of relief follows because a dangerous individual is removed from the road. When a police officer stops you for the same offense, the transaction is not a cordial one. Every excuse is used to avoid payment, and frequently the parties seek judicial settlement. There is little cooperation when political rules — otherwise supported by third parties — are imposed on us.

4. There is, as Tom Willett accurately points out, a time dimension to such interactions. Business practitioners may compete over market share using competitive strategies — as did Apple and Microsoft over operating systems following the introduction of personal computers (PCs) into the marketplace — and later revert a cooperative strategy — as reflected by Microsoft's loan to Apple to retain competition in that market. One possibility is that leaders select a competitive or cooperative strategy according to the situation. When threats to their market share are more extreme and immediate, they respond with a more competitive strategy. As Alsharabati (1997) argues, when power transitions are slower, the dominant power has more time to deal with the emerging threat, and consequently a cooperative response is likely. The victim of a successful competitive strategy must either discount losses in the short term and agree to the new cooperative principles, or, more likely, maintain the competitive strategy until the outcome is clear and time erases competition (as was the case in the Apple-Microsoft dispute). It is further possible that elites mix competitive and cooperative strategies to maximize their advantage. Such strategies, while conceptually plausible, would be detected in the long run, thereby nullifying the advantage that could be gained from them.

5. The distinction between complex interdependence and pursuit of national sovereignty has divided our field for some time. On the complex interdependence side see Keohane and Nye 1977; and Keohane 1984. On the national sovereignty side, see Krasner 1976; and Huntington 1997. Ineffective understanding of this continuum also divides practitioners who advocate an "internationalist" view and those who advocate a "national interest" first perspective (Organski 1990). Power Transition incorporates these alternatives into a single perspective.

6. Dissatisfied-dissatisfied interactions mirror the satisfied-dissatisfied patterns. The exception is collusion among dissatisfied nations to advance common goals. This possibility is rare and generally only applies to security matters (see chapter 1) and is thus omitted from this chapter's discussion for simplicity.

7. Adherence to a cooperative strategy does not resolve internal distributional problems. When such disputes fester and cannot be resolved, partners are likely to move to a competitive strategy. Note for example that successful companies that foster a cooperative relationship among internal divisions may over time diverge in aims because they cannot solve the distributional problems. A good example is the ongoing public debate between divisions of the Arthur Anderson Group regarding a possible split between associates and consultants despite enormous financial success. When not resolved, problems of internal distribution can move a relationship from cooperation to competition.

8. See Krasner 1976; Waltz 1979; and Huntington 1993.

9. See Grieco 1988; Powell 1991; Snidal 1991; and Grieco, Powell, and Snidal 1993.

10. This behavior produced a large literature concerned with "free riding" principles suggesting that Europeans unduly took advantage of the United States by spending less for defense (Domke, Eichenberg, and Kelleher 1987). Some authors even argued that the United States could be endangered by this principle since members of the coalition would grow faster than the dominant nation that paid excessively for defense (Keohane 1984). From the perspective of Power Transition such concerns are misplaced because even if an overtaking were created by such subsidies, the regime in place would continue as both nations would now defend the status quo. This is the case of the EU and Japan who support the status quo and are not a threat to the United States.

11. See Intriligator and Brito 1987 for a theoretical perspective on this issue. Military aid in the Middle East and Latin America followed similar principles, as in Organski 1990.

12. This is a mistake frequently made by analysts who profess to follow the precepts of realism and have a rigid hierarchy between "high" politics and "low" politics, which in effect shifts, based on the degree of satisfaction of the challenger. Such insights derive from the mistaken assumption of anarchy. Following Waltz (1979), realists typically argue that the only deterrent to war is the fear of its consequences. From a more liberal viewpoint Keohane (1986) argues that the hegemon could be challenged by members of its own coalition who previously benefit from security and economic transfers. Such arguments do not stand the test of time. No long-term allies choose to fight simply because they have the opportunity to do so (Russett 1988; Kugler and Organski 1989a). Instead, long-term allied nations reinforce each other and contribute to the preservation of common preferences as they become stronger. For a formal treatment of such results see Bueno de Mesquita and Lalman 1992; Abdollahian 1996; and Alsharabati 1997.

13. See Huntington 1993.

14. See Kindleberger 1973.

15. Feng 1994.

16. See Hunt 1990.

17. See Caves, Frankel, and Jones 1999.

18. Since the defender tends to dominate economic relations, international law has little value as a mediation device. The construction and particularly the enforcement of such laws occur in line with the preferences of the defender. Fair and impartial application of these laws would necessitate a more powerful, third-party enforcer, which can only be the nation at the top of the hierarchy.

19. See Rogowski 1989.

20. Feng 1994.

21. In a recent development, the British announced the decision to sell 60 percent of its gold reserves and switch into T-bills and Euro notes.

22. Kugler and Organski 1989a; and Russett 1985.

23. Implications of security externalities are elaborated in Gowa 1989, 1994; Gowa and Mansfield 1993; Mansfield 1994; and Mansfield and Bronson 1997.

24. Soviet MIGs, for example, relied on vacuum tubes rather than integrated circuits in part because of the technological restrictions imposed during the Cold War. Wilkins (1998) shows that sanctions restricted technical trade more than general trade. For related arguments, see Pollins 1989a, 1989b; and Mansfield 1994. For assessment of sanctions see Morgan and Schwebach 1997.

25. Given the sizes of China, India, and Russia it is not possible for the United States

to fundamentally alter their growth trajectories through trade sanctions. Moreover sanctions are effective only when applied universally.

26. For example, President Carter's efforts to restrict oil equipment transfers required to build an oil pipeline from the Soviet Union to Western Europe collapsed after sanctions were violated by EU members.

27. See Bueno de Mesquita, Newman, and Rabushka 1996 on the future of China's unity.

28. Power Transition and democratic peace advocates converge on the issue of satisfied, internally similar nations preserving peace. McNamara suggested three decades ago that economic performance is associated with democracy. In turn, the large literature on the democratic peace shows that democracies seldom challenge each other. Thus, the common sense and empirical literatures concur on the fact that economic growth accelerates democracy and that democracy enhances international stability. See Russett 1993; Bueno de Mesquita and Siverson 1995; and Feng 1997.

29. Endogenous growth theory makes a very plausible argument about convergence among developed and developing societies. For recent work on this subject, see Feng and Zak 1999; Feng 2000; and Feng, Zak, and Kugler 2000.

30. See the discussion on the developmental path in chapter 1.

31. Kugler 1999. Also see articles by Bueno de Mesquita et al., Feng and Sak, and Swaminathan in this special issue of *Journal of Conflict Resolution*.

32. For a formal model demonstrating this result with empirical support, see Feng and Zak 1999.

33. Exceptions are found in the oil-producing nations. Saudi Arabia and Kuwait rank among the richest in per-capita income, but autocratic rule persists despite sustained economic growth. These discrepancies are the result of geographic luck, as the wealth of these nations is based on resource endowments rather than the productivity of their populations.

34. The literature supporting this claim is vast. For a sampling, see Russett 1993; Ray 1995; Chan 1996; and Rummel 1997.

35. Indonesia, with a relatively high per-capita income, may be just starting a process of democratic development. The Philippines, another anomaly, has adopted democratic structures and a market economy but has yet to produce sustained growth.

36. See Chen, Dietrich, and Feng 2000. Also chapter 7.

37. For example, Europe has had to take more and more responsibility for NATO, both in terms of the provision of forces and funding. Similarly, the trade balance has shifted more in Europe's favor, as suggested by Kugler and Organski (1989a).

38. It is important to note that the dominant nation need not subsidize its partners. Rather, they should seek joint maximization of absolute gains that produce benefits for both the dominant nation and its allies.

39. A substantive argument revolves around the issue of whether integration is most effective among advanced nations, among nations that can complement each other's production functions, or among nations that are very underdeveloped and can gain market share. The integration of Europe suggests that complementary economies prompt integration among equals. The EU has shown by the introduction of Spain, Portugal, and Greece that economic parity is not a prerequisite for integration. Power Transition suggests that integration can be successful at several levels depending on the political attitudes toward the status quo by partners that drive this effort.

40. Stone (1995) shows that within the COMECON, patterns of interdependence evolved that were very similar to those noted by Keohane and Nye (1977) in the Western context.

41. The empirical finding of the Phoenix Factor is not just that states recover from wars, but that they recover to levels of power and growth they would have been expected to experience had war never occurred in the first place. Paradoxically, war appears to have no long-term effect on national power trajectories. If one recalls the original Power Transition argument that national power ultimately arises from domestic, and basically demographic, resources, this Phoenix Factor is less surprising. In order for a nation's power to be permanently changed by war, that war would have to permanently alter the demographic basis of the nation. Although wars are frightfully devastating, they do not (with startling exceptions such as Paraguay's experience in the War of the Triple

Alliance in the 1860s and that of various German principalities in the Thirty Years' War) generally make large impacts on population. The gruesome conflict on the Eastern front of World War II resulted in 7,500,000 Soviet casualties. This sounds terrifying, but was less than 5 percent of Soviet prewar population (Small and Singer 1982, 91). Under such conditions the demographic resources lost in the conflict can be reproduced in relatively short order by a postwar baby boom. As offensively dismissive as these speculations sound, they make explicable the observation of the Phoenix Factor. The literature on the Phoenix Factor includes Kugler 1973; Organski and Kugler 1977, 1980; Kugler and Arbetman 1989b; and Arbetman 1996. For a complementary, but less empirically established argument from economics, see Olson 1982.

42. This is demonstrated in Efird and Feng 1999.

43. Recent research identifies patterns of behavior whereby victors reconstitute the vanquished. Siverson and Starr (1994) describe the international consequences of losing wars where a losing state's pattern of international alliance commitments change to more closely reflect the international alliance commitments of their conquerors. Werner (1996) reports on the frequency with which victors impose a new government on their vanquished foes. Although this is uncommon, it is much more likely when the prewar domestic political systems of the belligerents diverge. Apparently, when victors reconstitute the vanquished they do it in ways that change both the domestic and international political characteristics of the reconstituted state. Although neither of the studies cited here are evaluations of Power Transition theory, both are consistent with arguments we would make about what dominant powers can and should do in the aftermath of wars to prevent recurrence of conflict.

Chapter 6: The Realignment Challenge

1. Goldgeier (1998) reports on the evolution of views in the Clinton Administration. For a discussion of Russian views of the inevitability of limited NATO expansion, see *Current Digest of the Post-Soviet Press* 1997; and Doherty 1997.

2. One of the more persuasive presentations of the opposition is Mandelbaum 1995a. A comprehensive review is Richard L. Kugler 1996. Other discussions of flaws in the expansion argument include Brown 1995; Dean 1997; McGwire 1997; *Arms Control Today* 1997.

3. Complaints include Pushkov 1997; and Fischer and Potter 1996.

4. A relatively early argument to this effect was Harries 1993.

5. The following review many of the current views about the possible evolution of Russian views toward the United States and NATO: Yanov 1997; Arbatov 1996; Kittfield 1997; and Pushkov 1997.

6. Recent proclamations along these lines include Baoxiang 1997; and Holloway and Bickers 1997. For a more traditional grand strategy view, see Brzezinski 1996.

7. See Goodby 1998. Leaders of the Democratic Choice Party in the Duma have formed a deputies group called "For the Atlantic Union." *Ria Novosti*, 28 May 1997.

8. See Snyder 1990; and Christensen and Snyder 1990. Snyder (1994) discusses emerging trends in Russia and their consequences for European Security. Walt 1987 is a standard citation on alliance politics.

9. Schweller (1994) addresses strategies for manipulating balancing versus bandwagoning behavior.

10. See Repko 1996.

11. See Ching 1996.

12. *The Current Digest of the Post-Soviet Press* 1997; and Holloway 1997.

13. Tyler (1996) writes of a supposedly secret deal to modernize Chinese Air Force with SU-27 fighter planes.

14. Koretsky (1996) points this out, and Fulghum (1996) addresses the issue of production rights for SU-27 fighters. Russia, for the first time since the 1960s, is ready to export military high technologies to China. This assumes great significance since the SU-27 is a transcontinental fighter and Moscow could come within its firing range.

15. Holloway and Bickers 1997.

16. Ukraine or Russia may sell SS-18s to China according to Erlanger (1996). This development is particularly dangerous given Chinese statements about developing regional deterrent strategies based on nuclear weapons systems they do not currently posses. See Johnson 1995. For a more optimistic view see Garrett and Glaser 1995.
17. From *Beijing Review* 1996. See also Shinkarenko and Malkina 1996.
18. Discussed by Zhilin (1996).
19. For the earliest discussions of this idea see Organski 1958. More recent treatments include Gilpin 1981 and Organski and Kugler 1980. Tests of the underlying propositions include Houweling and Siccama 1988; Kim and Morrow 1992. Further empirical studies and literature review can be found in Kugler and Lemke 1999 and Lemke and Kugler 1996.
20. For a discussion of what works and what does not in deterrence situations, see Huth and Russett 1993. China's reported theft of nuclear weapons secrets is but one example of the types of steps that rising states may pursue in their attempts to gain parity with the system leader.
21. Organski and Organski 1961.
22. These estimates are at purchasing power parity; calculations based on exchange rates would calculate the Chinese economy as much smaller.
23. Paus (1994) presents a skeptical view of the notion that economic liberalism can provide for long-term high-speed expansion.
24. See especially Esty 1997. Smil 1997 lays out China's current and coming environmental woes. Saywell 1997 addresses the problem of dwindling food stocks. As fleets compete for catches, the region may be heading into an era of fish wars. Niu and Harris 1996 also addresses China's coming environmental constraints.
25. Engardio (1996) discusses China's mercantilist tendencies.
26. See Campbell 1974; Perkins 1968; and Rock 1989, chap. 2.
27. For views that discuss the dilapidated core of the Russian army, see Loshak 1997 and Yurong 1995.
28. For specific and more general arguments that expansion increases demands more than the offsetting gains, see Kittfield 1996.
29. See Kelley 1995; Asmus, Kugler, and Larrabee 1996. On the DOD estimates, see Mann 1997. A comparison of the three estimates is Erlanger 1997. The chief author of the CBO study termed a recent estimate putting the cost at a mere $1.5 billion "ludicrous," Shenon 1998.
30. See Turner 1997.
31. See Schroeder 1994.
32. Helpful reviews of the initial phases of NATO development include Artner 1985. A nice review of the social changes in Germany at the relevant time is Park 1986. Also Baylis 1992 and Kirchner and Sperling 1992.
33. See Zelikow and Rice 1995 and Maier 1997, chaps. 5–6.
34. Posen (1984) provides a helpful exposition of the importance of civil control of military organizations. For a discussion of how the Soviets viewed U.S. policies, see Lockwood 1983.
35. See Ehrlich 1974; Markides 1977; and Mandell 1992.
36. Yeltsin insisted it was inevitable that Eastern and Western Europe be more unified and predicted that NATO will evolve into a single armed force for one free Europe. See *Current Digest of the Soviet Press* 1992a and 1992b.
37. Many in the United States viewed this as a clear signal of future Soviet intentions. See Gaddis 1997. As we know from the debate about the origins of the Cold War, intentions are very important but extremely difficult to divine.
38. See Keylor 1996, chap. 3.
39. For a discussion of U.S. and Russian space issues, and in particular the financial issues involving the Mir space station see Covault 1996; Lawler 1996; Reichhardt 1996.
40. On cooperation between Lockheed and the Russian firm, NPO, see Asher 1997. See also Scott 1997, which notes that this particular project is coming in on time and under budget, unlike many of the governmental programs such as the European space station and the Mir project.
41. Covault (1997) addresses some of the lingering concerns over this type of cooperation.

42. On the joint agreement with Russian Institute to supply electronic systems for aircraft, see *New York Times* 1992 and *Aviation Week & Space Technology* 1993.
43. On Portugal's role in NATO, see Bosgra 1969, and for a review of Greece and Turkey's entry and subsequent crises, see Hart 1990.
44. Secretary Albright's comments reflect her Senate testimony on 23 April 1997 and her House comments, 5 March 1997. See Albright and Obey 1997.
45. A volume that addresses some of the early integration issues in the context of German reunification and Russian democratization is Baranovsky and Spanger 1992.
46. The two contrasting policies for managing relations with China are known as containment and engagement, represented loosely by Bernstein and Munro 1997 and Nathan and Ross 1997. Most recently, see Nye 1997.
47. See Gaddis 1997.
48. See Mahbubani 1993.
49. For a pessimistic view, see Huntington 1996, and for a more optimistic one see Fukuyama 1992.
50. See Monk 1996.
51. See Russett 1993.
52. Alexandr Chudodeyev, Pavel Felgengauer, and Vladimir Abarinov, Russian political analysts, debate the possibility of an alliance between China and Russia, since the Chinese political climate has changed considerably following the death of Deng Xiaoping in *Current Digest of the Post-Soviet Press* 1996.
53. U.S. government estimates put China's military spending as exceeding Japan's for more than a decade. U.S. Arms Control and Disarmament Agency, *World Military Expenditures and Arms Transfers* 1997. In an interview, Chen Jian, spokesman for the Chinese Foreign Ministry, highlighted the tension between Japan and China by noting that Japan decided to stop aid to China for the rest of the 1995 fiscal year because it opposed Chinese nuclear testing programs. Cited *Beijing Review* 1996.
54. A novel view of future security concerns in Asia is Simon 1996. For a more traditional perspective, see Mandelbaum 1995b. Roy 1994 reviews growing fears of increasing Chinese power in East Asia. See also Dreyer 1996.
55. Cronin and Cronin (1996) argue that multilateral containment and engagement will be the only way to manage relations with China in the future — their key point being that not only the United States, but other states as well will have to cooperate in order to prevent future East Asian regional spats from flaring into potentially global crises.
56. Recent problems controlling technology transfers to China highlight the difficulties that the United States will face if it tries to forge ahead alone in its containment policy toward China. For discussion of these problems see Holloway 1996. China bought high-tech American machine tools, ostensibly for civilian use. Instead, it sent them to a weapons factory — exposing U.S. export controls as ineffective.
57. Biddle (1996) argues that a powerful interaction between a major skill imbalance and new technology caused the radical difference between the rate of casualties of Iraqi and coalition forces in the Gulf War. He points out that technology alone is not sufficient to guarantee victory, but that the combination of technological superiority and high skill levels will likely create stunning defeats for unprepared states.
58. The idea that there is a tradeoff between goods for domestic consumption and military security is frequently referred to simplistically as the "guns versus butter" choice. In actuality, the consequences are often complex, indirect, and vary over time and from country to country. Nevertheless, "The price of national vigilance will have to be paid somehow. It may be paid by foregoing current consumption, by depleting past savings, or by mortgaging future economic growth," quoted in Ward, Davis, and Chan 1993, 547. More generally, see Ward, Davis, and Lofdahl 1995 and Chan 1995.
59. See Oneal and Russett 1997 and Russett, Oneal, and Davis 1998. World War I is commonly identified as a counterexample on economic interdependence. Even if the interdependence point is correct, the cited articles indicate that the likelihood of war between two states rises with geographic contiguity, a deterrence situation of power balance rather than dominance, a conflict of alliance ties, autocratic governments in one or both states, and a thin or absent network of international organizations. All these other influences were present in 1914, leaving trade alone as a conflict-mitigating force.

60. Nolan (1996) argues that China cannot have it all — economic gains, political autocracy and a huge army.
61. See Qingshan 1992.
62. Brzezinski (1996) argues that China should be treated with the same great power respect that the Soviet Union was accorded during the Cold War. On the potential reaction to various U.S. policies directed toward China, see Shambaugh 1996.
63. An argument for just this sort of engagement policy is offered by Segal 1996.
64. Fukuyama 1992.
65. The common starting point in this literature is Olson 1971. For more recent treatments of collective action in NATO, see Oneal 1990 and Sandler 1993.
66. See Conybeare 1994. See also Oneal and Diehl 1994 and Murdoch and Sandler 1991.
67. In an interview, Japanese Prime Minister Morihiro Hosokawa argued that there is no present need for a NATO-like security organization in North Asia, reported in Chanda 1993.
68. Whether democratization raises the likelihood of interstate war is hotly disputed. The affirmative case is made by Mansfield and Snyder (1995). Challenges, rebuttals, and counterrebuttals include the correspondence in Mansfield and Snyder 1996; the exchange between Mansfield and Snyder (1997) and Thompson and Tucker (1997); Maoz 1998; and Ward and Gleditsch 1998.
69. See Krain 1997 and Rummel 1997.
70. Przeworski and Limongi 1997.
71. This type of expansion raises the obvious question, if NATO should be willing to include all states that meet certain criteria, why not just use the United Nations to accomplish the same goal of collective security? The key lies in the hierarchical nature of NATO, which matches the hierarchical nature of power in the international system.

Chapter 7: The Asian Challenge

1. We do not address Japan because in the future it is not likely to be able to compete with the United States or China and it is likely to be drawn even closer into the U.S.-led international order. See note 86. The European community also could join the superpower club, but this possibility is nonthreatening since the major and great powers there are satisfied.
2. See Organski, Kugler, and Abdollahian 1995, 169–92.
3. Kristof (1993) states: "The rise of China, if it continues, may be the most important trend in the world for the next century."
4. From Lord 1995, 775. For a parallel assessment by a key official of the U.S. intelligence community, see Gannon 1998.
5. From Jisi 1996, 41.
6. Figure 7.1 is our three-dimensional modification of the original. Mouhang 1995, 19–20. There are many other official and unofficial Chinese views of the U.S. See Pillsbury 2000.
7. It is no exaggeration to assert that any projection of Chinese GDP is fraught with peril. Anyone who has delved into the arcane issues surrounding purchasing power parity (PPP) and exchange rate calculations understands there is no agreed upon standard of measurement. Even among PPP advocates, with expenditure and production approaches, numbers may vary widely. Having examined IMF, World Bank, CIA, ACDA, Department of Commerce, CRS (DRI and McGraw-Hill), Maddison, and Penn World Tables data, we conclude that China, at current growth rates, will pass the United States in GDP in the middle of the first quarter of the twenty-first century. This GDP cross point should not be given inflated importance because it is only a very preliminary measurement of power. For a comprehensive description of estimating techniques and results for China, see Wu 1998; Maddison 1998; and Ren 1997, 28–32. In a 1995 analysis, the Rand Corporation extrapolated Chinese GDP from 1994 to 2015 using their version of PPP and two different scenarios. Assuming stable growth of 4.9 percent, they concluded China would exceed U.S. GDP by 27 percent in 2015. Wolf et al. 1995. The IMF, using PPP, puts the crossover point at 2007. Morrison 1998.

8. Even using our projections of economic parity with the United States by 2015, China per capita GDP, at one-fifth that of the United States at that time, will limit China's ability to convert potential into actual power. See Maddison 1998, 17, for the GDP per-capita projections; the conclusion is ours. Also see the World Bank 1997.

9. Figure 7.2 anticipates continued growth by China at 5.5 percent based on Lemke 1997a, 23–36; and Maddison 1998, 17.

10. There is a good deal of variance in Chinese growth rates depending on the source of the data and the method of calculation (exchange rate vs. purchasing power parity). Virtually all the data sets, however, indicate a decrease in real GDP growth rates year to year from 1992 to 1999. Some long-term Western projections forecast 8 percent growth rates through 2005 and 7 percent rates through 2015. Others, including Maddison and the authors of this volume, use 5.5 percent for the out-years. See Morrison 1996; Ren 1997, 108, 130; Wu 1998; and Maddison 1998.

11. Lardy (1998, 9) concludes that the official data are overstated by 1 to 2 percentage points.

12. Using official data, China's real GDP grew on an average annual basis by 9.4 percent from 1979 to 1998. State Statistical Bureau (various years). Also see Maddison (1998). Growth rate inflation in not just a function of manipulation at the national level. As one Chinese weekly newspaper put it: "The village deceives the township, the township deceives the country — in deception upon deception as a report moves up the hierarchy." Cited by the U.S. Embassy Beijing as from *Liaouang Weekly* #18 as reprinted in Wenzhai Zhoubao (Chengdu), 20 April 1998, 1.

13. Organski, unpublished, 1995.

14. Tax revenues for 1989 were 30 percent of GDP compared to 12 percent in 1998. See "China's Economy," *Economist*, 24 October 1998, 25. See also Maddison 1998, 18. In order to increase revenues, Chinese officials have issued orders to crack down on tax evasion by foreign funded enterprises and to step up collection of taxes from individuals and small businesses. These actions increased revenues in 1999.

15. John C. Gannon, chairman of the National Intelligence Council made the case against fragmentation in a December 1998 speech before the World Affairs Council. Gannon 1998. Also see Lardy 1994, 25–27 for an accurate prediction on this issue. For the interplay of economic and political factors influencing growth, see Arbetman and Kugler 1997 and Bueno de Mesquita and Stokman 1994.

16. The Communist takeover of China also had a profound effect on domestic politics in the United States. It was the second shock after the establishment of Soviet control in Eastern Europe and it fed the hysteria of the McCarthy years. We mention this because there is a strong potential for similar domestic fallout as China climbs the power ladder.

17. The same phenomenon showed up again almost a decade and a half later in Vietnam. The unlearned lesson of what occurred in Korea caused the United States to pay an unnecessarily high price in Vietnam. Organski and Kugler 1980, chap. 2.

18. There is some question how permanent such a change would turn out to be if government policy were to relax.

19. Mastel 1995, 373, asserts that "China's economic reforms will be judged the most important economic event of the (twentieth) century's latter half."

20. State Statistical Bureau 1994–97. *China Statistical Yearbook*: Beijing Statistical Publishing House.

21. A number of authors conclude that China currently is a dissatisfied power including Segal 1993; Roy 1994; and Nathan and Ross 1997, 230.

22. See Benson 1999.

23. This policy is subject to a number of diverse political vulnerabilities including the following: national security (helping to arm the enemy), human rights (placing economic interests above the rights of individuals and groups), religious (failure to open up China to religious freedom), abortion (not protecting the rights of the unborn), environmental (international environmental issues), and jobs (exporting high paying jobs abroad). This unusual coalition of interests, spanning the political spectrum, is showing signs of uniting for operational purposes and may pose a significant resistance point to an open policy of making the creation of a vibrant Chinese marketplace a priority for U.S. foreign policy. See Lee 1998.

24. See Lardy 1995, 1073. Lardy (1996, 12) also states: "Surprising as it might seem under the circumstances (China being awash in foreign capital) China has not been heavily dependent on foreign capital to finance investment and thus to generate the rapid economic growth of the 1990s." U.S. foreign investment in China has averaged about 7.8 percent of total foreign investment since the late 1970s.
25. Yong 1998, S2–3.
26. For a discussion of the role of foreign direct investment in China, see Rosen 1999.
27. See Prime and Park 1997. For geographical and sectoral analysis of foreign direct investment, see Broadman and Sun 1997. For the argument that direct foreign investment is overstated by including investment from Hong Kong firms, see Hayter and Han 1998. See also Yin 1999.
28. Morrison 1998, 3.
29. See Lardy 1998, 214, for the caution that extrapolating Chinese growth rates into the future "is highly problematic."
30. Maddison 1998, 17, 159; State Statistical Bureau, annually from 1991; and Morrison 1996, 5. The current Chinese strategy toward the private and state managed marketplace is called "wen zhu yi tou, fang kai yi pion," or stabilize one end, and let loose the other.
31. Despite this status, U.S. direct investment has been hampered by an apparent Chinese policy of denying U.S. firms contracts on the Yangtze River dam project and in the nuclear energy field, both multibillion-dollar opportunities.
32. Maddison 1998, 16; and Radelet and Sachs 1997, 46.
33. For the role of princelings, see Cheng and White 1998. See also Forney 1999.
34. See Karmel 1997; Joffe 1995; Bickford 1994; Woon 1993; Valdecanas 1995; Cheung 1996; Sun 1997; and Maddison 1998.
35. See Pomfret 1998a.
36. See Pei 1998.
37. China estimates its floating population at 80 million or more. Western sources cite 100 to 150 million. See West 1997; Tenent 1997, 3; and Prybyla 1996, 20. The U.S. Embassy in Beijing, citing Chinese sources, gives a range of 130 to 300 million. U.S. Embassy-Beijing 1997.
38. For a discussion of domestic disorder in China and its constraint on Chinese power, see Austin 1995.
39. This may in part account for the inflated official growth estimates for 1998.
40. See Yost 1997 for an outline of U.S. policies designed to produce incentives for Chinese internal policy reforms.
41. For supporting arguments, see Cable and Ferdinand 1994. For a critique of interdependence, see Roy 1994. For an alternative strategy called by its author "calm balancing," see Heilbrunn 1995.
42. A full list of foreign policy players would include intellectuals, social and religious leaders among others. Their power varies with the size of their constituencies and with the function that they perform. The three groups of players we focus on here are clearly the most important for our purposes. See Organski and Tammen in Kugler and Lemke 1996.
43. Such a coalition may not be impossible to achieve. Even the highly conservative Heritage Foundation published a paper arguing that "integrating China into the global economy is more likely to advance long-range U.S. interests by transforming the PRC into a more peaceful and prosperous member of the family of nations." O'Quinn 1997, 2. Despite its ominous title — *The Coming Conflict with China* — similar conclusions are offered in Bernstein and Munro 1997.
44. The evidence for this statement is both structural (creation of a National Economic Council at a level with the National Security Council) and behavioral (economic issues almost invariably win over security issues in the current political climate).
45. Recognizing, of course, that a portion of the business community profited from the increased military expenditures during that period.
46. Organski and Tammen in Kugler and Lemke 1996, 355.
47. See Garten 1997 for an assessment of the increasingly important role of commercial transactions in U.S. foreign policy.

48. For an appreciation of the importance of the U.S. business community as a component of U.S. foreign policy toward China see Bartley 1997. For the business role in the WTO vote, see Kaiser and Mufson 1999.

49. See the Weinberger tests outlined by Organski and Tammen in Kugler and Lemke 1996.

50. Cronin and Cronin (1996) make the case against containment.

51. L. Li (1997) explores the bargaining and bureaucratic maneuvering between the rich provinces and the central government.

52. The United States must resist the temptation to "assist" the decentralization process by any covert means. Difficult to carry out at best, if discovered, such U.S. assistance could lead to a resurgence of central government controls.

53. For a review of China's current legal reforms, see Pei 1998.

54. See Mufson 1998.

55. See Lardy 1998, 20; and Pei 1999.

56. For evidence of the territorial imperative, see Vasquez 1993; Hensel 1996; and Huth 1996. For the argument that positive economic relations and negative security relations cannot guarantee peace, see Benson 1999.

57. In addition, the United States also helped China expel an invader during World War II.

58. China shares multiple territorial claims with its neighbors including disputes over Diaoyu Island (Japan, China and Taiwan); Outer Mongolia (historical Chinese claims against Russia); the Spratley Islands (Taiwan, Vietnam, Philippines, Malaysia, Brunei); and boundary questions with Tajikistan and North Korea. This century China has engaged in conflicts with Russia, India, Japan, Vietnam, South Korea, Taiwan, and the United States, a formidable list. According to Nathan and Ross (1997), China's territory overlaps with that of twenty-four other governments. Also see Kim 1992, 248; Garver 1993; Sutter 1994; and Nathan and Ross 1997, 7–10.

59. See Johnston 1998.

60. See Tucker 1996.

61. This conclusion flows from the formal proofs and work of Abdollahian (1996) and Alsharabati (1997).

62. We share with most of the policy world the perception that these justifications for inaction are questionable. Chinese public and private statements, military preparations, and various historical and cultural imperatives weigh heavily on the other side of the equation. We should not overlook the possibility, however, that China may be prepared to wait out the development cycle until Taiwan can be reincorporated at little or no cost.

63. Tucker (1996, 177) early on suggested an accommodation might be engineered in discussions between the Taiwan Straits Exchange Foundation and China's Association for Relations Across the Straits. President Jiang Zemin met with Taiwanese businessman Koo Chen-fu in October 1998 as a conclusion to two rounds of cross-straits talks started in 1995. The United States supports this dialog. See Shirk 1998.

64. Leng (1998) provides an evaluation of the political context of Taiwanese investment in China.

65. By 1999 Taiwanese investment totaled $35 billion. China has eagerly sought Taiwanese investments and this economic relationship appears to exist outside of the contentious political arena but Chinese military threats and tensions do cause slowdowns in the investment stream. See Morrison 1995.

66. See Freeman 1998, which argues that Taiwanese leaders believe that the U.S. Congress would "quickly overwhelm a reluctant administration" when faced with Chinese military action even in the case of a declaration of independence.

67. As a consequence of the Taiwan Relations Act of 1979, Taiwan operates in the United States under the umbrella of the Taipei Economic and Cultural Representative (formerly the Coordinating Council for North American Affairs), an organization that absorbed the resources of the former embassy but is quite restricted in its official activities.

68. For example, see "Lawmakers Wooed by Taiwan Trips," in The Hill 3, no. 45 (13 November 1996): 1, 26. This article indicates that twenty members of Congress and 124 staffers took free trips to Taiwan in 1996 alone. Also see Lampton 1998. By way of full disclosure, one author of this book, Ronald L. Tammen, was a participant in one of these trips to Taiwan when chief of staff to Senator William Proxmire (D-Wis.).

69. Taiwan mounted a sophisticated $5 million lobbying campaign in support of a 396–0 tally in the U.S. House of Representatives that put pressure on the administration to allow this visit.

70. We recognize that there are sufficient signals coming from conservative political leaders and others that the Taiwanese may be seduced into thinking the United States will intervene under all circumstances including a declaration of independence. Balancing those perceptions, we believe private high-level messages from the United States carry a clear negative response. This then becomes a question of what evidence the Taiwanese choose to believe. The adoption of the "Three Nos" formula by President Clinton during his visit to China in June 1998 may have reinforced the conclusion that the United States is an unreliable supporter of last resort.

71. President Lee Teng-hui's 9 July 1999 statement that Taiwan and China should negotiate in the future on the basis of a "special state-to-state relationship" may be read as an incremental initiative. Other possible rationales for this statement are offered by Shambaugh (1999).

72. See Pomfret 1998b.

73. Downs and Saunders (1999) point out that the Chinese have taken the long-range view in the Diaoyu Island dispute with Japan — thereby demonstrating a willingness to be patient until growing Chinese power forces a change in Japanese resolve.

74. Chinese officials often make the observation that at present the United States is the world's only superpower. See Jisi 1996 and R. Li 1997, which also cites various Chinese scholars. For other views, see Pillsbury 2000.

75. Ironically, this is a derivative of a similar Japanese saying from 1868, from Godwin 1998, 172. This in turn may have a Chinese ancestry.

76. For an analysis of China's realist perspective which the author argues currently dominates political thinking, see Deng 1998. Also Garver 1996.

77. See Pomfret 1999.

78. Christensen (1996, 49) puts forward a strategic calculation: "Taiwanese democracy and Taiwanese independence are logically and morally separate issues.... China's a huge 55 times larger than Taiwan."

79. See Swain 1997.

80. Former Reagan administration Assistant Secretary of Defense Richard Perle draws the parallel by saying: "China is laying the foundation for an aggressive claim to preeminence in the Pacific. It ought to be very clear that this is a catastrophe for all of us, and could foreshadow a Cold War as bad as the last." Quoted in "Myths About China's Military Might," *Washington Post*, 18 May 1997, C4.

81. Chas. W. Freeman Jr. makes the point that following the collapse of the Soviet Union, the United States entered "a difficult period of what can be called *enemy deprivation.*"

82. Garrett and Glazer (1996) argue that "A tough confrontational stance toward China by the United States and Japan will likely be interpreted in Beijing as adoption of a containment strategy. This would likely fuel Chinese xenophobia and strident Chinese nationalism."

83. Davison 1999.

84. The U.S. business community, concerned about deteriorating U.S.-Chinese relations, has created a lobbying organization named the Business Coalition for U.S.-China Trade with a membership of more than one thousand multinational corporations and trade associations. See Blustein 1997. Official statements on U.S.-Chinese relations interestingly enough have been centered at the Department of Defense where several secretaries of defense have taken the lead.

85. Brinkley (1997) argues the case as follows: "Far into the next century the various trade agreements ... will advance Washington's global agenda while promoting American domestic renewal."

86. See Roy 1997, 134, for the argument that Chinese hegemony in the Asia Pacific region might be viewed by nations there as more peaceful than that of the United States. In contrast to defection by some nations, we expect Japan to move closer to the United States as Chinese power grows. Consequently U.S. influence over Japan also will increase in the next decades. For a supportive argument, see Garrett and Glaser 1997, 400.

87. Population estimates vary with the source and estimating technique, but based on the U.S Bureau of the Census International Data Base, India exceeded the 1 billion level in 1999.

88. Assuming a U.S. growth rate of 3 percent and an Indian growth rate of 4.5 percent, India's economy could jump to twice the size of the current U.S. economy by 2050, yet it would be restrained by a relatively low per-capita income of around $12,000. These calculations assume high economic and low population growth and thus are the most favorable of a larger range of possibilities including stagnation and modest growth. See Hammond 1998.

89. The Indian middle class is defined quite differently than that of the United States. The following table, based on an interview with Indian businessmen, provides one basis for defining the Indian middle class. Note that the totals do not match the 1 billion cited in the text. See National War College 1999, 116.

Classification	Households	Number of Persons	Purchasing
Very rich	1,000,000	6,000,000	all items
Consumers	30,000,000	150,000,000	furniture/car
Climbers	50,000,000	275,000,000	television
Aspirants	50,000,000	275,000,000	bicycle/radio
Destitute	35,000,000	210,000,000	food

90. Scalapino (1999) states: "India is a nation whose time is coming … the probabilities are that India will assume a much higher regional and global posture by the early part of the twenty-first century. And it may well be in South Asia where the highest risks of major conflict will exist."

91. The three primary disputes were NEFA (North East Frontier Province) in the east, the Indo-Tibetan middle sector, and Ladakh in the west.

92. The inflation rate had increased to 17 percent; the external debt had soared to about $70 billion; and the debt service ratio was 32 percent of GDP. The Nehruvian approach was the foundation upon which India's strategy of economic development was based. The key elements of this strategy were central planning, socialist ownership of the means of production through the nationalization of heavy industry and utilities and the prioritization of heavy industry over agriculture. Accordingly, investments went directly into capital goods production. Savings were encouraged by restricting the availability of consumer goods and imports were curtailed through the imposition of tariffs and quotas. The growth of heavy industry was slow, rates of savings and investment were not as high as anticipated, and agricultural performance was largely unimpressive. Levels of unemployment were high and deficit financing had created inflationary trends within the economy. In addition, the Soviet Union had collapsed, thereby depriving India of a guaranteed market for its goods when the international trend moved toward market reform.

93. Imports of technology, raw materials and capital goods were liberalized, the currency was devalued, there was a reduction in licensing and controls, capital threshold limits were removed, and a previously regulated economy was opened to foreign investment.

94. Both countries continue to engage in discussions via a Joint Working Group that meets periodically.

95. There is a wide range of scholarly opinion and policy options on this subject. For example, Segal (1996) offers a critique of both containment and engagement. He suggests that Chinese behavior can be moderated by outside pressure, a strategy he calls "constrainment." Segal (1995) also argues that multilateral agreements would best serve the purpose of integrating China into the world community. Heilbrunn (1995) concludes that "Neither the engagers nor the containers, however, capture the realities of the U.S.-China relationship. Both are frozen in fossilized cold war models of economic détente or military confrontation. They have merely replaced the old 'who lost China' debate with a 'who can win China' debate." He recommends a policy of "calm balancing." Shambaugh (1995, 245) categorizes three U.S. viewpoints on China as being: engagement, confrontation, and destabilization. According to Oksenberg (1991, 10), the Chinese remain skeptical if not hostile to the theory of interdependency with its acceptance of international norms and regimes developed essentially without Chinese

participation. For support of this argument note Wang Jisi's statement: "In essence, China's leading political analysts doubt the virtue of what is referred to in the West as interdependence and globalization. They tend to see the world as increasingly chaotic and assertive nationalism and fierce economic competition as the main features of international relations. In their eyes world politics continues to involve a zero-sum game, and a hierarchy of power inevitably exists within which the more powerful nations dominate the weak." Quoted in S. Kim (1996, 12). Shambaugh (1996) also argues that China will be difficult to engage because it is insular, defensive in character, and subject to the strong influence of nationalism.

96. Shambaugh (1995, 245) concludes that the "domestic politics in each country will continue to have a profound — even defining — impact on (U.S.-China) relations."

97. There is considerable evidence of rising Chinese nationalism. See Zhang and Qiang (1996). Xiaobo Zhang and Ming Zhang edited the widely popular nationalistic 1996 Chinese book *China Can Say No — Political and Emotional Choices in the Post-Cold War Era;* Also see Ming Zhang 1996 and Oksenberg 1987. Garver (1996) reviews the banned and recalled Chinese book, *China's Grand Strategy: A Blueprint for World Leadership,* which argues that China will be the world's leading power in the third decade of the twenty-first century as a result of its new market economy and rapid growth. The book also posits that the United States will be forced to abandon its protective position toward Taiwan as Chinese power grows.

Chapter 8: The World to Come

1. See the argument advanced by Organski and Tammen 1996 and the references therein.

2. We fully understand the political problems associated with realigning the Security Council. In order for it to be an effective institution, however, we believe its membership should be dynamic — reflecting the reality of actual power distributions.

3. See Russett 1993 and Ray 1995 for excellent summaries.

4. This finding is prominent in the work of Oneal and Russett 1997.

5. Lemke and Reed 1996.

6. The world population shares are as follows: North American 7 percent, South America 6 percent, Europe 11 percent, Africa 11 percent, and Asia 65 percent. This figure is adapted from a presentation at the Milken Institute's Global Conference, 19 March 1999.

7. The current world GDP shares are as follows: North America 30 percent, South American 4 percent, Europe 34 percent, Africa 2 percent, and Asia 30 percent. This figure is again adapted from work by the Milken Institute.

8. The future world GDP shares, based on projections for 2027, are as follows: North America 21 percent, South America 3 percent, Europe 22 percent, Africa 2 percent, and Asia 52 percent. This figure is again adapted from work by the Milken Institute.

Bibliography

Abdollahian, Mark Andrew. 1996. *In Search of Structure: The Nonlinear Dynamics of International Politics*. Ph.D. dissertation, Claremont Graduate University.

Albright, Madeleine, and David Obey. 1997. "Does NATO Enlargement Serve U.S. Interests?" *CQ Researcher* 7 (19): 449.

Aldrich, John H., and Forrest D. Nelson. 1984. *Linear Probability, Logit and Probit Models*. Sage University Paper 45 in Quantitative Applications in the Social Sciences series. Beverly Hills, Calif.: Sage Publications.

Alsharabati, Carole. 1997. *Dynamics of War Initiation*. Ph.D. dissertation, Claremont Graduate University.

Alsharabati, Carole, and Jacek Kugler. 1995. "Structural Deterrence: Dynamic Bargaining and the Stability of Deterrence." Paper presented at the Peace Science Society Meetings, Columbus, Ohio, 13–15 October.

———. 1996. "Prospects for Peace after Bilateral Deterrence." Presented at the Annual Convention of the International Studies Association, San Diego, Calif., 16–20 April.

Arbatov, Alexei. 1996. "Eurasia Letter: A Russian-U.S. Security Agenda." *Foreign Policy* 104 (fall): 102–17.

Arbetman, Marina. 1996. "The Consequences of the American Civil War." In *Parity and War*, edited by Jacek Kugler and Douglas Lemke. Ann Arbor: University of Michigan Press.

Arbetman, Marina, and Jacek Kugler, eds. 1997. *Political Capacity and Economic Behavior*. Boulder, Colo.: Westview Press.

Arbetman, Marina, Jacek Kugler, and A.F.K. Organski. 1997. "Political Capacity and Demographic Change." In *Political Capacity and Economic Behavior*, edited by Marina Arbetman and Jacek Kugler. Boulder, Colo.: Westview Press.

Arms Control Today. 1997. "The Debate over NATO Expansion: A Critique of the Clinton Administration's Responses to Key Questions," 27 (6): 3–12.

Artner, Stephen J. 1985. *A Change of Course: The West German Social Democrats and NATO, 1957–1961*. Westport, Conn.: Greenwood Press.

Asher, James R. 1997. "Lockheed Martin Buys Russian Rocket Engines." *Aviation Week & Space Technology* 146 (26): 24–25.

Asmus, Ronald D., Richard L. Kugler, and Stephen F. Larrabee. 1996. "What Will NATO Enlargement Cost?" *Survival* 38 (3): 5–26.

Austin, Greg. 1995. "China: Domestic Change and Foreign Policy." *Survival* 37: 7–23.

Aviation Week & Space Technology. "Russian Zhukovsky Facility Shows Flight Test Diversity," 138 (24): 66–67.

Bahl, Roy. 1971. "A Regression Approach to Tax Effort and Tax Ratio Analysis." *International Monetary Fund Staff Papers*, vol. 18.

Bairoch, Paul. 1976. "Europe's Gross National Product: 1800–1975." *Journal of European History* 2: 269–333.

Baranovsky, Vladimir, and Hans-Joachim Spanger, eds. 1992. *In From the Cold: Germany, Russia, and the Future of Europe.* Boulder, Colo.: Westview.

Barro, Robert J., and Xavier Sala-I-Martin. 1992. "Convergence." *Journal of Political Economy* 100 (2): 223–51.

Bartley, Robert L. 1997. "China: Taking a Long View." *Wall Street Journal* (10 June), 1, 18.

Baylis, John. 1992. *The Diplomacy of Pragmatism: Britain and the Formation of NATO, 1942–1949.* Hampshire, England: Macmillan.

Beijing Review. 1996. "Joint Statement by the People's Republic of China and the Russian Federation," 39 (20): 6–8.

Bennett, D. Scott, and Allan C. Stam III. 1998. "The Declining Advantages of Democracy: A Combined Model of War Outcomes and Duration." *Journal of Conflict Resolution* 42: 344–66.

Benson, Michelle. 1998. "Measuring the International Status Quo: The Hegemon vs. the Stag Hunt." Paper presented at the Annual Meeting of the American Political Science Association, Boston, Mass.: 3–6 September.

———. 1999. *The Ties that Bind: Status Quo Preferences, Democracy and Conflict.* Ph.D. dissertation, Claremont Graduate University.

Berstein, Richard, and Ross H. Munro. 1997. *The Coming Conflict with China.* New York: Knopf.

Bickford, Thomas J. 1994. "The Chinese Military and Its Business Operations." *Asian Survey* 34: 460–74.

Biddle, Stephen. 1996. "Victory Misunderstood: What the Gulf War Tells Us about the Future of Conflict." *International Security* 21 (2): 139–79.

Binnindijk, Hans, and Ronald N. Montaperto. 1998. *Strategic Trends in China.* Washington, D.C.: NDU Press.

Blustein, Paul. 1997. "U.S. Companies Lobby for More China Trade." *Washington Post* (18 March), D1–2.

Bosgra, S.J. 1969. *Portugal and NATO.* Amsterdam: Angola Committee.

Boulding, Kenneth. 1962. *Conflict and Defense.* New York: Harper and Row.

Bremer, Stuart A. 1992. "Dangerous Dyads: Conditions Affecting the Likelihood of Interstate War, 1816–1965." *Journal of Conflict Resolution* 36: 309–41.

Brinkley, Douglas. 1997. "Democratic Enlargement: The Clinton Doctrine." *Foreign Policy* 106: 111–27.

Broadman, Harry G., and Xiaolun Sun. 1997. "The Distribution of Foreign Direct Investment in China." *World Economy* 20: 339–61.

Brodie, Bernard. 1959. *Strategy in the Missile Age.* Princeton: Princeton University Press.

———, ed. 1946. *The Absolute Weapon.* New York: Harcourt, Brace and Company.

Brown, Michael E. 1995. "The Flawed Logic of NATO Expansion." *Survival* 37 (1): 34–52.

Brzezinski, Zbigniew. 1996. "Geopolitical Pivot Points." *Washington Quarterly* 19 (4): 209–16.

Bueno de Mesquita, Bruce. 1981. *The War Trap.* New Haven: Yale University Press.

———. 1984. "A Critique of 'A Critique of *The War Trap.*'" *Journal of Conflict Resolution* 28: 341–60.

Bueno de Mesquita, Bruce, and David Lalman. 1992. *War and Reason*. New Haven: Yale University Press.

Bueno de Mesquita, Bruce, David Newman, and Alvin Rabushka. 1985. *Forecasting Political Events*. New Haven: Yale University Press.

———. 1996. *Red Flag Over Hong Kong*. Chatham, N.J.: Chatham House Publishers.

Bueno de Mesquita, Bruce, and William H. Riker. 1982. "An Assessment of the Merits of Selective Nuclear Proliferation." *Journal of Conflict Resolution* 26: 283–306.

Bueno de Mesquita, Bruce, and Randolph Siverson. 1995. "War and the Survival of Political Leaders." *American Political Science Association* 89 (4): 841–55.

Bueno de Mesquita, Bruce, and Frans Stokman. 1994. *European Community Decision Making*. New Haven: Yale University Press.

Cable, Vincent, and Peter Ferdinand. 1994. "China as an Economic Giant: Threat or Opportunity." *International Affairs* 70: 243–61.

Campbell, C.S. 1974. *From Revolution to Rapprochement: The United States and Great Britain, 1783–1900*. New York: Wiley.

Caves, Richard E., Jeffrey A. Frankel, and Ronald W. Jones. 1999. *World Trade and Payments*. Reading, Mass.: Addison-Wesley.

Chan, Steve. 1995. "Grasping the Peace Dividend: Some Propositions on the Conversion of Swords into Plowshares." *Mershon International Review* 39 (1): 53–95.

———. 1996. "In Search of the Democratic Peace: Problems and Promise." *Mershon International Studies Review* 41 (1): 59–92.

Chanda, Nayan. 1993. "The View From Japan," *Far Eastern Economic Review* 156 (48): 14.

Chelliah, R. 1971. "Trends in Taxation in Developing Countries." *International Monetary Fund Staff Papers*, vol. 18.

Chen, Baizhu, J. Kimball Dietrich, and Yi Feng. 2000. *Financial Market Reform in China*. Boulder, Colo.: Westview Press.

Cheng, Li, and Lynn White. 1998. "The Fifteenth Central Committee of the Chinese Communist Party." *Asian Survey* 38: 231–64.

Cheung, Tai Ming. 1996. "Can PLA Inc. Be Tamed?" *Institutional Investor* 7: 41.

Ching, Frank. 1996. "Sino-Russian Pact a Good Sign." *Far Eastern Economic Review* 159 (21): 40.

Christensen, Thomas J. 1996. "Chinese Realpolitik." *Foreign Affairs* 75: 37–52.

Christensen, Thomas J., and Jack Snyder. 1990. "Chain Gangs and Passed Bucks: Predicting Alliance Patterns in Multipolarity." *International Organization* 44 (2): 137–68.

Churchill, Winston. 1955. "Defense Through Deterrents." *Vital Speeches* 21: 1090–92.

Conybeare, John A.C. 1994. "The Portfolio Benefits of Free Riding in Military Alliances." *International Studies Quarterly* 38 (3): 405–19.

Covault, Craig. 1996. "Mir Assembly Nears Finale," *Aviation Week & Space Technology* 144 (18): 29–30.

———. 1997. "Zenit Explosion Hits Military, Civil Projects," *Aviation Week & Space Technology* 146 (22): 34.

Cronin, Audrey Kurth, and Patrick M. Cronin. 1996. "The Realistic Engagement of China." *Washington Quarterly* 19: 141–69.

Current Digest of the Post-Soviet Press. 1992a. "Military Alliances: From Cold War to Security." 43 (51): 21–22.

Current Digest of the Post-Soviet Press. 1992b. "Military Alliances: Russia Wants to Join NATO." 43 (52): 19.

Current Digest of the Post-Soviet Press. 1996. "Yeltsin, China's Jiang Call for 'Multipolar' World." 49 (17): 1–5.

Current Digest of the Post-Soviet Press. 1997. "Russia, NATO Agree on Act Formalizing Relations." 49 (20): 1–5.

Davison, Sarah. 1999. "Anti-China Mood a Threat to Asian Security-Perry." *Reuters* (22 March).

de Soysa, Indra, John R. Oneal, and Yong-Hee Park. 1997. "Testing Power Transition Theory Using Alternative Measures of National Capabilities," *Journal of Conflict Resolution* 41: 509–28.

Dean, Jonathan. 1997. "The NATO Mistake: Expansion for All the Wrong Reasons." *Washington Monthly* 29 (7): 35–38.

Deng, Yong. 1998. "The Chinese Conception of National Interest in International Relations." *China Quarterly* 154: 308–29.

Dugherty, James E., and Robert L. Pfaltzgraff Jr. 1996. *Contending Theories of International Relations: A Comprehensive Survey*. New York: Longman.

Doherty, Carroll J. 1996. "Pact with Russia Eases Way for NATO Expansion." *Congressional Quarterly Weekly Report* 55 (20): 1149.

Domke, William K. 1988. *War in the Changing Global System*. New Haven: Yale University Press.

Domke, William K., Richard C. Eichenberg, and Catherine M. Kelleher. 1987. "Consensus Lost? Domestic Politics and the 'Crisis' in NATO." *World Politics* 39: 382–407.

Doran, Charles. 1991. *Systems in Crisis*. New York: Cambridge University Press.

Downs, Erica Strecker, and Philip C. Sanders. 1999. "Legitimacy and the Limits of Nationalism." *International Security* 23: 114–46.

Dreyer, June Teufel. 1996. "Regional Security Issues — Contemporary China: The Consequences of Change." *Journal of International Affairs* 49 (2): 391–411.

Economist. 1998. "China's Economy" (24 October): 25.

Efird, Brian. 2000. *Formal Dynamics of Power Transitions*. Ph.D. dissertation, Claremont Graduate University.

Efird, Brian, and Yi Feng. 1999. "Assessing the Economic Consequences of Conflict." Paper presented at the annual meeting of the Midwest Political Science Association, Chicago, 15–17 April.

Efird, Brian, and Gaspare Genna. 2000. "Power, Satisfaction, and Regional Integration." Paper presented at the annual meeting of the Midwest Political Science Association, Chicago, 14–16 April.

Efird, Brian, and Jacek Kugler. 1999. "Formal Dynamics of Power Transitions." Paper presented at the annual meeting of the American Political Science Association, Atlanta, 1–5 September.

Ehrlich, Thomas. 1974. *Cyprus 1958–1967: International Crises and the Role of Law*. Oxford: Oxford University Press.

Engardio, Pete. 1996. "Global Tremors from an Unruly Giant." *Business Week* 3465 (4 March): 59–62.

Erlanger, Steven. 1996. "U.S. Warns Three Nations on Missile Technology Sale: Is China Seeking Soviet Rocket Secrets?" *New York Times* 145 (22 May), A9.

———. 1997. "A War of Numbers Emerges Over Cost of Enlarging NATO." *New York Times* (13 October): A1.

Esty, Daniel. 1997. *Sustaining the Asia Pacific Miracle: Environmental Protection and Economic Integration.* Washington, D.C.: Institute for International Economics.

Fearon, James D. 1994. "Signaling Versus the Balance of Power and Interests." *Journal of Conflict Resolution* 38: 236–69.

Feng, Yi. 1994. "Trade, Conflict and Alliances: An Empirical Study." *Peace and Defense Economics* 5 (4): 301–13.

———. 1997. "Democracy, Political Stability, and Economic Growth." *British Journal of Political Science* 27: 391–418.

———. Forthcoming. *Democracy, Governance, and Economic Performance.*

Feng, Yi, Jacek Kugler, and Paul Zak. 2000. "The Politics of Fertility and Economic Development." *International Studies Quarterly.*

Feng, Yi, and Paul Zak. 1999. "The Determinants of Democratic Transitions." *Journal of Conflict Resolution* 43: 162–77.

Fischer, David A.V., and William C. Potter. 1996. "NATO Expansion: The March of Folly." *Moscow News* 14 (11 April): 5.

Foy, Colm, and Angus Maddison. 1999. "China: A World Economic Leader?" *OECD Observer* 215: 1–4.

Freeman, Chas. W., Jr. 1998. "Preventing War in the Taiwan Strait: Restraining Taiwan — And Beijing." *Foreign Affairs* 77: 6–11.

Fukuyama, Francis. 1992. *The End of History and the Last Man.* New York: Free Press.

Fulghum, David. 1996. "China Buys SU-27 Rights from Russia." *Aviation Week & Space Technology* 144 (7): 60.

Gaddis, John Lewis. 1987. *The Long Peace.* New York: Oxford University Press.

———. 1997. *We Now Know: Rethinking Cold War History.* New York: Oxford University Press.

Gannon, John C. 1998. *"The Outlook for China."* Reading, Pa.: World Affairs Council.

Garrett, Banning, and Bonnie S. Glaser. 1995. "Chinese Perspectives on Nuclear Arms Control." *International Security* 20 (3): 43–78.

———. 1996. "China and the Great Powers in the Asia-Pacific: Perspectives from Beijing." Paper presented at the Conference on China into the Twenty-first Century: Strategic Partner and/or Peer Competitor, Army War College, Carlisle, Pa., 23–25 April.

———. 1997. "Chinese Apprehensions about Revitalization of the U.S.-Japan Alliance." *Asian Survey* 37: 383–402.

Garten, Jeffrey E. 1997. "Business and Foreign Policy," *Foreign Affairs* 76: 67–79.

Garver, John W. 1993. *Foreign Relations of the People's Republic of China.* Englewood Cliffs, N.J.: Prentice Hall.

———. 1996. "China as Number One." *China Journal* 39: 61–66.

Gelpi, Christopher. 1997. "Democratic Diversions: Governmental Structure and the Externalization of Domestic Conflict." *Journal of Conflict Resolution* 41: 255–82.

Gibelterra, John. 1998. "Nuclear Proliferation, Technology, and the Status Quo." Ph.D. dissertation, Claremont Graduate University.

Gilpin, Robert. 1981. *War and Change in World Politics.* New York: Cambridge University Press.

Godwin, Paul. 1998. "Force and Diplomacy: China Prepares for the Twenty-First Century." In *China and the World,* edited by Samuel S. Kim. Boulder, Colo.: Westview Press.

Goldgeier, James. 1998. "NATO Expansion: The Anatomy of a Decision." *Washington Quarterly* 21 (1): 85–102.

Goodby, James E. 1998. *Europe Undivided: The New Logic of Peace in U.S.-Russian Relations.* Washington, D.C.: U.S. Institute of Peace Press.

Gowa, Joanne. 1989. *Closing the Gold Window: Domestic Politics and the End of Bretton Woods.* Ithaca, N.Y.: Cornell University Press.

———. 1994. *Allies, Adversaries, and International Trade.* Princeton: Princeton University Press.

Gowa, Joanne, and Edward D. Mansfield. 1993. "Power Politics and International Trade." *American Political Science Association* 87 (June): 408–20.

Grieco, Joseph M. 1988. "Realist Theory and the Problem of International Cooperation: Analysis with an Amended Prisoner's Dilemma Model." *Journal of Politics* 50 (3): 600–624.

Grieco, Joseph M., Robert Powell, and Duncan Snidal. 1993. "The Relative-Gains Problem for International Cooperation." *American Political Science Review* 87 (3): 729–43.

Hammand, Allen. 1998. *Which World? Scenarios for the 21st Century.* Washington, D.C.: Island Press.

Harries, Owen. 1993. "The Collapse of the 'West.'" *Foreign Affairs* 72 (4): 41–53.

Hart, Parker T. 1990. *Two NATO Allies at the Threshold of War: Cyprus, a Firsthand Account of Crisis Management, 1965–1968.* Durham, N.C.: Duke University Press.

Hayter, Roger, and Sun Sheng Han. 1998. "Reflections on China's Open Policy Towards Foreign Direct Investment." *Regional Studies* 32: 1–16.

Heilbrunn, Jacob. 1995. "The New Cold War." *New Republic* 213: 27–30.

Hensel, Paul R. 1994. "One Thing Leads to Another: Recurrent Militarized Disputes in Latin America." *Journal of Peace Research* 31: 281–97.

———. 1996. "Charting a Course to Conflict: Territorial Issues and Interstate Conflict, 1816–1992." *Conflict Management and Peace Science* 15: 43–74.

Hill. 1996. "Lawmakers Wooed by Taiwan Trips." Vol. 3 (45): 1, 26.

Holloway, Nigel. 1996. "Playing for Keeps." *Far Eastern Economic Review* 159 (6): 1416.

———. 1997. "Brothers in Arms: The U.S. Worries about Sino-Russian Military Cooperation." *Far Eastern Economic Review* 160 (11): 20–21.

Holloway, Nigel, and Charles Bickers. 1997 "China's Buying Binge in Moscow's Armory." *World Press Review* 44 (6): 10–11.

Houweling, Henk, and Jan Siccama. 1988. "Power Transitions as a Cause of War." *Journal of Conflict Resolution* 32 (1): 87–102.

Hunt, W. Ben. 1990. "Port Access and Arms Sales." *Journal of Conflict Resolution* 34 (2): 335–65.

Huntington, Samuel P. 1989. "No Exit: The Errors of Endism." *The National Interest* 17: 3–11.

———. 1993. "Why International Primacy Matters." *International Security* 17 (4): 68–83.

———. 1996.*The Clash of Civilizations and the Remaking of World Order.* New York: Simon and Schuster.

———. 1997. "The Erosion of American National Interest." *Foreign Affairs* 76: 28–49.

Huth, Paul K. 1996. *Standing Your Ground.* Ann Arbor: University of Michigan Press.

Huth, Paul K., and Bruce M. Russett. 1984. "What Makes Deterrence Work? Cases from 1900–1980," *World Politics* 36:496–526.

———. 1990. "Testing Deterrence Theory: Rigor Makes a Difference." *World Politics* 42: 466–501.

———. 1993. "General Deterrence Between Enduring Rivals: Testing Three Competing Models." *American Political Science Review* 87 (1): 61–73.

Hwang, Young-Bae. 1993. *The Search for Alliance Stability.* Ph.D. dissertation, Vanderbilt University.

Intriligator, Michael, and Dagobert Brito. 1981. "Nuclear Proliferation and the Probability of War." *Public Choice* 37: 247–60.

———. 1984. "Can Arms Races Lead to the Outbreak of War?" *Journal of Conflict Resolution* 28: 63–84.

———. 1987. "The Stability of Nuclear Deterrence." In *Exploring the Stability of Deterrence,* edited by Jacek Kugler and Frank Zagare. Denver: GSIS Monograph Series in World Affairs.

Jackman, Robert. 1993. *Power Without Force.* Ann Arbor: University of Michigan Press.

Jervis, Robert. 1991. "The Future of World Politics, Will it Resemble the Past?" *International Security* 16: 39–73.

Jisi, Wang. 1996. "China's Muscular Nationalism," *New Perspectives Quarterly* 13: 41–45.

Joffe, Ellis. 1995. "The PLA and the Chinese Economy." *Survival* 37: 24–43.

Johnson, Alastair Iain. 1995. "China's New Old Thinking: The Concept of Limited Deterrence." *International Security* 20 (3): 5–42.

———. 1998. "China's Militarized Interstate Dispute Behavior 1949–1992: A First Cut at the Data." *China Quarterly* 153: 1–30.

Jones, Daniel M., Stuart A. Bremer, and J. David Singer. 1996. "Militarized Interstate Disputes, 1816–1992." *Conflict Management and Peace Science* 15: 163–213.

Kaiser, Robert G., and Steven Mufson. 1999. "U.S. Business Lobby Poised for China Trade Deal." *Washington Post* (14 November): 1, 27.

Karmel, Solomon M. 1997. "The Chinese Military's Hunt for Profits." *Foreign Policy* 107: 102–13.

Kelley, Charles T. 1995. *Admitting New Members: Can NATO Afford the Costs?* Santa Monica, Calif.: Rand Corporation.

Keohane, Robert. 1984. *After Hegemony.* Princeton: Princeton University Press.

———, ed. 1986. *Neorealism and Its Critics.* New York: Columbia University Press.

Keohane, Robert, and Joseph Nye. 1977. *Power and Interdependence: World Politics in Transition.* Boston: Little, Brown.

Keylor, William R. 1996. *The Twentieth Century World: An International History,* 3d ed. Oxford: Oxford University Press.

Keynes, John Maynard. 1920. *The Economic Consequences of the Peace.* London: Macmillan.

Kim, Samuel S. 1996. "China's Quest for Security in the Post-Cold War World." Paper presented at the Conference on China into the Twenty-first Century: Strategic Partner and/or Peer Competitor, Army War College, Carlisle, Pa., 23–25 April.

Kim, Woosang. 1989. "Power, Alliance, and Major Wars, 1816–1975." *Journal of Conflict Resolution* 33: 255–73.

———. 1991. "Alliance Transition and Great Power War." *American Journal of Political Science* 35: 833–50.

———. 1992. "Power Transitions and Great Power War from Westphalia to Waterloo." *World Politics* 45: 153–72.

———. 1996. "Power Parity, Alliance, and War from 1648–1975." In *Parity and War,* edited by Jacek Kugler and Douglas Lemke. Ann Arbor: University of Michigan Press.

Kim, Woosang, and James Morrow. 1992. "When Do Power Shifts Lead to War?" *American Journal of Political Science* 36 (4): 896–922.

Kindleberger, Charles. 1973. *The World in Depression, 1929–1939.* Los Angeles: University of California Press.

Kinsella, David. 1994. "Conflict in Context: Arms Transfers and Third World Rivalries During the Cold War." *American Journal of Political Science* 38: 557–81.

———. 1995. "Nested Rivalries: Superpower Competition, Arms Transfers, and Regional Conflict, 1950–1990." *International Interactions* 21: 109–25.

Kirchner, Emil J., and James Sperling. 1992. *The Federal Republic of Germany and NATO: 40 Years After.* London: Macmillan.

Kissinger, Henry. 1957. *Nuclear Weapons and Foreign Policy.* New York: Harper.

Kittfield, James A. 1996. "A Larger NATO Means Bigger Headaches?" In *NATO and the Changing World Order: An Appraisal by Scholars and Policymakers,* edited by Kenneth W. Thompson. Lanham, Md.: University Press of America.

———. 1997. "A Larger NATO Means Bigger Headaches?" *National Journal* 29 (29): 1467–69.

Koretsky, Aleksandr. 1996. "China Will Build Russian Planes Itself." *The Current Digest of the Post-Soviet Press* 48 (8): 23–4.

Krain, Matthew. 1997. "State-Sponsored Mass Murder: The Onset and Severity of Genocides and Politicides." *Journal of Conflict Resolution* 41 (3): 331–60.

Krasner, Stephen D. 1976. "State Power and the Structure of International Trade." *World Politics* 28 (3): 317–47.

Kristof, Nicholas D. 1993. "China's Rise." *Foreign Affairs* 72: 59–74.

Kugler, Jacek. 1973. *The Consequences of War*. Ph.D. dissertation, University of Michigan.

———. 1984. "Terror Without Deterrence." *Journal of Conflict Resolution* 28: 470–506.

———. 1996. "Beyond Deterrence: Structural Conditions for a Lasting Peace." In *Parity and War*, edited by Jacek Kugler and Douglas Lemke. Ann Arbor: University of Michigan Press.

———, ed. 1999. *Journal of Conflict Resolution* 43 (Special Issue: "The Democratic Transition Process").

Kugler, Jacek, and Marina Arbetman. 1989a. "Choosing Among Measures of Power: A Review of the Empirical Record." In *Power in World Politics*, edited by Michael Ward and Richard Stoll. Boulder, Colo.: Westview Press.

———. 1989b. "Exploring the Phoenix Factor with the Collective Goods Perspective." *Journal of Conflict Resolution* 33: 84–112.

Kugler, Jacek, and William Domke. 1986. "Comparing the Strength of Nations." *Comparative Political Studies* 19: 39–69.

Kugler, Jacek, and Yi Feng. 1997a. "The Expected Utility Approach to Policy Decision Making: Assessments, Forecasts and Strategies." *International Interactions* 23 (3–4).

Kugler, Jacek, and Yi Feng, eds. 1997b. "Special Issue on Expected Utility." *International Interactions* 23 (3–4).

Kugler, Jacek, and Douglas Lemke. 2000. "The Power Transition Research Program: Assessing Theoretical and Empirical Advances." In *Handbook of War Studies II*, edited by Manus Midlarsky. Ann Arbor: University of Michigan Press.

———, eds. 1996. *Parity and War*. Ann Arbor: University of Michigan Press.

Kugler, Jacek, and A.F.K. Organski. 1989a. "The End of Hegemony?" *International Interactions* 15: 113–28.

———. 1989b. "The Power Transition: A Retrospective and Prospective Evaluation." *Handbook of War Studies*, edited by Manus Midlarsky. Boston: Unwin Hyman.

Kugler, Jacek, and Frank Zagare. 1990. "The Long-Term Stability of Deterrence." *International Interactions* 15: 113–28.

———, eds. 1987. *Exploring the Stability of Deterrence*. Denver: GSIS Monograph Series in World Affairs.

Kugler, Richard L. 1996. *Enlarging NATO: The Russia Factor*. Santa Monica, Calif.: Rand Corporation.

Lampton, David M. 1998. "China." *Foreign Policy* 110: 13–27.

Lardy, Nicholas R. 1994. *China in the World Economy*. Washington, D.C.: Institute for International Economics.

———. 1995. "The Role of Foreign Trade and Investment in China's Economic Transformation." *China Quarterly* 144: 1065–94.

———. 1996. "Economic Engine?" *Brookings Review* 14: 10–15.

———. 1998. *China's Unfinished Economic Revolution*. Washington, D.C.: Brookings Institution Press.

Lawler, Andrew. 1996. "Russian Deal Bolsters the Space Station — at a Price." *Science* 71 (5250): 753–54.

Lebow, Richard Ned. 1994. "The Long Peace, the End of the Cold War, and the Failure of Realism." *International Organization* 48: 249–77.

Lee, Jessica. 1998. "Religious-right Leader Sets Foreign Policy Goals." *USA Today* (14 April): 6A.

Lemke, Douglas. Forthcoming. *Regions of War and Peace.*

———. 1993. *Multiple Hierarchies in World Politics* Ph.D. dissertation, Vanderbilt University.

———. 1995a. "Toward a General Understanding of Parity and War." *Conflict Management and Peace Science* 14: 143–62.

———. 1995b. "The Tyranny of Distance: Redefining Relevant Dyads." *International Interactions* 21: 23–38.

———. 1996. "Small States and War: An Expansion of Power Transition Theory." In *Parity and War,* edited by Jacek Kugler and Douglas Lemke. Ann Arbor: University of Michigan Press.

———. 1997a. "The Continuation of History: Power Transition Theory and the End of the Cold War." *Journal of Peace Research* 34 (1): 23–36.

———. 1997b. "Is the Whole the Sum of Its Parts?: Aggregating Regional Analyses of War." Paper presented at the annual meeting of the Peace Science Society (International), Indianapolis, 21–23 November.

Lemke, Douglas, and Jacek Kugler. 1996. "The Evolution of the Power Transition Perspective." In *Parity and War,* edited by Jacek Kugler and Douglas Lemke. Ann Arbor: University of Michigan Press.

Lemke, Douglas, and William Reed. 1996. "Regime Type and Status Quo Evaluations: Power Transition Theory and the Democratic Peace." *International Interactions* 22 (2): 143–64.

———. 1998. "Power Is Not Satisfaction: A Comment on de Soysa, Oneal and Park." *Journal of Conflict Resolution* (forthcoming).

Lemke, Douglas, and Suzanne Werner. 1996. "Power Parity, Commitment to Change, and War." *International Studies Quarterly* 40: 235–60.

Leng, Tse-Kang. 1998. "Dynamics of Taiwan-Mainland China Economic Relations." *Asian Survey* 38: 494–509.

Levy, Jack S. 1987. "Declining Power and the Preventive Motivation for War." *World Politics* 40: 82–107.

Li, Linda Chelan. 1997. "Provincial Discretion and National Power: Investment Policy in Guongdong and Shanghai, 1978–93."*China Quarterly* 152: 778–804.

Li, Rex. 1997. "China's Investment Environment: The Security Dimension." *Asia Pacific Business Review* 4: 39–62.

Liao, Tim Futing. 1994. *Interpreting Probability Models: Logit, Probit, and Other Generalized Linear Models.* Sage University Paper 101 in Quantitative Applications in the Social Sciences series. Beverly Hills, Calif.: Sage Publications.

Lockwood, Jonathan Samuel. 1983. *The Soviet View of U.S. Strategic Doctrine: Implications for Decision Making.* New Brunswick, N.J.: Transaction Books.

Lord, Winston. 1995. "U.S. Policy Toward China: Security and Military Considerations." Statement before the Subcommittee on East Asian and Pacific Affairs of the Senate Foreign Relations Committee, Washington, D.C., 11 October 1995, *U.S. Department of State Dispatch* 6 (43): 775.

Lorenz, Konrad. 1966. *On Aggression*. New York: Harcourt, Brace, and World.

Loshak, Victor. 1997. "Army Bigger Threat than NATO." *Moscow News* (13 February): 2.

Lucas, Robert. 1988. "On the Mechanics of Economic Development." *Journal of Monetary Economics* 21: 3–32.

Maddison, Angus. 1998. *Chinese Economic Performance in an International Perspective*. Paris: Organization for Economic Cooperation and Development.

Mahbubani, Kishore. 1993. "The Dangers of Decadence: What the Rest Can Teach the West." *Foreign Affairs* 72 (4): 10–14.

Maier, Charles S. 1997. *The Crisis of Communism and the Collapse of East Germany*. Princeton: Princeton University Press.

Mandelbaum, Michael. 1995a. "Preserving the New Peace: The Case Against NATO Expansion." *Foreign Affairs* 74 (3): 9–13.

———, ed. 1995b. *The Strategic Quadrangle: Japan, China, Russia and the United States in East Asia*. New York: Council on Foreign Relations.

Mandell, Brian. 1992. "The Cyprus Conflict: Explaining Resistance to Resolution." In *Cyprus: A Regional Conflict and Its Resolution*, edited by Norma Salem. New York: St. Martin's Press.

Mann, James H. 1999. *About Face: A History of America's Curious Relationship with China from Nixon to Clinton*. New York: Alfred . Knopf.

Mann, Paul. 1997. "Clinton, Senate Duel over NATO Expansion." *Aviation Week & Space Technology* 147 (2): 38–39.

Mansfield, Edward D. 1994. *Power, Trade, and War*. Princeton: Princeton University Press.

Mansfield, Edward D., and Rachel Bronson. 1997. "Alliances, Preferential Trading Arrangements, and International Trade." *American Political Science Review* 91 (1): 94–107.

Mansfield, Edward D., and Jack Snyder. 1995. "Democratization and the Danger of War." *International Security* 20 (1): 5–38.

———. 1997. *Journal of Conflict Resolution* 41 (3): 428–54.

Maoz, Zeev. 1998. "Realist and Cultural Critiques of the Democratic Peace: A Theoretical and Empirical Re-assessment." *International Interactions* 24: 3–89.

Maoz, Zeev, and Bruce M. Russett. 1993. "Normative and Structural Causes of Democratic Peace, 1946–1986,. *American Political Science Review* 87: 624–38.

Markides, Kyriacos C. 1977. *The Rise and Fall of the Cyprus Republic*. New Haven: Yale University Press.

Mastel, Greg. 1995. "A New U.S. Trade Policy toward China." *Washington Quarterly* 19: 189–207.

McGwire, Michael. 1997. *NATO Expansion and European Security*. London: Brasseys.

Mearsheimer, John J. 1990. "Back to the Future: Instability in Europe after the Cold War." *International Security* 15: 5–56.

Merritt, Richard, and Dina Zinnes. 1989. "Alternative Indices of National Power." In *Power in World Politics*, edited by Michael Ward and Richard Stoll. Boulder, Colo.: Westview Press.

Meyer, Stephen. 1984. *The Dynamics of Nuclear Proliferation*. Chicago: University of Chicago Press.

Monk, Paul. 1996. "China's Power Trip." *Far Eastern Economic Review* 159 (12): 28.

Morgan, T. Clifton, and Valerie L. Schwebach. 1997. "Fools Suffer Gladly: The Use of Economic Sanctions in International Crises." *International Studies Quarterly* 41: 27–50.

Morrison, Wayne M. 1995. "China-U.S. Trade Issues." *CRS Issue Brief* IB91121: 1–15. Washington, D.C.

———. 1996. "China-U.S.-Taiwan Economic Relations." *Report for Congress* 96–498E (3 June): 1–41. Washington, D.C.

———. 1998. "China's Economic Conditions." *CRS Issue Brief*. Washington, D.C.

Morrow, James D., Randolph M. Siverson, and Tressa E. Tabares. 1998. "The Political Determinants of International Trade: The Major Powers, 1907–1990." *American Political Science Review* 92: 649–62.

Mouhang, Xue. 1995. "The New World Order: Four Powers and One Superpower?" *Beijing Review* 38: 19–20.

Mufson, Steven. 1998. "A New Day in China?" *Washington Post*, National Weekly Edition (29 June): 6–7.

Mulvenan, James. 1997. *Chinese Military Commerce and U.S. National Security*. Santa Monica, Calif.: Rand Corporation.

Murdoch, James C., and Todd Sandler. 1991. "NATO Burden Sharing and the Forces of Change: Further Observations." *International Studies Quarterly* 35 (1): 109–14.

Nathan, Andrew J., and Robert S. Ross. 1997. *The Great Wall and the Empty Fortress: China's Search for Security*. New York: Norton.

National War College. 1999. *U.S. Regional Security Strategies for 2020*. Washington, D.C.: National War College.

New York Times. 1992. "Allied-Signal's Russian Deal." Vol. 142 (13 October): C5.

Niu, Wen-Yuan, and William Harris. 1996. "China: The Forecast of Its Environmental Situation in the 21st Century." *Journal of Environmental Management* 47 (2): 101–15.

Nolan, Peter. 1996. "Large Firms and Industrial Reform in Former Planned Economies: The Case of China." *Cambridge Journal of Economics* 20 (1): 1–28.

Nye, Joseph S. 1990. *Bound to Lead*. New York: Basic Books.

———. 1997. "China's Re-emergence and the Future of the Asia Pacific." *Survival* 39 (4): 65–79.

O'Quinn, Robert P. 1997. "Beyond the MFN Debate: A Comprehensive Trade Strategy Toward China." *Asian Studies Center Backgrounder* 148, Heritage Foundation (16 May): 1–30.

Oksenberg, Elizabeth, and Michael Oksenberg, eds. 1999. *China Joins the World: Progress and Prospects*. New York: Council on Foreign Relations Press.

Oksenberg, Michael. 1987. "China's Confident Nationalism." *Foreign Affairs* 65: 501–23.

———. 1991. "The China Problem."*Foreign Affairs* 70: 1–16.

Olson, Mancur. 1971. *The Logic of Collective Action: Public Goods and the Theory of Groups.* Cambridge, Mass.: Harvard University Press.

———. 1982. *The Rise and Decline of Nations.* New Haven: Yale University Press.

Oneal, John R. 1990. "The Theory of Collective Action and Burden Sharing in NATO." *International Organization* 44 (3): 379–402.

Oneal, John R., and Paul F. Diehl. 1994. "The Theory of Collective Action and NATO Defense Burdens: New Empirical Tests." *Political Research Quarterly* 47 (2): 373–96.

Oneal, John R., and Bruce M. Russett. 1997. "The Classical Liberals Were Right: Democracy, Interdependence and Conflict, 1950–1985." *International Studies Quarterly* 41: 267–93.

Organski, A.F.K. 1958. *World Politics.* New York: Alfred A. Knopf.

———. 1965. *The Stages of Political Development.* New York: Alfred A. Knopf.

———. 1968. *World Politics,* 2d ed. New York: Alfred A. Knopf.

———. 1990. *The $36 Billion Bargain.* New York: Columbia University Press.

———. 1995. "Expected Utility Analysis: Stability in China." Unpublished paper.

Organski, A.F.K., and Marina Arbetman. 1993. "The Second American Century." In *Behavior, Culture and Conflict in World Politics,* edited by William Zimmerman and Harold K. Jacobson. Ann Arbor: University of Michigan Press.

Organski, A.F.K., and Jacek Kugler. 1977. "The Costs of Major Wars: The Phoenix Factor." *American Political Science Review* 71: 1347–66.

———. 1980. *The War Ledger.* Chicago: University of Chicago Press.

Organski A.F.K., Jacek Kugler, and Mark Abdollahian. 1995. "The Mosaic of International Power: Reflections on General Trends." In *Towards and International Economic and Social History: Essays in Honor of Paul Bairoch,* edited by Bouda Etemed et al. Passe Present.

Organski, A.F.K., Jacek Kugler, Timothy Johnson, and Youssef Cohen. 1984. *Births, Deaths, and Taxes: The Demographic and Political Transitions.* Chicago: University of Chicago Press.

Organski, A.F.K., and Ronald L. Tammen. 1996. "The New Open Door Policy." In *Parity and War,* edited by Jacek Kugler and Douglas Lemke. Ann Arbor: University of Michigan Press.

Organski, Katherine, and A.F.K. Organski. 1961. *Population and World Power.* New York: Alfred A. Knopf.

Park, William. 1986. *Defending the West: A History of NATO.* Boulder, Colo.: Westview Press.

Paus, Eva. 1994. "Economic Growth Through Neoliberal Restructuring? Insights from the Chilean Experience." *Journal of the Developing Areas* 29 (1): 31–56.

Pei, Minxin. 1998. "Is China Democratizing?" *Foreign Affairs* 77: 68–82.

———. 1999. "Is China Unstable? *Foreign Policy Research Institute Wire* 7: 1–4.

Perkins, Bradford. 1968. *The Great Rapprochement: England and the United States, 1985–1914,* New York: Atheneum.

Pillsbury, Michael. 2000. *China Debates the Future Security Environment.* Washington, D.C.: National Defense University Press.

Pollins, Brian. 1989a. "Conflict, Cooperation, and Commerce: The Effects of Inter-national Political Interactions on Bilateral Trade Flows." *American Journal of Political Science* 33 (August): 737–61.

———. 1989b. "Does Trade Still Follow the Flag?" *American Political Science Review* 83 (June): 465–80.

Pomfret, John. 1998. "Jiang Tells Army to End Trade Role." *Washington Post* (23 July): 1, 23.

———. 1998. "Taiwanese Negotiator Jiang Meet in Beijing." *Washington Post* (19 October): 1, 15.

———. 1999. "Protests May Change Chinese Policies." *Washington Post* (16 May): 1, 28.

Posen, Barry. 1984. *The Sources of Military Doctrine: France, Britain and Germany between the World Wars.* Ithaca, N.Y.: Cornell University Press.

Powell, Robert. 1990. *Nuclear Deterrence Theory: The Search for Credibility.* New York: Cambridge University Press.

———. 1991. "Absolute and Relative Gains in International Relations Theory." *American Political Science Review* 85 (4): 1303–20.

———. 1996. "Uncertainty, Shifting Power and Appeasement." *American Political Science Review* 90 (4): 749–64.

Prime, Penelope B., and Jong H. Park. 1997. "China's Foreign Trade and Invest-ment Strategies." *Business Economics* 32: 29–35.

Prybyla, Jan S. 1996. "China as an Asian Economic Power." Paper presented at the Conference on China into the Twenty-first Century: Strategic Partner and/or Peer Competitor, Army War College, Carlisle, Pa., 23–25 April.

Przeworski, Adam, and Fernando Limongi. 1997. "Modernization: Theories and Facts." *World Politics* 49 (2): 155–83.

Pushkov, Alexei K. 1997. "Don't Isolate Us: A Russian View of NATO Expansion." *National Interest* 47 (Spring): 58–62.

Radelet, Steven, and Jeffrey Sachs. 1997. "Asia's Reemergence." *Foreign Affairs* 176: 44–59.

Rathjens, George W., and George B. Kistiakowsky. 1969. "Limitation of Strategic Arms." In *Progress in Arms Control,* edited by Bruce M. Russett and Bruce G. Blair. San Francisco: W.H. Freeman and Company, 1979.

Ray, James Lee. 1995. *Democracy and International Conflict.* Columbia: University of South Carolina Press.

Ray, James Lee, and Bruce M. Russett. 1996. "The Future as Arbiter of Theoretical Controversies." *British Journal of Political Science* 26 (October): 441–70.

Ray, James Lee, and Ayse Vural. 1986. "Power Disparities and Paradoxical Conflict Outcomes." *International Interactions* 12: 315–42.

Reichhardt, Tony. 1996. "U.S. Deal Buys into Mir to Keep Russia on Board International Station Project," *Nature* 379 (6565): 476–77.

Reiter, Dan. 1995. "Exploding The Powder Keg Myth: Preemptive Wars Almost Never Happen." *International Security* 20: 5–34.

Ren, Ruoen. 1997. *China's Economic Performance in an International Perspective.* Paris: Organization for Economic Cooperation and Development.

Repko, Sergei. 1996. "We'll Never Be Allies." *The Current Digest of the Post-Soviet Press* 48 (30): 21–22.

Ria Novosti. 1997. "For the Atlantic Union" (28 May).

Richardson, James L. 1994. *Crisis Diplomacy.* New York: Cambridge University Press.

Rock, Stephen R. 1989. *Why Peace Breaks Out: Great Power Rapprochement in Historical Perspective.* Chapel Hill: University of North Carolina Press.

Rogowski, Ronald. 1989. *Commerce and Coalitions: The Economics of Discriminatory International Trade Policies.* Oxford: Basil Blackwell.

Romer, Paul M. 1986. "Increasing Returns and Long-Run Growth." *Journal of Political Economy* 94: 1002–1037.

Rosen, Daniel H. 1999. *Behind the Open Door: Foreign Enterprises in the Chinese Marketplace.* Washington, D.C.: Institute for International Economics.

Rosen, Steven J. 1977. "A Stable System of Mutual Nuclear Deterrence in the Arab-Israeli Conflict." *American Political Science Review* 71: 1367–83.

Rousseau, David L., Christopher Gelpi, Dan Reiter, and Paul K. Huth. 1996. "Assessing the Dyadic Nature of the Democratic Peace." *American Political Science Review* 90: 512–33.

Rouyer, Alwyn. 1987. "Political Capacity and the Decline of Fertility in India." *American Political Science Review* 81: 453–70.

Roy, Denny. 1994. "Hegemon on the Horizon? China's Threat to East Asian Security." *International Security* 19: 149–68.

———. 1997. "The Foreign Policy of Great-Power China." *Contemporary Southeast Asia* 19: 121–35.

Rummel, R.J. 1997. *Power Kills: Democracy as a Method of Nonviolence.* New Brunswick, N.J.: Transaction Publishers.

Russett, Bruce M. 1985. "The Mysterious Case of Vanishing Hegemony; or, Is Mark Twain Really Dead?" *International Organization* 39: 207–231.

———. 1993. *Grasping the Democratic Peace: Principles for a Post-Cold War World.* Princeton: Princeton University Press.

———. 1996. "Ten Balances for Weighing Reform Proposals." *Political Science Quarterly* 111 (2): 259.

Russett, Bruce M., John R. Oneal, and David Davis. 1998. "The Third Leg of the Kantian Tripod for Peace: International Organizations and Militarized Disputes." *International Organization* 52 (3): 441–67.

Russett, Bruce M., and Allan Stam III. 1998. "The Future of NATO: The Russian Role in the U.S.-China Power Transition." *Political Science Quarterly* (forthcoming).

Sagan, Carl. 1989. "Nuclear War and Climatic Catastrophe: A Nuclear Winter." In *The Nuclear Reader,* edited by Charles Kegley and Eugene Wittkopf. New York: St. Martin's Press.

Sandler, Todd. 1993. "The Economic Theory of Alliances: A Survey." *Journal of Conflict Resolution* 37 (4): 446–83.

Saywell, Trish. 1997. "Fishing for Trouble: Asia's Fish Stocks are Dwindling Because of Over-Exploitation and Pollution." *Far Eastern Economic Review* 160 (11): 50–52.

Scalapino, Robert A. 1999. "The American Response to a Changing Asia." Paper presented at the 1999 Pacific Symposium, National Defense University, Washington, D.C., 1–2 March.

Schroeder, Paul W. 1994. *The Transformation of European Politics, 1763–1848.* New York: Oxford University Press.

Schweller, Randall L. 1992. "Domestic Structure and Preventive War." *World Politics* 44: 235–69.

———. 1994. "Bandwagoning for Profit: Bringing the Revisionist State Back In." *International Security* 19 (1): 72–107.

Scott, William. 1997. "Lockheed Martin, Energomash Development of RD-180 on Track." *Aviation Week & Space Technology* 146 (14): 40–1.

Segal, Gerald. 1993. "The Coming Confrontation Between China and Japan." *World Policy Journal* 10: 27–32.

———. 1995. "Tying China into the International System." *Survival* 37: 60–73.

———. 1996. "East Asia and the "Constrainment" of China." *International Security* 20 (4): 107–135.

Shambaugh, David. 1995. "The United States and China: A New Cold War?" *Current History* 94: 241–47.

———. 1996. "Containment or Engagement of China? Calculating Beijing's Responses." *International Security* 21: 180–209.

———. 1999. "Two Chinas, But Only One Answer." *Washington Post* (18 July), B1–2.

Shenon, Philip. 1998. "Pentagon Report Plays Down Cost of Expanding NATO." *New York Times* (21 February).

Shinkarenko, Pavel, and Tatyana Malkina. 1996. "Yeltsin Visit Marks Closer Russia-China Ties." *Current Digest of the Post-Soviet Press* 48 (17): 6–9.

Shirk, Susan L. 1998. "The United States and Taiwan." Testimony before the House International Relations Committee, Washington, D.C., 20 May, 1–5.

Signorino, Curtis S., and Jeffrey M. Ritter. 1997. "Tau-b or Not Tau-b: Measuring Similarity of Alliances and Interests." *Center for International Affairs Working Paper 9–7.* Harvard University.

Simon, Sheldon. 1996. "Alternative Visions of Security in Northeast Asia," *Journal of Northeast Asian Studies* 15 (3): 77–99.

Singer, J. David, Stuart Bremer, and John Stuckey. 1972. "Capability Distribution, Uncertainty, and Major Power War, 1820–1965." In *Peace, War and Numbers,* edited by Bruce M. Russett. Beverly Hills, Calif.: Sage Publications.

Singer, Max, and Aaron Wildavsky. 1996. *The Real World Order: Zones of Peace/ Zones of Turmoil,* rev. ed. Chatham, N.J.: Chatham House Publishers.

Siverson, Randolph, and Harvey Starr. 1991. *The Diffusion of War.* Ann Arbor: University of Michigan Press.

———. 1994. "Regime Change and the Restructuring of Alliances." *American Journal of Political Science* 38: 145–61.

Small, Melvin, and J. David Singer. 1982. *Resort to Arms.* Beverly Hills, Calif.: Sage Publications.

Smil, Vaclav. 1997. "China's Environment and Security: Simple Myths and Complex Realities." *SAIS Review* 17 (1): 107–26.

Snidal, Duncan. 1991. "Relative Gains and the Pattern of International Cooperation." *American Political Science Review* 85 (3): 701–26.

Snyder, Jack. 1990. "Averting Anarchy in the New Europe." *International Security* 14 (4): 5–41.

————. 1994. "Russian Backwardness and the Future of Europe." *Daedalus* 123 (2): 179–202.

Solow, Robert M. 1987. *Growth Theory and Exposition*. Oxford: Oxford University Press.

State Statistical Bureau. 1994–1997. *China Statistical Yearbook*. Beijing, China.

Speed, R. 1979. *Strategic Deterrence in the 1980s*. Stanford: Hoover Institution Press.

Sun, Lena H. 1997. "U.S. is a Big Market for Firms Owned by Chinese Military." *Washington Post* (24 June): A7.

Sutter, Robert G., and Shirley Kan. 1994. "China as a Security Concern in Asia: Perceptions, Assessment, and U.S. Options." *CRS Report for Congress* 95–46S: 1–28.

Swain, Michael D. 1997. "Don't Demonize China." *Washington Post* (18 May): C1–4.

Tan, Qingshan. 1992. *The Making of U.S. China Policy: From Normalization to the Post-Cold War Era*. Boulder, Colo.: Lynne Rienner.

Tammen, Ronald L. 1973. *MIRV and the Arms Race*. New York: Praeger Publishers.

————. 1999. "The Policy Implications of Power Transition Theory." Paper presented at the annual meeting of the American Political Science Association, Atlanta, 1–5 September.

Tenent, George J. 1997. "China: Economics, Demographics, and Environment." Statement Before the Senate Select Committee on Intelligence, 5 February.

Thompson, William R., and Richard Tucker. 1997. *Journal of Conflict Resolution* 41 (3): 457–77.

Tucker, Nancy Bernkopf. 1996. "War or Peace in the Taiwan Strait?" *Washington Quarterly* 19: 171–87.

Turner, Stansfield. 1997. *Managing the Nuclear Genie: An American Challenge for Global Security*. Boulder, Colo.: Westview Press.

Tyler, Patrick E. 1996. "China to Buy 72 Advanced Fighter Planes from Russia," *New York Times* 145 (7 February): A3.

Urlanis, B. 1971. *Wars and Population*. Moscow: Progress Publishers.

U.S. Arms Control and Disarmament Agency. 1997. *World Military Expenditures and Arms Transfers, 1996*. Washington, D.C.: Government Printing Office.

U.S. Department of Commerce. National Trade Data Bank and Electronic Bulletin Board. "China: Economics, Demographics, and Environment." Washington, D.C.

U.S. Embassy-Beijing. 1999. "How Do Statistics Become Just a Numbers Game?" Beijing, China: U.S. Embassy.

U.S. Strategic Bombing Survey. 1945. *The Effects of Strategic Bombing on the German War Economy*. Washington, D.C.: Government Printing Office.

U.S. Strategic Bombing Survey. 1946. *The Effects of Strategic Bombing on Japan's War Economy*. Washington, D.C.: Government Printing Office.

Valdecanas, Maria Christina. 1995. "From Machine Guns to Motorcycles." *China Business Review* 22: 14–18.

Vasquez, John A. 1993. *The War Puzzle*. New York: Cambridge University Press.

Volgy, Thomas J., and Lawrence E. Imwalle. 1995. "Hegemonic and Bipolar Perspectives on the New World Order," *American Journal of Political Science* 39: 819–34.

Walt, Stephen M. 1987. *The Origins of Alliances*. Ithaca, N.Y.: Cornell University Press.

Waltz, Kenneth. 1979. *Theory of International Politics*. Reading, Pa.: Addison-Wesley.

———. 1981. "The Spread of Nuclear Weapons: More May Be Better." *Adelphi Paper 171*. London: International Institute of Strategic Studies.

———. 1990. "Nuclear Myths and Political Realities." *American Political Science Review* 84: 731–46.

———. 1993. "The Emerging Structure of International Politics." *International Security* 18: 44–79.

Waltz, Kenneth, and Scott D. Sagan. 1995. *The Spread of Nuclear Weapons: A Debate*. New York: W.W. Norton and Company.

Wang, Kevin, and James Lee Ray. 1994. "Beginners and Winners: The Fate of Initiators of Interstate Wars Involving Great Powers since 1495." *International Studies Quarterly* 38: 139–54.

Ward, Michael D., David R. Davis, and Steve Chan. 1995. "Military Spending and Economic Growth in Taiwan." *Armed Forces & Society* 19 (4): 533–50.

Ward, Michael D., David R. Davis, and Corey L. Lofdahl. 1995. "A Century of Tradeoffs: Defense and Growth in Japan and the United States." *International Studies Quarterly* 39 (1): 27–50.

Ward, Michael D., and Kristian S. Gleditsch. 1998. "Democratizing for Peace." *American Political Science Review* 92 (1): 51–62.

Washington Post. 1997. "Myths about China's Military Might" (18 May), C4.

Wayman, Frank Whelon. 1996. "Power Shifts and the Onset of War." In *Parity and War*, edited by Jacek Kugler and Douglas Lemke. Ann Arbor: University of Michigan Press.

Werner, Suzanne. 1996. "Absolute and Limited War: The Possibilities of a Foreign Imposed Regime Change." *International Interactions* 22: 67–88.

———. 1998. "Negotiating the Terms of Settlement: War Aims and Bargaining Leverage." *Journal of Conflict Resolution* 42: 321–43.

Werner, Suzanne, and Jacek Kugler. 1996. "Power Transitions and Military Build-ups." In *Parity and War*, edited by Jacek Kugler and Douglas Lemke. Ann Arbor: University of Michigan Press.

West, Loraine A. 1997. "Shifting Boundaries." *China Business Review* 24: 15–20.

Wilkins, Reginald Avery. 1998. "Trade and Security Externalities: A Disaggregated Approach." Ph.D. dissertation, Claremont Graduate University.

Wohlstetter, Albert. 1959. "The Delicate Balance of Terror." *Foreign Affairs* 37: 211–34.

Wolf, Charles Jr., K.C. Yeh, Anil Bamezai, Donald P. Henry, and Michael Kennedy. 1995. "Long-Term Economic and Military Trends 1994–2015, The United States and Asia." Santa Monica, Calif.: Rand Corporation, 1–57.

Woodward, Bob. 1991. *The Commanders*. New York: Simon and Schuster.

Woon, Eden. 1993. "Economic Reform and Defense." *East Asian Executive Reports* 15.

World Bank. 1997. *China 2020: Development Challenges in the New Century.* Washington, D.C.

Wu, Harry X. 1998. "How Rich Is China and How Fast Has the Economy Grown? Statistical Controversies." *China Economy Papers,* NCDS Asia Pacific Press: Australian National University.

Yanov, Alexander. 1997. "Russian Liberals and NATO." *Moscow News* (30 January): 1–2.

Yin, Xiangshuo. 1999. "The Impact of the Asian Financial Crisis of China." *1999 Pacific Symposium,* 1–2 March, 1–20.

Yong, Wang. 1998. "State to Trim Budget Deficit, Up Investment." *Washington Post* (25 May): S2.

Yost, Casimir A. 1997. "The China Challenge and the U.S. Response." *Institute for the Study of Diplomacy.* Columbia International Affairs Online (October).

Yurong, Chen. 1995. "Russia Distances Itself from the West." *Beijing Review* 38 (14–15): 22–25.

Zagare, Frank C. 1987. *The Dynamics of Deterrence.* Chicago: University of Chicago Press.

———. 1996. "The Rites of Passage." In *Parity and War,* edited by Jacek Kugler and Douglas Lemke. Ann Arbor: University of Michigan Press.

Zagare, Frank, and D. Marc Kilgour. 1993. "Asymmetric Deterrence." *International Studies Quarterly* 37: 1–27.

———. 2000. *Perfect Deterrence.* Cambridge, Mass.: Cambridge University Press.

Zelikow, Philip, and Condoleeza Rice. 1995. *Germany Unified and Europe Transformed: A Study in Statecraft.* Cambridge: Harvard University Press.

Zhang, Baoxiang. 1997. "NATO-Russia Talks over Expansion Remain Deadlocked." *Beijing Review* 40 (6): 8.

Zhang, Ming. 1996. "The Shifting Chinese Public Image of the United States," *Strategic Forum* 89: 1–4

Zhang, Xiaobo, and Song Qiang. 1996. "China, Too, Can Say 'No.'" *Los Angeles Times* (15 August): 11.

Zhilin, Alexander. 1996. "Rodionov to NATO: Don't Bait a Wounded Bear." *Moscow News* 51 (26 December): 1–2.

Index

About the Authors

RONALD L. TAMMEN is Chair of the Department of National Strategy and Professor of National Strategy at the National War College in Washington, D.C., where he also has served as associate dean of faculty, codirector of regional studies, and core course director. In prior positions, he was managing partner of public relations firm, chief of staff to Senator William Proxmire (D-Wis.), and staff consultant to the Congressional Foreign Policy and Arms Control Caucus led by Senator Mark O. Hatfield (R-Ore.). His publications and research have centered on U.S. foreign policy and national security issues; he is the author of *MIRV and the Arms Race* and editor of *The Economics of Defense Spending*.

JACEK KUGLER is the Elisabeth Helms Rosecrans Professor of International Relations at the School of Politics and Economics, Claremont Graduate University, where he has also served as director and chairman. He is the cofounder of Decision Insights, Inc. His publications in world politics and political economy are widely available in scholarly journals. He is the coauthor of *The War Ledger* and *Births, Deaths, and Taxes*, as well as the coeditor of *Parity and War, The Long Term Stability of Deterrence*, and *Political Capacity and Economic Behavior*.

DOUGLAS LEMKE is an assistant professor of political science at the University of Michigan. His research focuses on the causes of international conflict. He has published articles in *International Studies Quarterly, Journal of Conflict Resolution, International Interactions*, and other scholarly journals dedicated to the scientific analysis of world politics. He is coeditor of *Parity and War*, and has completed work on *Regions of War and Peace*, a book about regional hierarchies.

ALLAN C. STAM III is an assistant professor of political science at Yale University. His research focuses on initiation, escalation, and resolution of international disputes. He is the author of *Win Lose or Draw* and has published articles in the *American Political Science Review*, the *Journal of Conflict Resolution*, and other scholarly journals dedicated to the scientific analysis of world politics. He is now working on a book, *Search for Victory*, dealing with the issue of why democracies win wars, as well as a book-length project that explores why states fight the way they do during interstate war.

MARK ANDREW ABDOLLAHIAN is Vice President of Decision Insights, Inc., a New York consulting firm that forecasts political and economic events. He has lectured on decision making and foreign policy at Claremont Graduate University and UCLA. His work focuses on decision making, the dynamics of interstate relations, and the historic evaluation of international politics. He has recently published articles on the politics of Russia and South Africa in *International Interactions* and has contributed chapters to historical assessments of world politics.

CAROLE ALSHARABATI is an assistant professor currently teaching at the Balamand University Business School and on the Faculty of Law and Political Science of the University Saint Joseph in Beirut, Lebanon. Her work centers on game theoretical and formal approaches to the study of international politics. She specializes in operationalizing advanced computer-based policy evaluation tools using game theoretical approaches. She is working on a book dealing with the use of nuclear weapons in the Middle East.

BRIAN EFIRD is completing his Ph.D. in political science at the Claremont Graduate University and is an Associate at Decision Insights, Inc., in New York. His research focuses on interstate conflict, bargaining problems, dispute mediation, and the political economy of growth. His dissertation accounts for the dynamic relationship between the probability and severity of war, economic change, status quo assessment, and alliance formation. He has published articles in *International Interaction* and in books on political economy.

A.F.K. ORGANSKI was Professor of Political Science at the University of Michigan and a cofounder of Decision Insights, Inc. He pioneered work spanning several decades on several aspects of world politics, including political demography, political development, and grand strategy. His publications are widely available in scholarly journals. He was the author of *World Politics, The Stages of Political Development, The War Ledger, Birth Death and Taxes,* and *The $36 Billion Bargain.*